Corn-Fed

Corn-Fed

Cul-de-sacs, Keg Stands, and Coming of Age in the Midwest

MELANIE LAFORCE

BROOKLYN, NY

THOUGHT
CATALOG
Books

Cover illustration by @lehrerboys.

Published by Thought Catalog Books, a publishing house owned by The Thought & Expression Co., Williamsburg, Brooklyn.

Second edition, 2018

ISBN: 978-1-949759-00-6

Printed and bound in the United States.

10 9 8 7 6 5 4 3 2

For Dad.

CONTENTS

Introduction

I was born and raised in Painesville, Ohio without ever knowing that I was a Midwesterner. I didn't realize my true identity until my early 20s, when my saucy future husband knocked me down a few pegs. Dave hails from Indiana, and we were discussing my habit of over-apologizing, which he rationalized as a Midwestern trait.

"What do you mean?" I asked. "I'm from Ohio. That's not the Midwest."

Dave stared at me.

"What the hell do you think Ohio is, if not the Midwest?" he asked.

"The Great Lakes," I responded.

"Okay, that's not a thing. I mean, it is a thing, but Ohio is most definitely the Midwest."

I was stunned. I had made it all the way to young adulthood in denial of my Midwesterly roots. Whenever I thought of "Midwest," it conjured up images of Southern Iowa, agriculture, and people who shout about Hoosiers. Was I really one of them? I thought about my other potential Midwestern traits. I love a good fish fry, but my favorite meal is Velveeta and Ritz Cracker casserole. I say the word "aunt" like the insect. My hometown went apeshit in the mid-90s when we finally got an Applebee's. The women in my family bring slippers to house parties.

Yup. Shit. I'm a goddamn Midwesterner.

Living in Chicago for 18 years, I finally warmed to a Midwest identity. We are a diverse and empathic people (hence all of the apologizing) – the beating heart of the United States. We win awards for our food and drink. (Ever heard of a Los Angeles hot dog? That's because it's NOT A THING.) We weather cold winters and humid summers. The coasts may see us as bland, but we are *rich* with corn syrup and saturated fat.

This book is a tribute to the comfortable constant that is growing up in the Midwest – my Midwest. You may find some of my experiences similar, because you were right there with me in the breadbasket of the United States. Or you might not – it's important to note that my experiences are by no means universal. I wanted to call the book "A lower-middle-income-mostly-straight-cis-white woman's experiences with casseroles and Schlitz," but I was told it wouldn't sell.

My life and experiences reflect my context: I am a French vanilla white woman, and I've been proudly toting a vagina since birth. This body, despite my juvenile rheumatoid arthritis and subsequent hobbling around in discount acid-washed jeans, continues to afford me a life that many have not had. Which is a great selling point for reading the rest of this book, right? Another white cis-girl story, how novel! I know you are thinking, "LET ME AT IT." There's also recurring themes of debilitating anxiety and self-pity. Get stoked!

But. There are also boobs. Try to hold out for the boobs.

In addition to my specific experiences and various bodily extremities, this book is about conformity, social identity, friendship, and vintage taxidermy. Themes that, I hope, you may occasionally see yourself in, regardless of color, gender, or religious persuasion. I don't want to sugarcoat any privilege or the attitudes that were fostered because of it, nor do I want to offend. I probably did both, but we'll see where I landed. Could wind up being a helluva book burning.

A Brief History of my Qualifications to Write This Book

As much as I'd love to pass myself off as a bold, sinewy, seamlessly graceful woman, like Robin Wright in *Wonder Woman*, or even a female Legolas[1], my personality is really more of a cartoon ladymonkey that plays with herself inappropriately. I first realized that I liked to make people laugh when I was about four. I was sitting on the almond-colored shag carpet in my parents' inherited Cape Cod house in Willoughby, Ohio. There was some sort of party or gathering happening, because I remember being surrounded by adults. My mom knelt down and told me "Guess what? We're going to Chuck E. Cheese!"

I looked up at the warm faces around me and said, "Well, I guess I better go put on some underwear!" Everyone laughed and laughed, and I gleefully basked in the joy of being a star.

I continued on this path for many years. In 7th grade I became briefly middle school-famous for writing "hysterical" (according to my teacher Ms. Lehman) fictional essays about my classmates' capers at the mall. When you're 12 in 1990 in Northeast Ohio, the mall is pretty much your Las Vegas. My mall stories were a pre-adolescent version of *The Hangover*, minus cameos from convicted rapists.

I continued this strategy through high school, writing zines and sharing them with 10-15 of my closest friends. My longest-running zine was titled "To Anyone Who Cares" and featured culturally important quizzes (e.g. "Who should you go to prom with?"), running lists of companies that didn't use animal testing, poignantly awkward Lightning Seeds song lyrics, and ongoing rants about homeroom teachers. This book is a (mostly?) adult version of those zines. However, I promise I

---

1. Although he was basically a chick anyway, right?

won't make you read about losing my virginity or getting my first period. There are already plenty of those stories around. You will, however, be treated to plenty of vulvalicious content.

A Sample of Important Topics Contained Herein

1. *Childhood awkwardness.* Gobs and gobs of it.

2. *Nesting.* The fine art of domesticating with shitty taste and not much money.

3. *Winter.* Everyone loves to read about weather, right?! It's gonna be great.

4. *Human behavior and social psychology.* I'm such a big ol' nerd about this that I went and got a doctorate.

5. *Unrequited love.* No Midwestern memoir could be complete without unrequited love stories. Fortunately, I've got loads.

6. There's also an unreasonable number of references to *dairy products.*

So why the Midwest? Well, I live here, and all my other themes were rejected. LA and New York tend to permeate a lot of popular stories for women as of late (Think Lena Dunham, *Sex and the City,* and Bridget the animated mouse from *American Tail).* I would like to see the Midwest get its due. People often call us the heart of America; we pride ourselves on being real, salt of the earth folks who help each other out, swap creamed corn recipes, have euchre tournaments, and debate good-naturedly over who makes the best deep dish pizza. (Seriously, only tourists eat that shit.) For me, growing up in the Midwest was about finding my people. I won't say "finding my tribe" because I'm not comfortable with that particular form of cultural appropriation. Let's go with "finding my pack," because it's okay to metaphorize canids, and white people have never systematically oppressed the wolves, run them out of their territory, or hunted them to oblivion. Wait.

OK, we're just gonna go with "pack" anyway. In the Midwest, and really anywhere, it takes trial and error to determine your place in the world and your status in the pack. With any luck, you will find a good pack that will watch out for you, protect you, howl with you, and toss you a scrap of dead possum meat from the side of the road. Over time, I was lucky enough to find a few pretty great packs. They wove in and out of my life and helped me figure out who I am.

I hope that these stories inspire you to embrace your roots and inner weirdo, however that manifests. And obviously, I hope that this book allows me to reach my ultimate goal: developing a cult-like following of worshippers to do my evil bidding.

Thanks for reading.

—Melanie

1

HARRIET THE SPY

I've lived in Chicago for almost 20 years. Whenever I fly into O'Hare, especially at night, I marvel at the seemingly endless city grid opening up like a giant checkerboard carefully outlined in Christmas lights. The grid system is not only beautiful, but practical. It makes Chicago easy to navigate. Almost all streets are north-south or east-west and run from end-to-end of the city. If someone gives you an address in Chicago, you can picture where it falls. This is one of the many ways Chicago is superior to cities such as Boston, which had no urban planning whatsoever and whose streets resemble a bowl of spaghetti. Being eaten by Satan. (I really dislike Boston.)

I grew up in the rural suburbs of Cleveland. Until Lebron James showed up, Cleveland was best known for its failing sports teams and filth so extensive that the Cuyahoga River actually caught on fire in 1969. More specifically, I was raised in Painesville Township, which is bordered on the east by very suburban Mentor and on the west by very rural Leroy, which is as farm country as it sounds. Painesville Township is the land of cul-de-sacs. From an airplane, it resembles a series of asphalt amoebas, with skinny bodies and fat round heads. Suburban amoebas became popular in the 1960s as a stark contrast to urban grids. The cul-de-sac model kept through traffic out. Limited traffic made it safer for little kids to ride their tricycles and Big Wheels, have impromptu lemonade stands, and generally socialize with other little kids. The American Dream.

Our cul-de-sac was unlike many of the others in Painesville Township, in that it was built on the edge of a forest. Mom and Dad fell in love with my childhood home solely because it sits atop a ravine and has large living room windows overlooking acres of untouched woods. Recently, these woods became officially protected by the county, preserving the view forever.

The other aspects of our house itself are fairly forgettable. It was built in the 1950s with the standard awnings and lack of reliable central climate control characteristic of the era. My bedroom was in the top corner of the second floor, next to the attic. It overlooked the woods, which made the stifling summers tolerable. I fell asleep with the windows open, listening to rain on the trees.

In our circle driveway there were two multi-story pine trees that my mother hated and my younger brother Dusty and I loved. The pines dripped buckets of brown sap on the roof of our car, but provided Dusty and I with a killer hideout. They were great for climbing, leaving most of our warm weather clothes stained with sticky patches. Between the trees was a little bed of fallen amber pine needles, perfect for picnics and naps and hatching elaborate schemes. My dear departed guinea pig Sammy was also buried between the pines, as well as an infant blue jay that had fallen from its nest. (Dusty and I had tried desperately to keep the baby bird alive by feeding it raw hamburger, but it died after only a couple of days.)

Our cul-de-sac, however lovely, was isolated. Unlike the

housing developments that proliferated just a short distance away, we were a solitary street with few children. This had some perks: trick-or-treating meant we *always* got FULL BARS of chocolate. It also meant that I didn't have to pretend to be friends with any Podunk Northeast Ohio rubes who wanted to play with Barbies all afternoon. (The only thing I liked about Barbies was that their knees crunched like mine when you bent them—thanks, juvenile rheumatoid arthritis!) Despite all this, the drawbacks were also sharp: I didn't have a cadre of little kids in the neighborhood with whom I could stage elaborate dance performances. No one to help me find and categorize caterpillars or fry eggs on the asphalt on a hot day[1]. Any lemonade stands were operated by me alone and scarcely patronized. Dusty was more lucky. A little boy his age lived on the street. My parents' college roommates also lived close by and had two sons.

The relatively constant presence of Dusty and his friends facilitated my becoming an eight-year-old boss bitch. I am three years older than Dusty and therefore permanently in charge. This professional relationship trickled down to his friends. I loved conceiving detailed summer day camps and forcing them to attend. Camp Funshine Bear was the best. (Camp names were usually based on whatever cartoon I was regularly watching. Other camp names included Camp Baby Miss Piggy, and Camp SheRa.)

A typical summer day camp schedule might look like this:

Arts & Crafts: 10:00am – 11:30am. I stole several spools of the most brightly colored thread from Mom's sewing kit.

---

1. Mom was right. Frying an egg on hot asphalt doesn't actually work; it just wastes a perfectly good egg.

a cassette tape that appeared unimportant enough to record over[3]. At dusk, I quietly slipped through the pines to the Panzanettis' back deck. Silently, I placed the boom box on the edge of the deck—out of sight but within earshot of the open kitchen window. I hit record and fled.

Night fell. It was a particularly humid August evening. I struggled to fall asleep. I listened through my open window to the trees moving in the wind and imagined the Panzanettis' conversations.

Mr. Panzanetti: Tonya, baby, the spaghetti is delicious today. Nobody makes a meatball like my Tonya.

Mrs. Panzanetti: Tony, you're a gem. Such a good provider of the money and diamond jewelry!

Teen Boy Panzanetti: Say, Pop, what should we do with that dead body collecting dust in the cellar?

Teen Girl Panzanetti: Yeah, Pop it's starting to smell as bad as Tony Junior's gym bag!

Teen Boy Panzanetti: Ayyyy, shut up Tonya Junior!

Mr. Panzanetti: Well I'm gonna kill at least three more people this week but then at the end of the week we should just dump the bodies and frame some unsuspecting family.

Mrs. Panzanetti: Sounds good to me, my sexy husband. Who should we frame this time?

Mr. Panzanetti: Let's frame the LaForces, they'll be perfect!

Teen Boy Panzanetti: I don't know, Pop, that daughter Melanie seems like a pretty smart cookie.

Mr. Panzanetti: (long, evil cackle) Trust your Pop, Tony Junior. I'll handle it.

The next morning, excited to collect an earful of juicy

---

3. When my brother and I were very young, Mom loved to tape us saying our first words, singing songs, and quoting McDonald's commercials. A few times I got into trouble for taping over these most precious memories.

Panzanetti intelligence, I went to retrieve my boom box. The sun warmed my arms and I felt quite satisfied as I crept along the edge of the Panzanettis' house toward the back deck.

My pink boombox was gone.

My heart fell into my stomach. I quickly scanned the deck, looking all the way to the edge of the ravine. Nothing. The mission had been compromised.

Panicked, I ran back to my room, avoiding interaction with my family. I sat on my bed and stared at the wall. My tiny brain ruminated over the "world of hurt" (as Dad would say) that I knew I was in for. I strained my ears, listening out the open window for any potential signs of Panzanetti movement. I spotted *Harriet the Spy* on my nightstand and stuffed it angrily under my mattress. Time crept by. I tried to read some *Beezus and Ramona* to distract myself but couldn't focus. After about an hour, our front doorbell rang. I held my breath, terrified, trying to make out the muffled conversation. A few moments later, Dad knocked at my door and opened it. He held my pink boombox. I began to sob, humiliated. The Panzanettis had caught me spying. They had returned the boom box and even left the tape in it, as if to taunt me. They had spoken to my Dad. Everything was over. I could not possibly survive this level of extraordinary shame.

Dad's moods were unpredictable—he might be cackling hysterically at Monty Python one moment, then cursing violently at a bill collector the next. Dad loved his kids more than anything, but his anxiety and depression led to surprising and occasionally traumatic verbal outbursts. Sometimes my brother and I accidentally got on the wrong side of Dad's "bad mood." I didn't know how he would react today – I feared deep anger over this unforgivable treason. Dad towered over me and tossed the boom box on my bed. I held my breath.

I got lucky. Dad looked at me with concerned, yet confused warm blue eyes. The buildup of anxiety from the past hour erupted like a volcano. I buried my face in my pillow and tried to stifle my tears.

"It's OK, look – it's fine," he said, awkwardly touching the boom box.

I *hated* showing emotion to my parents. Dad patted my back silently, unsure how to make things better. Why the hell was I so upset about a misplaced toy? What a garbage spy. I couldn't even withstand basic torture.

Of course, none of the adults knew I had been spying. I was just a kid who left a toy in the neighbor's yard. Adults are tall simpletons, and they tend to give kids the ethical benefit of the doubt.

And so my dastardly spying career died in secret. No conversation could be deciphered on the cassette tape. It was just a 90-minute Memorex whir of white noise. And by the grace of God, my position was never revealed, but I never attempted another mission. A good spy knows to leave the game when things get too hot.

So many summer adventures unfolded deep within my brain, never making it to the real world. This was probably for the best, as the drama in my head was not an accurate reflection of reality. A lack of age-appropriate friends had left me to retreat into my own imagination. I didn't mind. I wasn't lonely. I had E.T. and Herbert the stuffed elephant, Cabbage Patch Kids, and occasional human boy minions. I liked being alone—alone, there was no chance of conflict or disappointment. It would be a few years before I realized the critical importance of human friends.

Mom had the pine trees cut down after I moved to Chicago. A little bit of Dusty and me died that day. Mom replaced the space with a garden, crawling with succulents and cleomes that she painstakingly weeds herself. It is a beautiful garden, and there is no more pine sap to clean off the car. But the yard still looks naked without the towering pines. The space under those trees was a camp and a cool apartment and a jungle gym and a spy lair. Even though I aged out of fake camps and spying on neighbors, I found comfort under the pines. They reminded me of a safe place, a time when I was happy enough with the company of my imagination. It was a place where I didn't doubt myself and the world was my oyster. Mom's garden, while lovely, just isn't the same.

2

CAMP GIRL MEETS BOY

"CAMP, glorious CAAAAAMP. Cute boys and bonfiressss!" Two weeks before I headed to overnight camp, I sang this song to the tune of *Oliver!*'s "Food, Glorious Food."[1] *This summer would be DIFFERENT*, I thought. No more fake day camps in the backyard. I was finally going to REAL, OVERNIGHT CAMP deep in the exotic foothills of Geauga County, Ohio. A critical rite of passage, camp presented infinite opportunities. But most notably, camp presented the opportunity to smooch a boy.

I dedicate a fair amount of page space to the quest for boys. Oh, it's gross, for sure. It's needy and kind of pathetic. It only took me until now, at age (*Author's note: Age redacted*) to realize this. After seemingly millions of hours of therapy, I now, in 2018, actually feel some sense of self-worth derived from sources other than dude attention. Maybe. I'm working on it. It's a difficult vice for me to shake because acknowledgment from a dude-object-of-desire is the brain chemical equivalent of snorting heroin while water-skiing with a litter of puppies. If you'd like more details on my lifelong quest for dude atten-

---

1. *Oliver!* should be required watching for all Millennials/Gen Z. It contains critical life lessons on survival and wits. Artful Dodger remains a worthy idol.

tion, that's another book—probably one my therapist is writing as you read, in addition to her groundbreaking self-help book for algebra sufferers (see Chapter 4).

By the summer after 5th grade, popular media had taught me that hooking up was the preeminent purpose for camp. I had watched all three *Meatballs* movies and internalized the value of horny outdoor parties. I longed for short-shorts covered with mosquito repellent, crop tops, and breasts large enough to flash delighted male campers. I already spent at least 90% of my waking consciousness strategizing how to get boys to like me. Have you ever seen that video where the dog owner puts a dog treat on the sofa, just out of reach of a little French bulldog, and the dog claws and claws at the edge of the sofa, trying to get the treat? I craved boys like a dog treat, yet they stayed persistently out of reach. In addition to *Meatballs*, my other camp scripture was a YA paperback entitled *Camp Girl Meets Boy* by Caroline Cooney. The *Publishers Weekly* synopsis reads:

Marissa is a counselor because she loves the rituals and cama-raderie of summer camp. Violet disdains most camp activities; she has signed on as a counselor solely in the hope of meeting guys. At scenic Camp Menuncheokogue, familiarly known as "Camp Men" and even "Camp Girl-Meets-Boy," the two find a summer of surprises.

Camp Girls Meets Boy had a marginal subplot concerning personal growth, blah blah blah, but the main theme was clear: Go to camp, meet a preppy rich white-boy penis. I knew that camp would be *it*—a magical land full of boys who didn't know that I was not cool and somehow couldn't tell that I wasn't an 11-year-old version of a *Playboy* centerfold. I was more excited for camp than I had been about my first pair of acid-washed jeans.

A week before camp, a basic list of necessities arrived in the mail. Lest any idiots forget, Camp Sue Osprey recommended underwear, a flashlight, and bug repellent. Mom took me to Marc's to buy my camp supplies. Marc's was a discount store located in Painesville Shopping Center strip mall, which was also home to establishments like Little Caesar's, Just Closeouts (the trashiest of all the dollar stores), and second-run theater Cinema 20. Nowadays, Marc's has moved down Mentor Avenue to a bigger location, but they still sell my beloved Mt. Olive pickles. Marc's manages to slightly undercut other big box discount stores via hand-painted signs, modest selection, and (I'm convinced) black magic. It was where we purchased 99% of all household goods. It was like a giant Rite-Aid without all the goddamn pretentiousness.

I scoured the wire shelves of each aisle, spending the most time in the back corner where the Wet & Wild makeup taunted me. I searched for the perfect tiny mirror, the perfect travel toothbrush.

"We should buy maxi pads," Mom said absent-mindedly. She shook back her blonde bangs and stood on her tiptoes to reach the Teen Spirit deodorant in my signature scent, Caribbean Cool. (Mom, like me, clocks in at just under 60 inches tall.)

I was mortified and said nothing. My poor mother would try over the course of my life to get me to discuss a range of body troubles, like cramps and constipation and gas pains. I would always remain silent. The rubber shopping cart handle had become loose, and I instead fixated on slowly pulling it out. Up until this point, I had lived a blissful, menstruation-free life. Certainly, the universe wouldn't strike me down during my first overnight camp.

Maxi pads went into the shopping cart, but I distracted Mom from further puberty conversation in the travel-size products aisle, talking her into a fancy pink travel hairbrush. When I pressed on the reverse side of the bristles, the brush collapsed into a neat pouch; it is the most accomplished feat of modern engineering I've seen to this day. With my allowance, I also procured a small set of purple stationery, briefly forgetting that I had no one, other than my lame family, to write to from camp. The feather-soft stationery paper tickled my skinny fingers. The envelope sealflap seemed decadently oversized. I imagined penning a beautiful poem on a sheet of purple stationery, scenting it with Caribbean Cool, and hand-delivering it to my new Camp Boyfriend.

Over the next few weeks, I packed for camp early and often like a true Midwesterner, strategically cycling through key tank tops and edgy ankle socks. I considered every possible disaster and miracle:

- What would I wear to casual cafeteria breakfasts?
- Would I need a special outfit for sitting on the grass? (Yes. I am an acute sufferer of Summer Rash Legs.)
- Should I bring a curling iron? Will Mom let me borrow hers?
- Is camp BYO-God's-Eye-yarn?
- Will the camp cafeteria stock and reheat microwave French fries for me?
- Should I pack extra pencils in case camp doesn't have a pencil sharpener?
- What if I'm the only one without a bra? Should I steal some of Dad's Ace bandages for a DIY bra?

Everything went into Dad's old suitcase. In the 80s, all luggage took the form of The Suitcase, which was essentially an over-sized briefcase. Dad's suitcase was lined with dirty taupe satin, protecting my delicate unmentionables (scratchy cotton briefs printed with the name of the week). After a dozen repackings, my parents packed me into the Chevy Cavalier wagon and we headed to Camp Sue Osprey.

I had not yet seen many teenagers. (A reminder that my everyday social circle, up until that point, was largely limited to Cabbage Patch Kids.) My teen camp counselor, Jessi, was 80s beautiful: big brown eyes with eager lashes, legs as tall as me, and the most perfectly curled bangs I had ever seen and ever will. She had the artificial-nice but slightly cold presence that I associate with traditionally attractive white girls. I gripped Dad's suitcase in one hand and kept one palm safely on our Chevy Cavalier wagon as she approached. Jessi towered over my child-troll body. My shoulders loosened when she knelt down, parting her mauve lips to reveal brilliant teeth. "Hi, Melanie! You're the first to arrive for Brown Owl cabin," she said, squeezing my shoulder. Poor Jessi. She was at this stage unaware that I was about to become the bane of her camp-counseling existence. Over the next week, when anxiety hit, my only comfort would lie in clutching her tanned forearm and staring at her perfectly permed Sun-In-kissed hair.

Slowly, a group of six girls assembled. Most of the girls have faded in my mind—except for a girl named Anna, who in ret-rospect I think had a crush on me. And Jessi. And probably on most of the girls in our cabin. With her pixie hair and an ever-present backwards cap, I labeled her a tomboy, because I had no idea that lesbians were a thing. One of my best friends from my AT (academically talented) class at school, Lisa Fowler, was also at camp, but unfortunately, she was not placed in my cabin. Lisa had enviably long blonde hair—enough for a killer French braid—and a gap in her front teeth that caused a very slight lisp. Lisa and I were tight. In 4th grade I caught plantar warts from her and generally loved to watch her chew. She chewed like a beautiful Jersey cow, her mouth making slow, clockwise circles. Lisa's bedroom had a large, doublewide full-length mirror. When I went to her house to play, she locked her door so we could stare at our naked bodies, giggling in utter confusion and wonder. Once, she pointed out that my "thing" was hanging out.

(Henceforth, I tuck my clitoris to this day.)

Drop-off was late afternoon, so after a tour of the camp and bunk assignments, it was time for dinner. In a large shiplap-lined cafeteria, I ate a respectable amount of food. Pasta with meat sauce, an apple, a blue and white carton of 2% milk, organized neatly on a melamine tray. My cabinmates giggled throughout the meal. Jessi told a story about a high school boy. She heavily inflected key words.

"He has a *Camaro,* which *I* think is kind of like, show-off, you know?"

We nodded.

"And like, he used to have really *loooong* hair when he went to Catholic school, but when he came to *Chardon,* he cut it all off."

More fervent nods.

"But, I *love* him, you know? We will probably get married in a few years."

Jessi's life, her face, her boyfriend, her teeth, her bangs—she was *perfect*.

I observed everyone else in the cafeteria quietly, mentally ranking how attractive I was amongst all of the girls, and scouting the cute boys. I was prepared for camp to be a brutal meat market, the 5th grade equivalent of *Road House*. I also generally preferred observation to conversation, particularly with new humans.

After dinner ended and all the trays had been dropped with a clatter in the kitchen window, we were marched out of the cafeteria and across camp to a well-fed bonfire. An alpha male counselor with a blonde crew cut and wisps of peeking chest hair shouted over the din of early pubescent squeaking. It was a song, with the counselors repeating each line after him.

The other day
I met a bear.
Out in the woods
A way out there.
The other daaaay I met a beaarrrr, out in the wooods a way out therrrre.

We sat around the fire in a neat circle. My legs began to itch. I was grateful for the group singing. Much easier than actual conversation. I stared at the base of the bonfire where the embers glowed red. A quiet stress tickled my brain. I realized I wouldn't be going home tonight. I would go back to a crowded cabin and would be forced into interacting with six other humans. Homesickness washed over me. It was not unlike the brief wave of fear I would feel nearly a decade later, on my first day at college. I didn't really miss my family or my few friends. I missed my bedroom and its locking door—its comforting promise of solitude and safety.

That night I was restless. I was too pee-shy to go at our last opportunity before lights out. I willed my urethra to open the fuck up, but it stubbornly refused. Camp rules dictated that a counselor was required to accompany us to the lav during the night, but I felt guilty about waking Jessi and instead wove my legs tightly together all night, stifling my angry bladder. I could hear the other campers breathing. I knew that something was wrong with me because they could sleep and I could not. My thoughts raced:

Could this be a brain tumor, making it impossible for me to sleep?

No, it's probably just that I have to pee.

God I have to pee so much. What if my pee smells funny in the morning and everyone notices?

What if I fall asleep and pee my pants?

What if Jessi announces to all of camp that I peed my pants?

No, I've never peed my pants at night. It will be OK.

BUT I've never had to pee this bad. This might be different.

Who is snoring? I miss my stuffed elephant. If I had my stuffed elephant, I could pee on it and it would soak up all the pee.

By the third day of camp, I stopped eating altogether.

This was not unusual; most mornings, my brother and I both had such anxious knots before school that we couldn't ingest solid foods. By late elementary school, Mom discovered Carnation Instant Breakfast Drink, which we could actually force down our throats in the morning, only to subsequently suppress nervous, vitamin-fortified farts throughout the school day. But camp didn't have Carnation Instant Breakfast.

I stared at the cafeteria's shiplap walls, trying not to cry, and methodically ripping apart plain toast. I couldn't define exactly what I was afraid of: I just wanted to curl up in my bunk and bury my face into my pink sleeping bag alone, maybe with a comforting Sweet Valley Twins book. Instead of eating during camp breakfasts, I ruminated[2].

What if they make me play sports today?

What if I have to poop during sports?

What if I am required to swim in the POND? (They called it a lake, but it was small and cold and slimy and I knew a goddamn pond when I saw one.)

After my non-breakfast, Brown Owl cabin joined a few other cabins to play Prison. Prison is like dodgeball, but when people are tagged out with the ball, they go to "Prison" behind the opposing team. They can escape from Prison via the assistance of a brave teammate, who must shuffle undetected across enemy lines and run, holding hands with the inmate, back to safety. It is violent and provides heartbreaking opportunities for ostracization. I can't tell you how many times I languished in prison because my nerd friends were too physically weak and frightened to rescue me, and/or no boys wanted to hold my hand. Despite this, I enjoyed a good game of Prison, because it's not really sports and I liked the way dodgeballs smell. Having unsuccessfully convinced Jessi to let me go back to nap in my bunk, I resigned myself to the game.

AND THEN.

---

2. After decades of practice, I have become a champion ruminator. There is no rational argument that I cannot outworry. Just try. Someday, Individual Freestyle Worrying will become an Olympic sport and it will all pay off.

A VERY IMPORTANT THING HAPPENED.

Like a newborn infant, I can be distracted from my anxiety when something shiny is dangled in front of me. The shiny thing *most effective* against inner-facing nihilism was boys.

The Prison game became heated. Dodgeballs were flying like fireworks. My competitive nature and desire to look tough in front of the boy campers briefly usurped anxiety, propelling me into playing with effort. I targeted the weakest-looking girls. *Skinny arms? Vulnerable. BLAMMO.*

There was suddenly a boy in front of me. I recognized him from my earlier visual survey of eligible pre-teen bachelors in the cafeteria. His olive skin gave off a sexy Chachi vibe. He had dark hair, dark eyes a tantalizing Mediterranean aura.

Now he was standing in front of me, staring intently from just across the boundary separating my team from his. At me! Like a good deferential female, I looked down awkwardly at the patch of clover at my feet.

PHWAP! The side of my face burned from the impact of textured rubber, and I fell to the ground.

"OUT!" screamed the skinny-armed girl I'd taken down earlier, who had escaped from Prison to take her vengeance. *Bitch,* I thought, splayed awkwardly like a downed rodeo clown. My glasses had flown off my face and I awkwardly felt around the grass for them.

And then, a fucking miracle. The Mediterranean boy *crossed* the team boundary line, a *cardinal sin* in Prison, making one immediately out—to help me to my feet.

"Thanks," I uttered awkwardly, my hand flying up to cover my rapidly swelling face. He bent over and plucked my glasses from the ground. I stared at his remarkably clean fingernails.

He smiled silently, and we jogged back separately to our

respective Prisons. My feet felt light; my generic Keds floated through the damp grass. Despite being in the line of fire, he continued to catch my eye. He was looking. AT. MEEEE.

For the next hour, all my anxiety pissed right away. The climax of every romantic comedy I had seen (*Mannequin, Overboard, Coming to America*) flashed before my eyes as my brain pulsed with the power of impending courtship. This was my drug; I had found it. This is what could temporarily quell the scaries. BOYS. For one blissful hour, I was happy. Instead of palpitating, my heart danced to the reverb of Jefferson Starship's "Nothing's Gonna Stop Us Now" which throbbed in my cerebral cortex and flowed down into my nerves. We made eye contact approximately eight times.

During the relative peace of a group nature walk after the game, I found Lisa Fowler and dragged her to the back of our group to whisper furtively. (I could not have cared less about trees.)

"I SAW," Lisa whispered. She had not missed my many pointed looks each time the boy and I made eye contact.

"I wish I could remember what his hands felt like," I whispered. "Do you think we'll see him again?"

At the next bonfire, I thought, *he will find me. He will sit next to me, cross-legged, and our knees will touch. Suddenly, the counselors will offer free ice cream sandwiches to all. Everyone around the campfire will leave. He will look at me with those venison-brown eyes and say "I don't need an ice cream sandwich." He will take my head in his hands and put his lips on mine…*

Too young to identify the addictive drug that is the Pursuit of Men, I didn't realize the significance of the day's events. Like all drugs, however, it only lasts while it's in one's system. That evening, anxiety circled back, returning me to my diet of hand-pulled white bread.

———————————

By next morning I had devolved into downright grim. One of the most frustrating things about anxiety is how vague and diffuse it can be. Especially for a child. For reasons unknown to myself or my counselors, I couldn't force myself to do anything. I pushed myself through breakfast, unable to eat, with a terrible rot in the pit of my intestines.

What if I barf What if I barf What if I barf What if I barf

What if I barf then pee my pants What if I barf then pee my pants

My hands shook as I played with an unopened carton of milk. All I wanted was to be alone in bed. Being surrounded by strangers made the entire situation more difficult. I wished desperately that Lisa was in my cabin. A regular familiar face would certainly make me feel safer. I wasn't making any new friends at camp, withdrawing as much as I could from my cabinmates without causing a scene. I felt constant pressure to be "on"—to maintain some semblance of social normalcy. I was able to force minimal responses to other campers when they directly addressed me; otherwise, I quietly fretted and watched. The lack of control over my days gave me endless stress.

Playing with my milk carton, I listened to the camp director announce morning awards. The gleeful winners skipped to the front of the cafeteria to receive their brightly colored certificates.

"An award to Joey Collins for the best dive! From his counselor Sam."

"Lily Bontrager gets an award for helping clean up the arts and crafts cabin, from counselor Marie."

Their success only made me feel worse. *Why the hell did Lily Bontrager get to be happy when I was so miserable?* I began to cry silently for no real reason.

GET YOUR SHIT TOGETHER, LAFORCE. MAN UP. THIS ISN'T 5TH GRADE ANYMORE. THIS IS FUCKING CAMP. YOU SHOULD BE GETTING READY TO MAKE A KACHINA DOLL OUT OF A TOILET PAPER TUBE RIGHT NOW.

Over the course of my life, crying has become a great comfort. I hate that crying is such a social taboo because it's an excellent way to expel shitty feelings. When I was young, I hid tears more times than I could count. Anxiety builds up destructive adrenaline and cortisol in the bloodstream; literally pushing these shit hormones out of my swollen eye ducts is often the only way to make me feel better.[3] In adulthood, when my panic disorder peaked, I finally accepted crying in front of others because I sure as hell couldn't stop it. When I stopped being able to control my tears, it was a relief. Crying in front of another human can create a strong bond—a level of empathy and understanding that may not be possible when you are hiding.

Jessi, seeing my quiet tears, took pity on me, like a pathetic baby robin who had fallen from the nest. She pulled me aside after breakfast. "Do you want to hang out with me for a while?" she asked. I sniffled gratefully. "I just wish I could go home," I said.

---

3. Scientist Rose-Lynn Fisher (2017), inspired by her own period of traumatic tears, studied different types of tears under a microscope. She found that tears of joy, irritation, onion-chopping, and grief all had different structures. Onion tears looked like snowflakes, grief tears like a computer board, and laughing tears like a Jackson Pollock painting.

"If you decide you need to go home, you can," Jessi says. "But let's try to give it another day and see how you feel." I nodded. One more day. That felt manageable.

There are four cures for my anxiety.

1) Cute boys with no visible boogers, which had gotten me through at least six hours of camp.

2) Pharmaceutical and/or street drugs, which I was unfortunately too young to discover.

3) Crying so hard for so long that I have absolutely no adrenaline left to torment my brain.

4) THE THEATRE! (Said with a British accent and intensive arm gesturing.)

Jessi announced the camp talent show after lunch.

This was not a drill. Did you say…talent show? Let me crack my knuckles and prepare a stage event that will knock you on your fucking ass.

The world suddenly became a tolerable place to live again. Another enigmatic quality of anxiety is that it can ebb and flow with frustrating inconsistency, particularly when distractions ebb and flow. But let's not look a gift horse in the mouth. The announcement of the camp talent show was enough to make me forget all of my unexplained self-loathing, and at that moment I didn't really care why.

I love theater. I discovered this around kindergarten, at church, a place I generally hated. Sunday school and sermons were boring at best and terror-inducing at worst, what with all the sin-punishing-fires-of-hell talk. However, whenever a random cardigan-ed Sunday School teacher stuck me onstage for a reenacted Bible scene, I was in my element. I recognized the irony of being unable to stomach conversations with my peers, yet perfectly willing to take a microphone in front of a hundred people and pretend to be a leper.

I was going to fucking own this camp talent show.

Each cabin was to perform one act. Jessi took any guesswork out of a cabin debate and chose our talent.

Here's the thing about the 80s—the sexualization of children was not yet demonized. In fact, it was generally seen as downright *cute*. Nowadays you can't put lipstick on a 10-year-old without being turned in to social services, but back then you could dress young girls scantily and parade them around onstage for the sheer adorableness of it all. Thus, Jessi decided that our cabin's talent show piece was to be a lip-sync rendition of Karen Kamon's "Manhunt" from the iconic film *Flashdance*.

I'm goin' on a manhunt, turn it around!
Women have been hunted, now they're huntin' around
Manhunt, we all got the need!
The one that's been waitin' has taken the lead.

Brown Owl cabin embraced *Manhunt* perhaps a little too hard. Jessi howled as we twitched and gyrated our child hips. I like to think it was a slight, if not age-inappropriate, call for feminism from our juvenile loins. I channeled Tina Tech, tilting my chin down and looking seductively at the empty chairs lining the rehearsal hall. I was in the *zone*.

I'm going on a manhunnnnt, I'M OUT FOR THE KILL!

At the climax of the song, we finished with a gratuitous

open-arm twirl and simultaneously tossed our hairbrush microphones sassily upstage. Today, I still channel Tina Tech when I give work presentations to a roomful of researchers. (Minus the gyrating. Usually.)

I ate dinner that night. A bologna sandwich. Jessi gave me a hug. I powered through the next two days, eating a reasonable amount of powdered eggs and only crying six times.

———————————

On the last day of camp, *one more day left,* after lunch and before the talent show, we were allowed to nap. *This* was the camp activity I'd been waiting for all week. The best possible use of my time. But I couldn't sleep. Coated with sweat, I laid in my top bunk awake, frustrated. The cabin was humid and baked from late afternoon sun. My body began to twitch once again with adrenaline jitters.

I felt so confused. Anxiety was about as easy to predict as Pompeii. One minute I was a blossoming sex dancer, the next minute I was hiding alone on a mildewy lav toilet until some adult dragged me out.

Jessi eventually sensed me and stood next to my bunk until I opened my eyes.

"Melanie?"

"I'm awake," I said. I looked at her. Jessi was so tall that her eyes hovered above the metal bar of my bunk.

"Are you nervous for the talent show?"

"No," I said, squeezing my eyes tight again. "It will be fun." Was I nervous? Was that what was wrong? I wasn't sure.

"Let's get up," she said, "and we can all get ready for the talent show before dinner! Do you know what you're going to wear?"

Fucking obviously. I had mentally picked out my sexiest yellow tank top as soon as Jessi announced our talent.

Jessi smiled at me. "Want me to do your bangs?" she asked.

I brightened up. Grooming! I hadn't seen the Mediterranean boy in a few days, although I learned through Lisa over in Red Squirrel that his name was Ethan Parson. He was bound to be at the talent show. Within minutes, the cabin went from a roomful of post-nap groggy girls to a tornado of talent show outfits and rusty curling irons. Jessi's curling iron was one of the new skinny ones, about the diameter of a Magic Marker. I stood patiently for a half hour while Jessi curled my bangs. Some wisps of hair were wrapped up in the curling iron toward the crown of my head, other wisps were curled down. There was teasing with a pick. Spray. More teasing. Spray. Aerosol Rave hairspray coated my throat. (I am deeply convinced that 80s/90s hairstyles will ultimately give me cancer.) I coughed repeatedly, almost landing a hair pick to the eye.

"Oh, you're gonna like this," Jessi said, gently touching a final curl to test the heat of the iron. A final spray-tease-spray and she was done.

I turned to face my cabinmates through a cloud of chemicals. They *erupted* into applause over Jessi's art. Jessi put a hand-held mirror in front of my face. My bangs were a masterpiece. They sat gently atop my forehead like a dirty blonde bouquet of miniature roses. I even felt a little pretty, although I didn't love how my beautiful bangs kept getting caught in my blue plastic glasses.

At the camp reception hall, I fidgeted uncomfortably in a metal folding chair, performance anxiety replacing the vague feeling of dread that had been my shadow all week. I watched a cabin of boys tell knock-knock jokes, and then a duo of counselors perform awkward improvised comedy. When it was nearly time for our act, we quietly shuffled out of the hall to behind the stage. Jessi allowed us all a dab of her mauve lipstick. I stared at the checkered linoleum floor and rehearsed the moves in my head. We were all sweating. It was another hot, humid day, and with a hundred campers and counselors packed into the hall, I felt a bit faint. And then it was time.

Unlike rehearsals, when the brightest stage lights are kept off and you can see everything in the room, the blinding glare of spotlights during a performance causes the stage to feel otherworldly, almost ethereal. The inability to see more than two inches in front of your face quells the nerves—like performing into a heavenly void. Sometimes the heat from the lights stokes the scent of everything around you—you can smell the wood in the floorboards and the metal in the rafters. A kinetic energy permeates the room. The quietest audience still manages to give off an energy that buzzes the blood in your veins. This entire sensory overload tricks your brain into moving almost without conscious thought. It sparks you to just sort of *go*. Something about this strange, celestial ambiance always calms me.

The camp director was the emcee. His outfit was the same RELAX T-shirt he had worn all week. Before each act, he tried to tell jokes. He slurred slightly, sounding like my dad after he came home from hanging out with the other prosecutors at the LuTucci's Bar & Lounge.

"Want to hear my pizza joke? Never mind, it's too cheesy. Okay guys- I know it's hot in here and you have been very patient, but you need to quiet down."

"Quiet down."

"Quiet down."

"OK, this is our last act. We have Brown Owl Cabin…and they will be performing Mandunt? Mandunt. ManHUNT. Let's give them a hand!"

An insufferable pause hung while we waited for the cassette tape to cue up. Finally, the music started and we shouted, "1,2,3,4!" to begin our dance.

The adults in the room *ate it up*. Hooray for sexy tweens! I felt my bangs bounce on my forehead and sweaty hairspray ran into my eyes, burning. I didn't care. At the climax of *Manhunt*, I finally spotted Ethan the Mediterranean boy in the audience. He was looking at me directly! He was smiling! In retrospect, probably most of the boys in the audience had their first boners. God bless *Flashdance*.

———————————

When I woke up the next morning, hallelujah bells chimed in my head. This was it. My parents would be here this afternoon. No more lonely nights in a bunk, crying silently and listening to my cabinmates masturbate.

At breakfast, I felt good enough to eat an apple and piece of bread. The cabin director read the daily awards, and suddenly I heard my name.

"An award to Melanie LaForce, from her counselor Jessi, for eating food and staying at camp!"

I walked to the front of the cafeteria as campers applauded politely. It was a nice gesture, but I was wildly aware that I had just been given the most pussy award possible. Other kids got awards for actually *doing something*, and I got an award for basically not dissolving into a lump on the floor. But still. It was the last day. I made it. I didn't fail out of camp.

But alas, camp sucked. Despite a few silver linings, all of my pop culture preparation had failed me. It was an unambiguously terrifying life event. I did subconsciously learn a lot about myself that week. I learned how severe my anxiety could be, and I learned some of my favorite coping mechanisms. I learned the power of the Y chromosome and the power of the stage. It was the first time I had ever had to fend for myself. And if I've learned anything about anxiety over the years, it's that I always survive it. As long as there's *Flashdance* in the world, everything will ultimately be okay.

3

MATERNITY WARD

A surefire way to ensure you will never want children is to volunteer at a hospital maternity ward during your most vulnerable, formative years. I recommend that all young vagina owners consider spending four hours a week serving soup to brand-new moms.

When I was 12, I wanted some work experience to prepare me for a job. I knew there would come a time to compete with other teens for elusive convenience store cashier positions, and I wanted a leg up. Volunteering at the local hospital was one of few ways to achieve this, plus it was an opportunity to do some good.[1] I became a candy striper at Lake East Hospital in downtown Painesville. Candy-striping felt like a super old-school Midwest tradition even then. I had to wear all white clothes and a borrowed red and white vertical-striped smock—hence the name. Volunteers were required to commit to one four-hour shift each week and had zero control over placement. When I interviewed, the volunteer coordinator mentioned that there might be a coveted Maternity Ward position available. The Maternity Ward was the Cadillac of hospital volunteer

1. Prior to this, the only opportunities I'd had to "do good" included proselytizing under the guise of Christmas caroling. Because that's how organized Christianity rolls.

assignments: less death, objectively better odor. Plus, cute babies!

On my first night in the Maternity Ward, I received a set of strict rules:

1. You can't feed the babies.
2. You can't hold the babies. (I totally did once.)
3. You can't touch the babies at all. (I totally did on a number of occasions.)

It is widely accepted in current times that newborn babies are a Cthulhu level of ugly. When they hit three or four months old, they graduate to the cuteness equivalent of a bearded tamarin monkey or pygmy hippopotamus. But newborns are firmly in otherworldly sea monster territory. When I first visited the nursery, I asked one of the nurses "where the cute babies were." She laughed but did not explain further, so I assumed that everyone in my town just produced distinctly ugly babies. I figured it was probably because of Lubrizol, the chemical plant in Painesville that my mom also blamed for her thyroid and breast cancers. Regardless, I made a mental note to move to a different town prior to procreation.

My shifts were Friday evenings. Middle school had very limited extracurricular activities, namely sports. I wasn't into that, so Friday nights my schedule was generally open. A four-hour shift (even with a 30-minute meal break), however, was a *fucking eternity*. It was the first time I had ever done "work," and quite frankly, work was not winning me over. Most of my role entailed folding laundry (burp cloths, receiving blankets) and putting "take-home" bags together for new moms. Take-home bags contained items that had been donated by corporations

(Tylenol, a few disposable diapers, sample size butt wipes) with the occasional strange element like dog food or canned tuna.

It was boring, so I would touch the babies. The nursery usually contained anywhere from five to ten babies. The babies, safely organized like little human Matrix pods in plastic cribs, were constantly being left unattended for a few minutes at a time. When a nurse ducked out to visit the neighboring supply closet, I could sneak in and prod them gently. I was careful not to touch their skin, which somehow felt too taboo. I was never caught. Once, after I had been volunteering for a few weeks, a nurse allowed me to hold a baby. She made me sit in one of the hospital chairs, and I held the baby for about 38 seconds. It was underwhelming and made my arms tired.

My other task involved organizing meal trays for dinner and delivering them to new moms. This task required a tiny amount of actual brain use. Most of the women had meals assigned to them, but when they didn't, I had to put together a tray based on the food products in the ward fridge. Some women were on liquid diets only. Other women were on *clear* liquid diets. They couldn't even have red Jell-O. They could only have broth, ginger ale, or yellow Jell-O. Once I got to be on shift when my best friend Mindy's mom had her fifth and final baby. She was clearly in a lot of pain and very exhausted. Mindy's mom was put on a clear liquid diet, but she begged me to smuggle her in a Diet Coke. I felt terrible, for this was the woman who had fed me Kix and cleaned my vomit and let me sleep under her roof on at least a hundred occasions. But I refused, because I didn't fully understand the clear diet and was afraid that a Diet Coke might kill her.

Most of the new moms were incredibly nice and often asked me simple questions, like what grade I was in, or if I liked working at the hospital. Rarely, a new father would tip me for delivering food. Usually a dollar. I never asked anyone if it was OK to accept the money because I really wanted to keep it. The dads always seemed awkward and confused, trying their best to do everything they should be doing. Or sometimes there weren't dads. Many moms had no one there with them. Some of them cried, I assumed out of pain.

That was what scared me the most: the crying and the pain. Some moms could stand up and use the bathroom, but others had to use *bedpans*. For having a baby! That alone was enough to turn me off. I also became vividly aware of the amount of blood after childbirth. I spotted giant, blood-soaked maxi pads in corner garbage cans, sometimes with what looked like small intestines clinging to them. One time a young mom was walking down the hall in her gown, barefoot. She walked very, very slowly like she had just ridden a horse, leaving a trail of blood behind her. "Oops, I blooded!" she said to me, smiling. I tried to smile back but was screaming internally.

All of this for those ugly babies? It was definitely not worth it. I began to wonder what all the fuss over the maternity ward was about. Maybe I would've been a better fit somewhere else, somewhere with less genital bleeding. I met another candy striper on my way in for a shift once, and she asked if I wanted to have a meal break together. I didn't but felt bad saying no. It turns out she worked on a long-term care ward. In other words, cancer.

"Sometimes they smell like poop," she whispered to me over steamed broccoli and baked chicken in the cafeteria. "And they moan all the time."

I felt sad for her and wondered aloud what it would be like to find out that one of the patients had died.

She shrugged. "Sometimes someone is just gone the next week, and you don't know if they got released or if they died. But most people don't get released." Her response made me feel faint. I felt that she was doing a far nobler volunteer job than my inappropriate prodding of newborns.

I only volunteered for four months, the minimum required commitment. A blip in my pre-teen years that lingered only in my long-term fear of childbirth.

The only other part I remember was actually my favorite aspect of candy-striping. If things were slow and babies were unavailable for scrutiny, I would go into a vacant hospital room, shut the door, and spin around in circles. The vacant rooms were totally empty, as beds and equipment were all transported from the delivery room when a new patient came in. I felt safe in the empty room, away from all the people and whirring and beeping and crying and blood. It was almost as pleasant as retreating to my bedroom. The empty rooms were very clean. Often I would pretend that it was my grown-up apartment, and I would mentally decorate it. A nice table by the window, a kitchen catty-corner from the bathroom. Maybe a sofa bed so my mom could visit.

I knew I wasn't supposed to pee in the vacant room bathrooms, because they needed to be clean for the next patient. But sometimes I did. It was decadent.

4

ALGEBRA IS A PESTILENCE

When I graduated with a Ph.D. at age 28, I looked myself in the mirror.

"You did it," I told myself.

"I know," my reflection whispered back, joyful tears shining in her eyes under a rented maroon doctoral cap.

"We never have to take another math class again," I said to her, trembling with borderline disbelief.

"Promise?" she asked.

"I swear to you," I said grimly. "I will never do that to you again."

She paused.

"Unless for some reason we got paid a lot of money to do it," she countered. "Or like, we could take a math class on a remote Portuguese island. But we don't get graded, and the class is taught by a hot mythical centaur that we get to have sex with."

"OK," I agreed.

Portuguese Island Centaur Math 1 is not yet an offering, so I have managed to avoid as much new math learning as possible. This is not an easy feat given my line of work, which is inherently quantitative. I am an education researcher at a Fancy University. I also sometimes teach social psychology at another Equally Fancy University. More dedicated academics take special regression discontinuity or hierarchical linear modeling seminars. (These phrases alone set off my gag reflex.) LOL, what suckers! I stumble through what I can, cite whoever I can, and ask someone smarter than me to do the rest of the work. This is how the weak but manipulative survive.

When took my first timed test as a child, I was immediately stricken with Math Sickness. It is well known that timed tests were developed by adults solely to prevent kids from ever truly feeling at ease. Timed tests were designed to be given after recess to ensure that students' spirits were sufficiently broken, and they would thus be well-behaved for the remainder of the school day. School was not intended to be *fun*. Enjoyed that game of dodgeball, did ya? Here, let's give you 90 math problems to solve in four minutes, that should take the wind right out of your sails. Timed tests also do not pair super well with anxiety disorders.

Math Sickness metastasized to Stage II in 5th grade, when I had the most unforgiving teacher in all of elementary school in the history of the universe. Mrs. McCloud was in her 50s with an unnaturally delicate sparrow-like body. She was as stern and forced as her post-beehive hairstyle, an early predecessor of "Can I speak to the manager?" hair. Like any good demon, Mrs. McCloud disguised herself with a different cardigan each day. She had clearly engaged in a deep level of sorcery to convince the district she qualified as a school teacher. I imagined how she must've cloaked her tiny, feathered imp body with a soft taupe chenille cardigan and suppressed her horns beneath her plastic wig just long enough to interview with the principal. Mrs. McCloud always paired her cardis with conservative calf-length skirts, under which she certainly hid a forked tail. I watched her skirt *swish, swish, swish* as she click-clacked with heavy block heels around the classroom.

Mrs. McCloud was a huge disappointment for all of us in class, having just come from two years with the delightful Mrs. Stirling. Unlike Mrs. McCloud, Mrs. Stirling resembled a human woman who let us perform scenes from *Macbeth*, lip-sync to George Michael for talent shows, and even held a screening of the movie *Innerspace* where we got to see Dennis Quaid's naked butt. (The last was easily the most profound learning experience of our elementary careers.) We left Mrs. Stirling spoiled and with high hopes for 5th grade. Again, interspersing a kind and innovative teacher with Mephistopheles may have just been another strategy for the school district to break our spirits.

A key strategy for preventing math stomachaches (one of the most common symptoms of math sickness) was to completely tune out the lesson. The secret to enduring math and other horrible life events, I learned early, was blissful avoidance. I accomplished this by hiding *Sweet Valley Twins* books under my desk and reading them when Ms. McCloud began to drone about fractions. This went on successfully for months and I was quite proud of my creative genius. It worked perfectly as long as I remembered to look up *just frequently enough* that I appeared to be paying attention. Alas, it was a sweet temporary denial, for never in the history of the universe has a young child survived when up against Satan. One fateful day I became too absorbed in Jessica and Elizabeth Wakefield's crusade to rid Sweet Valley Middle School of a terrible bully, and forgot to look up at the board for a solid five minutes.

I felt a tight silence cast over the room. A split second of elephant-like pressure on my chest gripped me before the screaming started. Mrs. McCloud had caught me. Incensed, she march-clacked over to my desk with a stream of angry word salad.

"ARE YOU READING THAT PINK BOOK MATH CRIT-ICAL HONOR FRACTIONS DISRESPECTFUL GIFTED NOTHING IDIOCY?" she screamed. Snatching my beloved paperback, she threw it to the floor, stamping a block heel right through Jessica Wakefield's face.

I was a child master in averting my eyes at the first sign of any conflict, but even so, I swear I saw her irises flicker from hazel to bloody red. She raged for eternity[1], hovering danger-ously above my miniature desk, steam emanating from her bird body. It was utterly humiliating, worse even than that time the previous year when I slightly pooped my pants while running a quarter mile from the bus stop to my house. What the ever-loving hell had I been thinking? I had awakened a rage in Mrs. McCloud so deep that the other kids were stunned, unable to even shuffle their papers awkwardly and look away. They stared wide-eyed.

I somehow managed that day, probably through the grace of some heavenly interceder, to suppress the heaviest tears until I got home. A few lone droplets trickled down my right cheek, but I loathed to give that monster the satisfaction of total breakdown.

Other days, I was not so lucky. Fifth grade was absolutely plagued with timed tests, no doubt the doing of the Evil One Disguised as Amateur Golf Enthusiast. Or perhaps fifth grade was a weedout grade. Any kids who failed fifth grade would be sent to the steel mill.

---

1. In fifth grade time this is about two minutes.

On yet another day in an endless stream of shitty 5th grade days, Mrs. McCloud gave us a timed test for decimals. Fractions get all the buzz for being difficult, but decimals are equally heinous—or worse. Decimals wait secretly in the wings until you think you've left fractions safely behind. When the start buzzer went off, I had my first conscious panic attack. My heart burned and my brain froze. I stared at the page, completely unable to transcend terror to concentrate on the problems. I didn't understand why I just couldn't process what was in front of me. The blue carbon-copy numbers may as well have been written in Early Cyrillic. That day, the panic would not allow me to suppress tears. I fell into hysterics so dramatic that the whole test had to be stopped. I shuddered violently; waterworks soaked my sleeves and left snail-snot trails over my not-quite-yet-developing breasts. Kids stared at me, horrified, assuming that I was having a cataclysmic seizure. Rather than interrupt the class to support me, God forbid, the horrible Mrs. McCloud's eyes flashed red briefly and in a terrifyingly calm voice, she sent me to the principal's office. Despite the mortification of being sent away, I was so relieved to be fleeing the evils radiating in that classroom that I ran.

The principal, Mrs. Benin, immediately received me upon seeing my crazed face. Mrs. Benin had salt and pepper hair, cut not unlike Mrs. McCloud's, but appeared profoundly more kind. Mrs. Benin's eyes crinkled warmly even when she wasn't smiling, giving her a pervasive sense of welcome. As my hysterics continued, Mrs. Benin scrunched up next to me on a tiny child's chair and held my hand. She told me that there is a thing called "math anxiety" and all kinds of kids *and* adults could have it. She was a wonderful human being. Years later, I heard that Mrs. Benin got breast cancer and died at an unreasonably young age. Heartbreaking. I didn't typically have much interaction with principals over the course of my school career. Mrs. Benin was a gift, and somehow her comfort got me through the rest of the year more or less unscathed.

Sixth and seventh grade math passed relatively uneventfully. Math in middle school was no picnic, but the timed tests had dwindled in frequency. I managed to press on under the tutelage of less-evil teachers, and even earn the occasional B.

Until eighth grade. In eighth-grade they funneled the honors kids into algebra. Even my therapist knows all about eighth grade math; I hope that she writes a book and saves masses of children forever from the sheer *pestilence* that is algebra. I had thought nothing could top fifth grade, that I had left the worst math sickness behind me. Certainly, transitioning from a child to a young teen gave me some sense of control and maturity. I no longer feared that math might actually kill me. However, algebra probably came closer to killing me than any binge-drinking college blackout.

Susan Nelson taught honors eighth-grade algebra. She was the only teacher I ever had to call "Ms.;" the others were strictly Mrs. or Miss. Ms. Nelson had crunchy yellow platinum curls and a round face ripe with acne scars. It was widely known that her boyfriend was Mr. Schneider, the honors 9th grade history teacher. This was a thrilling scandal for our middle school, because Mr. Schneider's ex-wife Mrs. Schneider also taught there! Mrs. Schneider remained Mrs. Schneider even though they had divorced. I never had Mrs. Schneider, though my brother did and thought she was quite pleasant.

Ms. Nelson was not the type of person who would ever want to be known as Mrs. Schneider, even if she ever married Mr. Schneider (which she did, years later). It seemed to suit her just fine to date a coworker (and fellow coworker's ex-husband), all while maintaining her own nomenclature. Mr. Schneider and Ms. Nelson ate lunch together, walked the halls together, and even attended the occasional school function together. It was no big deal to them, but I always wondered how Mrs. Schneider felt. Had there been an affair? Was she trapped into her pension? Did she harbor deep resentment for algebra? All the kids craved secret drama.

If Mrs. Schneider did harbor a deep resentment for algebra, she and I had something in common. One day early in the fall, at the end of a lesson, I asked Ms. Nelson if we could write a journal entry about the assignment instead of actually solving the equations. Ms. Nelson shook her head at me in sheer disbelief.

"Oh, Melanie," she said. "You are the most right-brained person I've ever met."

A self-defined thespian and writer, I took it as a compliment, although in retrospect she clearly meant "Girl, you suck at math." But I generally liked Ms. Nelson. She talked to kids like adults, arming herself with a constant biting but not unkind sarcasm. It worked well on stupid teenagers.

The kids in my class were no help when it came to algebra. Tutoring in my childhood was a concept that only existed for very rich and simultaneously very stupid kids. Most of the kids in my class were smarter than me, but I was neither rich nor stupid. My classmates were the "gifted" and "A.T." (academically talented) kids I had grown up with. There was Jill Thompson, who later fought a brutal battle to become valedictorian and was crushed when she landed salutatorian. There were James Berton and Gene Moore, who cheated constantly[2]. James became my boyfriend in 10th grade; we had epic public fights at my locker. Jessica Mayer and Kristin Ackerman were so quiet that I never felt like I knew them. They played brass instruments. There was Ashley Wolf, who was far too pretty to be as smart as she was, and thus a constant source of jealousy for me. And finally, my closest friends: Mindy Quinn and Kate Kupstas. While we were in some ways a tight-knit orb of nerds who came of age together, I was typically known as the loud one, and not ever the smart one. My frame of reference was all these advanced kids, so I constantly felt myself at the bottom rung of the intelligence ladder.

Especially in eighth grade algebra.

I slogged through equation after equation like a tour of Vietnam, managing to horrifically maim each one yet never fully annihilate it; I left them to languish and die slowly on the page. I could identify patterns in what solutions were right and wrong, but could never fully comprehend their rules. To this day, I can pull off statistics, but when I need to actually write an equation for a federal grant proposal, I pass it to the student workers, who are far more eager to bury their faces in notation. Why does every goddamn symbol have to have three associated symbols attached to it? Why are they all in Greek? Wait, is this one supposed to be superscript or subscript gamma? WHY CAN'T I JUST WRITE WORDS IN A PARAGRAPH LIKE A HUMAN BEING? LANGUAGE IS WHAT DISTINGUISHES US FROM THE APES, FOR FUCK'S SAKE.

Every Monday morning, ye olde math stomachaches came back 'round. My math sickness had not been this significant

---

2. Really, they were the smartest. If I'd had the guts to cheat my psyche probably would've been a lot calmer. Moral of the story: JUST CHEAT, KIDS! Math is not worth the stress.

since Mrs. McCloud, but in 8th grade progressed to a potentially fatal Stage IV. On days when my symptoms were moderate, I was pushed into going to school. It was not uncommon for my brother and me to be sent to school with a sandwich baggie full of Tums and the ever-present "You'll be fine." Mom knew we could do it if we just showed up. She thought we were beautiful geniuses. And she was usually right: While it was sometimes difficult, her attitude is one of the reasons I fought through anxiety all those shitty-ass years.

"I'm not smart enough at algebra," I would tell Mom. "I bet I would do much better in all my other classes if I could drop math."

"You are so smart," my mom would reply, shaking her head. She dumped a packet of Carnation Instant Breakfast into a plastic cup. "Drink your breakfast and go to school."

Usually, I could only manage a half cup. Algebra class was right after lunch, too, so often my stomach was too knotted to eat then either. It's no wonder I was so skinny that year. (The algebra diet would do wonders for Hollywood awards season prep.)

Eighth-grade algebra was so vicious that I could regularly exaggerate my discomfort enough to be allowed to miss school on several occasions each semester. I became a master manipulator to an extent that I didn't even recognize in myself.

"I really, really just don't feel good," I would say.

(It wasn't a *total* lie; I definitely had a stomachache. I just also maaaaybe happened to have an algebra quiz that day.)

"HOW don't you feel good?" my mom would ask.

(Parents ask this question a lot. It means they recognize you are full of shit.)

"My stomach hurts."

"You don't have a fever."

"I never get fevers."

(Pause.)

"It's really bad," I would say.

She then squinted at me, half concern and half skeptical appraisal. "Are you *really* sick enough to miss school?"

"I just don't wanna go."

"I shouldn't let you do this again."

(Silence. Sometimes silence was the best manipulator.)

"OK. You can stay home."

Deep down Mom knew something emotional was going on, but in the early 90s she didn't have an extensive mommy blogosphere to tell her what it was. Like clockwork, as soon as I was granted permission to miss school, my stomachache miraculously disappeared and I would watch Katie Couric raze politicians and judge spring fashions on *The Today Show* until noon. I did feel guilty and stressed about missing school. But the memory of an anxious kid is short, and every time the math sickness came back around again, I was convinced that it was legitimate.

After calling in sick on a Monday for at least the third time in the fall semester, I showed up for algebra class on Tuesday and settled in for an hour of semi-cognizant battle.

Suddenly, shock and dismay. The enemy launched a surprise attack.

"Take out a plain sheet of paper," Ms. Nelson said forcefully. "We're having a quiz."

A FUCKING POP QUIZ. I was wholly unprepared. My hand trembled as a fumbled through my desk for a reasonably sharp pencil. My palms began to sweat and the desk lid crashed down.

"Factor this equation," she said. "$36x^2 + 120x + 100$."

DID SHE SAY X SQUARED? We never had to factor exponents before.

Where the hell was this coming from? I put my head down—violent nearsightedness had trained me to position the paper an inch from my eyeballs—and started solving the parts I knew. I showed my work. Then I showed my work some more. If there was one thing I could do, it was show my work. I could scribble on and on for pages, perhaps mixing in a bit of Marx or Nietzsche with my multiplication if it made my work seem more complete. "X times Y over C but only if C truly exists but like really how can we know if anything truly exists?" I showed about a half page of work but couldn't come up with a solution.

"Number. Twooooo." Ms. Nelson went on dramatically, "Factor $18x^3 + 3x^2 - 6x$."

I gulped. Completely flummoxed, I dared to question the content.

"Um, where is this from?" I asked innocently. *Certainly,* we hadn't covered this yet. There had to be some mistake.

"It's in. Your Notes. Melanie." Ms. Nelson had a rhythmic way of speaking, each syllable punctuating the air like an ominous war drum.

I scrunched up my face to reveal my deep pain and turned my head down to my paper to show more work. I divided and multiplied and added some random letters and numbers together. My temples warmed as I realized that, at best, I could scrounge up a 30% on this quiz, maybe, if I wrote enough bullshit on the paper and then annotated it in the margins. I frantically tried to force my brain to understand.

The silence was suddenly punctuated by a large boom. Like a cannon, James Berton shouted:

"PSYCH!!!"

The rest of the kids erupted in laughter. James was doubled over. I looked around, confused. Gene Moore laughed so hard that he fell out of his chair.

"There's no quiz." I stated it as a fact, but with hope.

"There's no quiz," Ms. Nelson said, smiling mischievously. The entire class had been in on the prank. This was their way to "teach me a lesson."

My therapist was horrified when I recounted this story a few years ago. She expressed disbelief that a certified teacher would go along with an entire room of adolescents to pull such a cruel prank. That my friends of many years, who knew my neuroses better than even my parents, could mock me in such a soul-crushing way. But when I had realized the prank, I felt only respite from the terror of not knowing how to factor with exponents. Relief washed over me and covered my insides like a shot of whiskey. I didn't care that the entire class had gathered to mock my math sickness and constant absences. I felt only gratitude that the quiz itself, so much like *The Taming of the Shrew* that we were reading in English class, was a farce. I may have even felt a bit popular. That I was enough of a "thing" to make a "thing" out of.

I got a D that semester. Finished the year with a C minus average. They pulled me out of honors math the following year. I didn't complain.

5

UGLY

Let's talk about physical attractiveness and lack thereof.

I know this is a minefield. Many could say—because I've seen it said on the interwebs—that as an able-bodied white woman I have no business talking about feeling ugly. I disagree and maintain that self-perceived ugliness is equal-opportunity. I talk more about social comparison theory in Chapter 11 but essentially—we, as humans, develop perceptions of ourselves via comparison with others in our peer groups (i.e., your BFFs) and/or another largely accepted standard of beauty (i.e., Beyoncé). And as we all know, since time immemorial, women of the world have been comparing themselves to an unattainable and ever-shifting standard of beauty. The world as a whole currently expects us to look like a Kardashian-Jenner, with perfectly symmetrical facial features and the hip-waist ratio of a sexy flamingo. Many women, even the most seemingly beautiful, regularly feel like shit about their looks.

Contrast this with my husband, who has repeatedly told me that he is pretty sure he's in the top 5% of attractive humans. Oh, to be a white man.

So there. I'm justifying my right to talk about it. In retrospect, of course my childhood looks were fine. They were the looks of your very average kid. Take a gander at this seventh-grade photo. My lack of a smile is an attempt to hide my large crooked teeth while sporting the thickest glasses money could buy. The glasses and Cadillac-sized crooked teeth were most definitely the features I honed in on during my bouts of physical self-loathing. My family wasn't particularly helpful on this front.

Aunt Caren: "You've got teeth like my sister Connie."
Me: "I do?"
Aunt Caren: "I used to call her 'Chiclets.'"

This must be why I started grinding my teeth at night. I was subconsciously trying to wear them down.

I was called ugly to my face on plenty of occasions and cried alone in my room all the time about my looks. Once I was so vocally distraught over my appearance that Mom overheard me and intervened. I gave in, allowed her to see my vulnerability, and sobbed about how ugly I was.

Sandy LaForce is extremely quick-witted. In this situation, she knew exactly what I needed to hear. She knew that my rational brain would need objective evidence to convince me that I was not, in fact, grotesque.

"You think you're ugly? That's crazy," she said. "Look at the ugly girls in your class! Hannah Sonnenheim, Tanya Bingham. *Those* are the ugly girls."

I sniffed. "Really?" I asked through a pool of nasal mucus.

"Sara Roberts!" she added. "With those weird moles? You're not ugly at all compared to a lot of those girls."

For the next half hour, she detailed why so many of the girls in my class were uglier than me. I felt comforted. Even if I wasn't quite Miss Ohio, I wasn't the worst. It was, in my opinion, some of her best parenting ever.

Starting in second grade, I had this really pretty, cool friend named Ashley Wolf. We met after school at my Melridge Elementary latchkey program before we both transferred to the gifted class at Hadden Elementary. Ashley was new (she came from private school). I don't remember this initial meeting well, but Ashley says I gave her some sort of popsicle stick craft that she cherished until it fell apart after a year. Ashley had everything I didn't: money, long eyelashes, dance lessons, ice-skating lessons, a dope animal surname, and really cool Halloween costumes. She had curly brunette hair and dark facial features that made me feel downright spectral when I looked at myself next to her in a mirror. I loved Ashley very much, but she definitely highlighted my ugly. She was in the gifted class with me, but with her *Charlie's Angels* looks, managed to not be immediately classified by outsiders as a nerd.

Me and Ashley in her bedroom. (I borrowed her clothes.) I couldn't even get the hand position right.

Ashley always stole the show. Ashley, Mindy Quinn, and I performed the "Three Little Witches" in 3rd grade for our class, and Ashley was objectively the hottest child-witch this side of the Mississippi. That girl would've been an ace Mouseketeer-turned-Justin-Timberlake- backup-dancer had she not had the one fatal flaw of living in Ohio. During a talent show in third grade, she and I both performed dances. Well, mine was less of a "dance" and more of an awkward, bouncy lip-sync to Debbie Gibson's "Out of the Blue." The desks in our classroom were pushed to the side, creating a small stage next to Mrs. Stirling's desk. I wore my lucky (only) leotard and relied on my theat-ahh skills and large mouth to carry me through.

Ashley dressed in her finest brand name, slightly shimmery leotard over tights, and nonchalantly *killed* a dance performance to Madonna's "Into the Groove." She picked the cooler song, had the cooler look, and could spin in circles repeatedly without falling down. It was emotionally moving. The only performance that day to overshadow Ashley was Matt Applaun's leather-jacket-wearing, soulful, stationary lip-sync of George Michael's "One More Try."

Ashley and I went to the same high school and even the same college. In high school she was cheerleading captain. In college she danced for the award-winning Ohio University dance team. She never joined a sorority but managed to go to all their parties. Despite my jealousy, Ashley was nice enough to me that I never attempted to maim her, even after we pooled our money in 6th grade to purchase the "Like a Prayer" cassette tape, and she got to keep the original. (I had to keep the recorded copy.) She was chill, not remotely catty or patronizing, and didn't typically take sides in girl arguments amongst our circle of friends.

All the boys had crushes on Ashley. This was the most detrimental part of my perceived ugliness; we've established that I was (am) boy-crazy as all hell. Any given school year I bounced through at least a dozen crushes. None of the boys ever liked me back. At least, none of the good ones. None of the *athletes*.

Remember in *Can't Buy Me Love*, when Patrick Dempsey throws $1,000 at a gorgeous, popular cheerleader to make him cool? There's a series of tumults, and lo and behold, ultimately, he does get to be cool.

Consider also the underrated 1990s Tony Danza project, *She's Out of Control,* where Danza's daughter gets contacts and goes from nerd to Ace Babe overnight.

A similarly misogynist yet lovable *She's All That* finds that a girl can go from arthouse lame to prom court with the help of tight clothes and white male social capital. There's *Clueless's* Tai, *Mean Girls'* Cady, *Maid in Manhattan's* JLo. Shit, ugly-to-babe is even the premise of *The Princess Diaries.* Except Anne Hathaway not only gets to be cool *and* bone a hot Schwartzman, she also gets to inherit a fucking European country. Nerd-to-cool/ugly-to-babe makeover themes were particularly common across 80s and 90s movies.

They are a LIE.

There is no escaping the Ugly Orb. Lord knows I tried.

The summer after eighth grade, I finally got contact lenses. There are no words to describe how big of a moment this was for me. It was, in my opinion, the last remaining ugly holdover—I had gotten my braces off at the end of 7th grade. (My teeth were still the size of luxury sedans, but they were *straight.* Well, straight enough. Like Neil Patrick Harris in *Gone Girl.*) The first morning I put my contacts in on my own, it took me a half hour. My friend Heather Henlea had spent the night, and she patiently flipped through *Sassy* while I assaulted my eyeballs, attempting to get the tiny invisible lenses to stick. Once the contacts were finally in, my eye sockets were as pink as a chafed bikini line, but I couldn't believe how BIG my eyes were. After years of only being able to see my face through my thick, size-diminishing glasses, I believed I looked like a very sensual meerkat.

"Are these proportions weird?" I asked Heather. "Should my eyes look *this* big?"

"Your eyes are just, like, very normal," she said.

I didn't believe her. *I must begin researching petite modeling careers,* I thought. *I'm fucking gorgeous.* I was so excited to have my climactic makeover-reveal moment! Everything was about to change! I HAD GIGANTIC MOVIE STAR EYES.

I eagerly awaited going back to school that fall and having the boys line up daily at my locker. I picked out my first-day-back outfit to highlight the delicate worn-asphalt blue-grey hue of my ginormous eyeballs. The first day back sans goggles, I made direct eye contact with all the boys I typically considered far out of my league.

They continued to avoid my gaze like a dog that just pissed all over the kitchen floor.

I didn't understand it. I had lost the braces AND glasses—wasn't I pretty enough yet? Was I just branded as an ugly nerd who could never have access to the hottest dudes? Where was the equity in all of this? Instead of a scarlet letter A emblazoned on my chest, I had a scarlet letter U. And Ugly would forever be my lot in the universe.

It was true. For the remainder of time in the universe of the Painesville Township local school system, I continued to be undesirable to the opposite gender. I could occasionally get some boyfriends with a good old-fashioned nipple slip, but the only *really quality* dudes to like me were outside of my school system. I became that girl at school who talked about her boyfriend from theater camp—he really exists! I promise! But my dreams of landing *the* quarterback, or even *the* all-state 400-meter-dash champion, had faded.

Boys were my entire life, and I weighed my value nearly

100% in terms of whether or not they liked me and found me attractive. I cared much less about grades and jobs and even theater than I did about boys. Boys were all I ever talked about, all I ever thought about. I wanted so desperately to be pretty enough that boys liked me.

It was kind of sad.

Teens today have been more successfully raised with the message that they don't necessarily need to be hot or have a mate to succeed at life. We raise kids more and more to embrace the notion that success is about actual skills and abilities, like critical thinking, and making art, and being able to touch the tip of your tongue to the tip of your nose!

My good friend Renee, a bang-up social psychologist and author of the acclaimed book *Beauty Sick*[1], might not like how much real estate I've given to physical attractiveness in this chapter. Renee and I fight a lot about beauty. Her research has consistently shown that having a culture so focused on beauty is detrimental to women's self-esteem. I certainly agree with this to an extent, largely because the standards of beauty are so high in our society that it's difficult for most women to come close. Renee wants to see less societal focus on physical attractiveness as a whole. I also agree with this to an extent—particularly in contexts such as the workplace.

The problem with the concept of physical attractiveness is that it's rooted in evolution and thus largely inescapable. In a strictly Darwinian sense, our foremost goal as animals is to ensure the survival of our species—i.e., to bump uglies with the best possible mates. And we use physical features to identify the most fertile mates and healthy genes. This is a key reason

---

1. Engeln, R. (2017). *Beauty Sick: How the Cultural Obsession with Appearance Hurts Girls and Women.* HarperCollins.

that so much of our energy is devoted to romance and maximizing our physical attractiveness. Obviously, this is not the whole story. It doesn't neatly account for relationships other than strictly hetero. However, I feel comfortable saying that physical attractiveness a big part of sexuality in general.

For me, the biggest concern is that society has bastardized beauty standards to extremes. This is why women's waistlines are regularly Photoshopped to the edge of invisibility. In addition, attractive people consistently get benefits that less attractive people don't. (This is a major reason why Olympians are so goddamn hot. Classically hot people are fostered and supported over their whole lives to achieve this pinnacle of success. This is also why I hope that when I die, heaven is Naked Olympic Village.)

Rather than ignore physical attractiveness, I want to see society shirk the unreasonable standards we've come to embrace. There *are* self-esteem benefits that come with feeling attractive. The problem is that these are fleeting because you can only feel so hot for so long until you are confronted with yet another story about how a gaggle of Kardashians weighs only 98 pounds. In my ideal world, I would see a broad definition of beauty so that all women can maintain an appropriate, consistent level of feeling context-appropriate babelicious. I love *beauty*, but I hate *beauty standards*. Look at any *National Geographic* portrait spread and you will see the beauty inherent in the human condition. Let's get better about embracing all the beauty, not just the *Sports Illustrated* Swimsuit Edition beauty.

It's unreasonable to think that we can completely escape the power of physical attraction. It's just not how we are wired. Nature is a dick. This is why even the prettiest birds get the most play.[2] But we are, as humans, slowly taking away the narrowness (and thus unattainability) of beauty. We have a long way to go. But I dream of a world where little Melanie can feel just as gorgeous and confident as little Ashley. And well beyond.

I ran into Ashley last year at our high school reunion. She hasn't changed. She still has a beautifully symmetrical face and large, lash-lined eyes—the kind of face that looks like she had *really expensive* work done when she probably hasn't. Despite her beauty, Ashley didn't end up as a model or a brand ambassador for tequila. She doesn't even post selfies! Perhaps because Ashley was able to always be confident in her looks, she never had to think so much about them. Her lack of insecurity took up less space in her brain and allowed it to be full of other valuable information, like business things. (She's CEO of her own recruiting company.) And thus she feels less of a need to put her beauty in everyone else's face. Ashley and I talked about old times and I admitted to her that she'd always been my childhood standard of beauty. Ashley laughed and shared some of her own beauty woes, as well as the fact that her stunning looks led her to be bullied in high school by jealous girls. While I genuinely love to see the privileged suffer, Ashley certainly didn't deserve this. Getting shit for being pretty is as bad as getting shit for being ugly. We could all benefit from paying less attention to physical attractiveness as a measure of worth.

Now! Check out this hot selfie of me on a hotel toilet!

---

2. In birds, it's the ladies who get to call all the shots on mates. But I mean, just try to watch a bird of paradise (*Cicinnurus respublica*) do its mating dance without getting aroused. (Fanning self.)

6

THE MALL

The mall needs to make a comeback.

I know, I know—malls *do* still prosper in certain areas, like Dubai and Atlanta and holiday romcoms. Hell, it's even socially acceptable to go for exclusive foodie dinners at malls in L.A. But for much of the Midwest, the mall has fallen by the wayside. With the advent of online shopping, malls have become obsolete, vacant, and even a primary source of ironic art and photography—competing closely with Detroit's feral housing and dilapidated amusement parks for failed bastions of capitalism and/or systematic racism. IN THE FUTURE, the Midwestern malls could rejuvenate and perhaps even reinvent themselves in some sort of tech-y, South Korean-influenced space. Elite robots will perform makeovers and AI chimpanzees will pierce your ears for $500. However it happens, we need to get more teens into malls. If I can put on my old lady hat for a moment, I will say that teens spend too much time on screens and not enough time making out behind Sbarro dumpsters. Oral herpes rates have dropped to a disturbing all-time low!

OK, sure. There were not-great things about the Midwest malls of the 80s and 90s: The sheer space they took up, the way they contributed to urban sprawl, their facilitation of a consumptive and materialistic society, the fact that they produce enough garbage to necessitate additional landfills…

But people. THINK OF THE CINNABON.

And the Claire's Earring Club cards. I have held onto my Claire's card for twenty years and will probably be eligible for a free pair of blue zircon birthstone earrings by 2028![1]

Think of the literal glass ceilings and elaborate water features, which make you feel not like you've entered Tower City mall in downtown Cleveland, but instead as if you've floated into some sort of shiny, leather-scented fairyland. I think Wilson's Leather pumped their store scent into the air, like Subway and their goddamned signature bread scent. Think of the kiosks with dreamcatchers and glass figurines. The Sharper Images! The Hot Topics! THE VICTORIA'S SECRETS, FOR FUCK'S SAKE. At the mall, you can simultaneously sip a Gloria Jean's Latte and peruse the latest Bath and Body Works spring scents, *while* you massage your freshly punctured ear cartilage hole.

Once upon a time, the mall was the pinnacle of cool in the Midwest. (Unless you were a cool-enough teen to get invited to those parties where people drove their pick-up trucks to a field and drank Coors.) The mall deserves a comeback for modern Midwest teens who have jack shit else to do but get drunk and pregnant. The Mall of the Future will be due for some necessary adaptations, like gender-neutral restrooms. Some other Gen Z updates—think cat cafes and Tide pod buffets—will also help move the mall into the 21st century. It could be so great! Adolescent America will thank me.

---

1. *Author Note:* I was informed after initial drafts of this chapter that Claire's has, heartbreakingly, filed for bankruptcy. RIP Claire's, Long Live Itchy Earrings.

My mall addiction began at age five, with my first gymnastics show at Euclid Square Mall. I did gymnastics until age six when my little brother broke his arm on a balance beam and I peaced right the fuck out. Doing a gymnastics show in the middle of the mall was the five-year-old equivalent of having a Las Vegas concert residency at the MGM. The lights, the people! I was in love with this joyful, purple-carpeted wonderland. Other important mall milestones followed. In second grade, I bought my first cassette tape (Beastie Boys' *Licensed to Ill*) at Camelot Music at Great Lakes Mall, where I would one day contemplate shoplifting a VHS *Heathers*.

I wanted so badly to be a shoplifter. With little spending money, I spent most of my mall time power-walking up and down the massive halls, looking for boys. Sometimes I did my homework in the food court. But I longed to pocket the infinite commerce that surrounded me. I knew that I could *probably* shoplift without getting caught but was simply too afraid. I had only shoplifted once when I was six. I stole a single piece of gum from the convenience store on Walnut Street when Mom wasn't looking. Someone, possibly a more daring six-year-old, had opened a gum package and relieved it of a piece. The open package of tantalizingly grape Bubble Yum stared me down from the wire shelf, right at my tiny person eye level. I gave in and pocketed a piece. We drove home. Wracked with guilt, I made it five minutes before creeping into the kitchen to reveal my stolen treasure to my mother. Mom tossed me back into the car and marched me up to the convenience store cash register to return the piece of Bubble Yum, along with a whispered apology to the bewildered adolescent store clerk.

When *Heathers* was released on video, I faced my biggest moral dilemma since Bubble Yum. I wanted desperately to see

Heathers, having fallen in love with Winona Ryder the year prior in *Beetlejuice*. I felt that Winona was a kindred anti-establishment heroine. By the time *Heathers* was finally released on video, I was twelve. Alone in Camelot Music, I stared intently at the video cover of Christian Slater manhandling Winona, waiting for God to give me some sign that I had permission to shoplift.

God didn't, and I didn't. When I was thirteen, I finally purchased *Heathers* with long-saved allowance money. Mom watched it once and confiscated it. She had also confiscated my Beastie Boys tape when I was seven. In retrospect, both of these actions were probably reasonable.

At age fourteen, at Tower City in downtown Cleveland, I visited my first Body Shop and was euphoric as a mini-donkey on MDMA—an entire store of products that didn't engage in the Draize eye irritancy test! (You'll learn more about this in the next chapter.) At the Body Shop, I could purchase perfume oil that made me smell like a Georgia peach farm. You can't test-drive peach farm body oil on Amazon Prime! Take that, Jeff Bezos![2]

There are just some things that only a mall can truly provide on an emotional level. I didn't get invited to alcohol parties, and I didn't play sports. But why did I need social events and a healthy outlet for my hormonal adrenaline when I had the B. Dalton's Bookstore President's Day sale? Everything good I wanted to do, I could find at the mall. It was basically a pop culture art museum, with the cleanest public restrooms east of the tollway rest stop!

---

2. If he figures out a way to do this I will absolutely lose my shit. Have you ever noticed Costco in *Idiocracy*? They got it exactly right, except it's Amazon.

My two best friends, Mindy and Kate, typically frequented the mall along with me. Mindy and I became friends initially in first grade. We even competed for the same boy—Chris Ferrari. (I maintain that he liked me better.) He was my first official boyfriend, which I can totally prove because my mom saved the love note he wrote me. Chris grew up to be a wildlife scientist. He studies wolves.

Mindy was the first-born child of Irish-Catholic Jack Quinn and Jackie O'Leary Quinn. She and I became friends mostly because we were the shortest in our class, with matching dirty blonde hair and thus were constantly mistaken for one other. Teachers typically grouped children by height for photos and miscellaneous line formations, so Mindy and I spent a lot of time together at the front of the line.

The Quinn family was something of a Wes Anderson movie. Jack and Jackie were adorable humans; Mr. Quinn's permanent smile twinkled with stereotypical Irish mischief, and Mrs. Quinn had a mop of permed curly hair atop her barely-five-foot figure. For a while, when leotard-based fitness became wildly popular, Mrs. Quinn taught aerobics classes. Mr. Quinn owned and ran a homemade ice cream store and drove a school bus on the side to provide his family with union health insurance. After Mindy was born, four little boys followed her. By the time the fourth brother came along, Mindy and I were young teens. She was devastated that her mother had chosen to produce yet another Y chromosome; her only solace was that she was allowed to choose his name. I was naturally concerned, given how distraught Mindy was, that she was about to be the older sister to Buttface Wienerpunch Quinn. But Mindy didn't hold a grudge and named her final brother Tyler. All of the Quinn children were also fucking adorable; elvish moppets with twinkle eyes and cackling laughs. Somehow you couldn't get mad at the boys, even if they refused to stop farting into your cassette player.

My first ever sleepover was at Mindy's. It was her 6th birthday. Mrs. Quinn successfully wrangled a posse of five girls into making homemade pizzas. The next morning, I came down with a dramatic case of the flu and barfed it all up. I cried while Mrs. Quinn scrubbed vomit-laden linoleum on her hands and knees. There was so much red, so much regurgitated Ragú. It took me years to stomach pizza or sleepovers again.

So many of my formative memories took place with Mindy. We partnered up on every school project possible, crushed on all the same boys, and practically lived at each other's houses. I spent so much time at Mindy's that her house and backyard still show up in my dreams. Mindy had a streak of danger running through her veins. I found this out the hard way when her family got a snowmobile.

Depending on where in the Midwest you live, you have differential proportions of snowmobiling in your blood. If you live in southern Illinois, you may not be much of a snowmobiler. If you are a northern Michigander, however, there's a good chance your parents skipped the hospital and just birthed you on a snowmobile. While sharing a can of Stroh's.

Another important factor in determining your snowmobiling blood level is how hillbilly you are. As a Mid-level Hillbilly with Virginian ancestors raised in Northern Ohio, I have been on a snowmobile about a half dozen times. Riding a snowmobile is very safe; it is on par with bungee jumping onto a moving bicycle, and then riding said bicycle into a crocodile tank.

If you are an avid snowmobiler and have survived childhood sans concussion, you are indeed a lucky human.

When the Quinns got a snowmobile, there was no such thing as helmet safety, and children were generally left unsupervised to engage in dangerous motor vehicle activities. (When I was a kid, the primary cause of death for children under ten was go-kart accidents.) Mindy ensured me that she was an *excellent* snowmobile driver, and so I reluctantly climbed on board, holding her waist tightly. The Quinn's house bordered an old farm, so Mindy shot us off through the snow-covered corn fields. The Quinn boys had paved a circular snowmobile trail, and about halfway around the circle was a giant mud bump. Mindy went faster and faster. Each time we went over the mud bump and landed, my tailbone sang with pain. Finally, Mindy took us over the bump so fast that we went airborne and crashed dramatically sideways, pinning us underneath the snowmobile. I laughed maniacally as we waited for Mr. Quinn to come rescue us. Having witnessed the crash, he was already headed to us as fast as the tractor could carry him.

Mindy (and Kate) went to college at the University of Dayton, and through a coincidence, my Dad took a job in Dayton for about a year at the same time. Dad traveled home to see Mom on weekends and frequently offered my high school best friends a ride with him. (I was attending Ohio University on the other side of the state.) Occasionally, my dad allowed Mindy or Kate to drive so he could nap.[3] He recalled an incident wherein he awoke to hear Mindy screaming "Oh, hell no," and revving the gas as hard as she could to prevent a truck from merging in front of her on the highway. In this way, several

---

3. LaForces are champion nappers.

LaForces have fortunately avoided near-death experiences with Mindy at the wheel.

Kate was much more mild-mannered. She was our class valedictorian and was raised a more devout Catholic (Roman Catholic) than Mindy's family. Kate attended private Catholic school until middle school. I went to a few St. Gabe's summer festivals with her. Catholics, thank god, are drinkers, so the festival vibe was always less church-y than my equivalent Protestant experiences. About half of the county attended the gigantic St. Gabe's, so the church had enough money to pony up for rides and carnies peddling fried food. But we never had any money and mostly went to look for cute private-school boys.

Kate was the voice of reason in our trio. She frequently talked us down from the nerd-level of mischief I tried to start, i.e., calling boys and hanging up, ringing boys' doorbells and running away, and hiding behind the bleachers to spy on boys. Although I always took Kate as the most prudish of our group, she did lose her virginity before Mindy and me—to an *older boy*, nonetheless. A telling Kate anecdote: Her bra strap busted when our 7th-grade class visited Washington, D.C. Poor Kate spent the entire day uncomfortably cross-armed and quiet, and only admitted the situation to us late in the evening. Rather than just whip the damn thing off, or drag a friend into a restroom to help jerry-rig a new strap, she suffered, ashamed and silent. I hope that in her adult life, Kate is able to enjoy some brazen free-boobin'. She deserves it.

The three of us celebrated Kate's fifteenth birthday at the mall, because where else would we be able to pull off a multi-layered feminine celebratory extravaganza? First, we went to the Prescriptives makeup counter and forced the staff to give all three of us complete makeovers, purchasing only a single blush for Kate (it cost $18; Mindy and I split it as our gift). We followed our makeovers by dancing to the juniors section of Dillard's, where we tried on Zum Zum black prom dresses and forced the paid-less-than-living-wage clerks to take photos of us. Finally, we paraded to the water fountain in the center of the mall under the skylight. It had the most pre-Instagram-Instagram-worthy lighting in all of greater Cleveland. Again, we forced strangers to take our photo.

When I asked Kate if I could use this photo, she said, "That would be fine. That may be one of three photos from 1992—1997 that I wouldn't mind people seeing."

I was old for my grade—the result of a December birthday. However, I was too afraid to be a new driver in the middle of lake-effect-snow Ohio winter. So I waited until June to get to get my driver's license. I was still the first of our trio—Kate and Mindy didn't turn sixteen until the following August and September, respectively. So I was always our driver that summer. Eventually, my parents would get the dead 1986 Chevy Cavalier station wagon (which had been collecting pine sap and bird feces in our driveway for years) working for me. Until then I borrowed my mom's car, a 1994 Plymouth Voyager minivan. My dad had leased the car and surprised my mom with it for Christmas. She cried, warmed by the sheer size of the gift, and then whispered to me out of the corner of her mouth that she had no idea how we were going to make the payments.

Driving rules did not come naturally to me. The first time I drove solo, sitting in the van at the top of the hill connecting my street to the busy Route 84, I watched the cars fly by and tried to remember the right-of-way rules.

If I'm turning right, I need to make sure no cars are coming from either direction, I thought. *Is that right? I mean, correct? And if I'm turning left, I only need to yield to cars coming from the left.*

I considered this rule for several minutes and decided that I did have it correct. I then proceeded to cut off a car trying to turn left into my street by pulling out right in front of them. They honked and looked back at me like I was an insane person, and it took me two days to figure out what I had done wrong.

The accident was really kind of the mall's fault if you ask me. If you want to keep people driving in certain places, you should put LINES on the asphalt. Why don't malls paint lanes in the parking lot? I had picked up Mindy and Kate and driven us to the mall shortly after getting my license. It was summer, and we were all wearing our cutest new shortalls. I played for them my favorite song of all time as loud as I could on the radio: OMD's "If You Leave" from *Pretty in Pink*. We knew all the words by heart and sang at the top of our lungs as we searched for a parking spot near the food court—our preferred entrance.

Distracted by our anthem, I plowed the shiny red nose of my mom's minivan directly into a rusty Honda Accord. I had been cutting across the empty parking spaces rather than driving straight up and down the rows. Just like the movies, everything felt like it happened in slow motion. The crash, the aftermath, the guilt. I turned in panic to Mindy and Kate and asked, "Do you guys know whose fault this is?" I had no idea. It was a small impact, although it felt like an earthquake. Luckily, as a trio of anxious nerds, we had all fastened our seatbelts securely.

A middle-aged woman got out of her worn sedan, looking more sad than angry. "I just had this car fixed up for my son," she told me, slamming the driver's-side door behind her. I burst into tears. She sighed, hugged me, and told me to go call my parents. I wiped my eyes and tried to be calm, but as soon as I had my dad on the payphone next to The Great Steak Escape, I couldn't stop bawling. Worse than wrecking my parents' car, worse than wrecking the nice lady's son's car, I knew that Mindy and Kate's moms would never let me drive them to the mall again. I was heartbroken. I had killed our only hobby.

The nice lady with the worn sedan let us pay her $200 cash for her son's car repair. More fortunately, Mindy and Kate's moms had been teen drivers once, too. There was never a question of me driving them again—at least, if there was, neither Mindy or Kate told me. Our mall outings continued with biweekly frequency. We were free to covet $2 earrings and leave armpit stains on every dress in the junior's section of Dillard's. One day of mild whiplash was a small sacrifice to pay to the Mall Gods. Long may they reign.

7

MEAT IS MURDER!

I'd love to say I didn't care about high school popularity, but I *really* wanted to be popular. I come from a long line of women on my mother's side who care a lot about what other people think. My maternal great-grandmother Julia was so upset about how the community might perceive her daughter Elsie marrying a hobbit-sized older man that she threatened to kill her.[1]

The women in my family like to be well-considered. Unfortunately, destiny had sealed my fate as a nerd early on. Had I known that one's lifelong social status is cemented by third grade, I would've swapped the advanced reading lessons and community theater for bullying and electric guitar. (That is what makes you cool, right?) Also, it would've been fine if I'd been born in the 2000s—nerds are super cool now! Y'all don't know how lucky you've got it. While I'm pleased that all of you smart, hard-working kids are finally getting your due, I

---

1. This particular great grandmother was also known for casting spells.

My murder-inspiring hobbit Grandpa, Carl Fanslow.

am more than a bit resentful and certainly talking about you behind your back.

I tried to be popular. I even tried out for ninth grade cheerleading, which was[2] the most guaranteed way up the social ladder. I had several friends who cheerled (cheerleaded?) and figured, I'm petite, not 100% ungraceful, and had taken three months of jazz dance lessons culminating in a group dance to Paula Abdul's *Straight Up*. I could totally do this. Cheerleading wasn't *hard*. You just had to yell and propel your extremities in various directions on cue. Smugly, I attended several of our middle school's cheerleading clinics and sweated for possibly the first time in my life. At the audition, I was paired with Cori Cardania. Cori was our school's teen girl equivalent of John

---

2. And perhaps still is, in some sectors of the Midwest as well as Dawson's Creek, Massachusetts.

Cena. She had a deep, booming voice like a boxing announcer and was approximately nine feet tall. By contrast, I was 4'11" and had the voice of an intoxicated dormouse. I thought I had it in the *bag*. Finally, my diminutiveness would come in handy. Next to Cori I would appear so adorably nimble, there's no way I wouldn't make the team or the squad or the herd or whatever a group of cheerleaders is called. And I did *theater*. I could *project*. I was an *actresssss*.

Cake. It was going to be a piece of cake.

After tryouts, I sat on the floor of the gymnasium with a group of girls, all of whom had curled hair tied back in ribbons and were pretending to be friends. We held hands as they announced the 1993 9th Grade Football and Basketball Cheerleading Squads. Yep, there were two squads.

I made neither. Cori made the football squad. I began openly mocking the institution of cheerleading the very next day.

Another great way to ensure that you are not popular, ever, is to become a rabid activist for a cause that absolutely none of your peers gives a shit about. First, activism had yet to really arrive in rural and suburban Midwest, particularly amongst teens. Northeast Ohio was not the wokest part of the nation. We were beyond sleepy, perhaps even comatose. Second, I chose a cause that made all of my friends think I was a crazy person: animal rights.

My open-minded parents taught me that all humans should have the same rights regardless of sexual orientation, skin color, or gender identity. (Although at this time, our only frame of reference for anything remotely in the realm of transgender was the occasional nod to "drag queens," specifically Divine.) However, even my reasonably socially conscious parents thought I was off my rocker when I picked up animal activism.

I became the only vegetarian at John R. Williams Junior High School. Sure, everyone's a vegetarian now.[3] Today there's a respectable movement against Big Meat and factory farming. Fuck, even Painesville's Discount Marc's has a variety of plant-based edible proteins. I bet your grandma's entire bingo team is vegetarian. But back then, *everyone* ate at least six pounds of meat at *every* meal. Unless it was Lent, when half the town then switched to six pounds of McDonald's Filet-O-Fish, at least on Fridays. Vegetarianism, and caring about things in general, was rare. I am not sure if I would've ever had an animal rights awakening had it not been for another traumatic away-from-home trip: the class trip to Washington, D.C.

My entire seventh-grade class boarded rented charter buses and rode seven hours down to Washington, D.C. This doesn't sound like long for a road trip, but try spending a whole day trapped on a bus full of hormonal, foul-smelling teenagers. It felt like 500 years. The entire week-long trip cost each kid about $200, including transportation, sack lunches, lodging, and borrowed bright yellow jackets to ensure that no one got lost. These same jackets had were worn by middle school students in the 1970s. Wearing one felt akin to being a piece of plastic-wrapped deli meat. We were required to wear the jackets at all times on our trip so we could be easily spotted if pulled into a limousine by a predatory congressman. The first night in D.C. all the kids were sectioned off into pre-established roommate groups. We were allowed to sleep *unattended*, although chaperones made frequent rounds to ensure we were safely contained in our respective Motel 6 rooms.

The idea of insufficient sleep makes me incredibly anxious

---

3. Sort of in the same way that everyone is now a proud introvert, which as a social psychologist, I can firmly say is a load of horseshit.

to this day. It wasn't until my late 20s when I started taking Lexapro, which gave me insomnia for the first six weeks, that I realized one can, in fact, survive on less than eight hours without spontaneously combusting. Unfortunately, sleep paranoia does not jibe well with camps (where I metaphorically melted into a pile of helpless dodgeball rubber), overnight parties (where I frequently called my parents to pick me up), or class trips (where I threw tantrums).

I got anxious the evening we arrived in D.C., thinking about the following day. It was to be a long day, with trips to multiple Smithsonians *and* the Vietnam Veterans Memorial. We would form two single-file lines wearing our yellow jackets and march around town for hours and hours.

My roommates Mindy, Kate, and Charla, showed zero interest in sleep the night we arrived. They were understandably giddy; it was essentially a slumber party in an exotic land where you could access a machine that distributed *unlimited ice.* We had just finished our in-room dinner of pizza. (I made it really difficult for them to like me that evening. They had let me choose the pizza toppings, and I picked broccoli and peas. I had never seen broccoli and peas as pizza toppings! The things you can get in the big city!) Mindy and Kate shared a bed and began giggling when I shut off the lights at 10. They took turns flexing their armpits and laughing at how this exercise pushed their breasts forward. Charla, my bedmate, added an occasional giggle. A legit hour of these impish shenanigans passed. My nearsightedness prevented me from seeing the digital clock without my glasses, so I kept grabbing them off the bedside table to check the time pointedly, voicing my displeasure via loud sighs. When this passive-aggressive move didn't work, I summoned the courage to ask them to be quiet. The last straw came when Mindy began mimicking the sound of her armpit flexing. "AH AH AH!" she cried.

"IF ANYONE NEEDS ME I WILL BE SPENDING THE NIGHT IN THE BATHROOM," I finally screamed. I grabbed my pillow and stomped out. Stabbing laughter followed.

I laid in the bathtub angrily for about 10 minutes. There was no way in hell I would fall asleep there; the cold porcelain pressed uncomfortably into my neck. Yet I was unwilling to swallow my pride. Thankfully, Kate appeared at the bathroom door. She was still giggling in her Gap pajamas.

"Are you really going to sleep in here?" she asked, trying unsuccessfully to suppress a laugh. I appreciated her effort, even if she was laughing at me, and began to feel the shame and stupidity that usually comes after an irrational anxiety tantrum.

"We'll be quiet," she promised.

I tossed my crisp white pillow (D.C. had much better pillows than Ohio) to the floor, and Kate reached down to help pull me out of the tub. I followed her back into the main room to awkwardly apologize and try to make a dumb joke out of it, per usual.

"I mean, I understand that you guys were doing some critical science experiments, so I really should've just been cool," I said, faking a laugh. "*Srryy,*" I added through gritted teeth.

My friends benevolently let it go, and I managed about six and a half hours of sleep. Amazingly, I did not die the next day.

What does any of this have to do with animal activism? Nothing, really. It's mostly just another neurotic story to fill space. However, that next day, at the Smithsonian museum, is where I get to a real point. The Smithsonian Museum of Natural History, a beautiful institution of this country, is ripe with gorgeous exhibits and rich learning content. BUT PEOPLE. THEY HAD THE *BEST* GIFT SHOP WE HAD EVER SEEN.

As rube kids from the sticks, we gleefully drank in the delightful merchandise. It was a thinly veiled toy store. Oh, the colors! The *quality* of T-shirts and stuffed animals! What a magical place. I floated immediately to the book section where I picked up a paperback called *Save The Animals!* by PETA president Ingrid Newkirk. It caught my eye because it was illustrated by Berke Breathed, creator of my dad's favorite Sunday comic *Bloom County.* (Moment of silence for print media. And Dad.)

The book also had a foreword by Linda McCartney. She was the wife of Beatles legend Paul McCartney! (Back then we were still only recognizing women by the accomplishments of their husbands.) Turns out Linda was also a fierce animal activist and killer photographer. Who knew? Ladies, man. They're pretty all right. I had enough money for one small souvenir, and I chose this book.

By the following week I was a proud, card-carrying member of PETA.[4] I wrote a membership letter and convinced my mom to include a check for a $15 a year commitment. PETA was only about a decade old and probably wasn't even on the FBI's terrorist watchlist yet.

Horrified by the atrocities I learned from *Save the Animals,* it was now my duty to make the rest of my friends aware of all the world's crimes against living creatures. Man, would they be disgusted when they found out! They would be so grateful to me for opening their eyes!

Right?

Starting my activism small, I wrote animal rights facts in my

---

4. I am still a practical champion for animals, but not for PETA. They are bat-shit crazy.

widely popular (widely popular amongst three of my friends) zine, *To Anyone Who Cares.* I maintained the focus of my zine – zinging one-liners[5] ("Why do the Catholics call it mass? Is it some kind of weight?"), helpful lists of "natural highs" (e.g., flannel boxers, tongue kissing, raspberry Lipsmacker, and Rolanda Watt's talk show), as well as running commentary on boys in our class and/or Christian Slater. (e.g., "I would like to call it to anyone's attention that I have a massive crush on Eric Heck and am proud of it. Will Doug Siegfried ever get a decent haircut?") Slowly, however, I began to intersperse the jokes with animal activism facts. Perhaps my strategy might work subliminally, and my friends would say "Huh, for no apparent reason I renounce meat forever." Not getting the reaction I wanted, I became more blatant, adding lists of meat additives and companies that did and did not test on animals.

Next, I began circulating animal rights tracts—like those pamphlets Jehovah's Witnesses pass out, but with slightly more blood. I wrote to several animal activism organizations and requested a few brochures to hand out to my friends.

"You got a package," Mom said to me one day, suspiciously. As though some anonymous middle-aged man was sending me gifts or I had stolen her credit card to order a case of Malibu Musk.[6]

Thrilled, I ripped open the heavy box. Inside, one thousand bright yellow flyers emblazoned with a photo of a sick cow stared out at me. The Downed Cow fliers described a vivid case study of a factory-farmed bovine. I won't go into it here, but I was prettttty unpopular in school that week.

Although my passion for animal welfare was legitimate, it

---

5. I've been tweeting since 1991, bitches.
6. Little did she know, I had stopped using Malibu Musk because....they tested on animals.

had a secondary social silver lining: having realized I couldn't be popular, I began to warm to the identity of being An Outsider. The year of peak animal activism I was downright *weird*. I was worse than a religious nut; I was a nut pushing pictures of rabbits with ulcerated bloody eyes.[7] Which I sort of loved. Hell, anything was better than being *solely* a nerd! The next year I continued with my avoidance of animal products and animal-tested cosmetics but chilled out on trying to convert others to my plight. It wasn't working. To my peers, a little animal cruelty was worth a delectable Beef Supreme or California beach-scented body spray.

Being An Outsider started to feel more comfortable. I procured a PETA "Fur is Dead!" T-shirt which was sooooo anti-establishment rad. I increased my zines' circulation and frequency and dyed my hair all black for a semester—unheard of in my Nerd Orb. I wanted to wear all black but didn't have enough clothes, so I could only wear my sole all-black outfit one day a week. My mother worried about me, assuming I was depressed. (Joke's on her! I had mind-numbing anxiety, not depression!) Being that I'm vampirically pale with near-invisible eyebrows, the all-black backdrop caused my facial features to retreat into a diffuse ivory vacuum. I still felt ugly. I still felt nerdy. But I started to feel like I was *someone.* Even if that someone was a maverick wackjob—I liked it.

---

7. The Draize Eye Irritancy Test. It's how your shampoo is made. Google image search it if you want to ruin your day. (And it's not even the worst one.)

8

BABY, REMEMBER MY NAME

The summer after ninth grade, I *begged* my parents to send me to the six-week program at Willoughby Fine Arts Association. Still shell-shocked from overnight Camp Sue Osprey, a theater day program felt much safer. I had already done some after-school children's theater productions at Fine Arts—most notably, playing King Arthur in *Sir Gawain and the Green Knight* and a talking candy cane in a holiday performance of *The Nutcracker.* The latter required method acting to maintain a strict candy-cane persona throughout the season. *What does the candy cane FEEL,* I asked myself. *What is the candy cane's MOTIVATION?*

Unlike these plays, the summer theater camp cost actual money, so it required some parental bribery. (Around this time I became the default toilet-cleaner in the family. Worth it.) Mom and Dad were pleased with my love of performing—that I had found something to make me happy besides reading Lurlene McDaniel paperbacks in bed "all the damn time." The-

*My teen haircut lent itself well to sixth-century male
royalty roles.*

ater camp meant six weeks that I wouldn't be mooning around
the house, throwing adolescent tantrums and eating all the
microwave French fries.

On the first day, I showed up in full Melanie-mode. I knew a
few friends from prior Fine Arts plays would be there, quelling
my social anxiety enough to go hardcore into my best self: a
Sassy-magazine-touting, classic-rock-educated, Payless-brand
Doc Martens-wearing, anti-establishment teen. My throwback
tie-dye shirts and ironic children's accessories (i.e., a rubber rat
bracelet, viciously uncomfortable vintage jelly shoes), seen as
weird at my school, were suddenly cool at theater camp. All of
my old friends and a ton of new friends went out of their way
to push through other kids in the auditorium…to talk to ME. I
had a sudden surge of curious self-satisfaction.

Theater camp was broken up into several classes: singing, acting, and dance/choreography. "Acting class" focused on getting the kids reasonably intelligible for stage. One of the first activities was reciting song lyrics as loud as possible. One of my best friends from *The Nutcracker*, Ryan Paulson, had also come to theater camp. For this particular exercise, he chose lyrics from The Beatles' "Happiness Is a Warm Gun." This didn't translate well to spoken word, but it further cemented him to me as a kindred spirit. Ryan and I were tight for several years, although we never hooked up.[1] My parents liked him because he went to the high school they had attended—Willoughby South High. (It took Willoughby South High School until 2017 to drop their confederate "Rebel" troll mascot. I'm hopeful that they choose to bring on something less offensive, like a Crips member or a child bride.)

Ryan became such a good friend that he performed in my ninth-grade mythology project for English class. He and I played Hades and Persephone. In this particular myth, the god of the underworld, Hades, falls in love with Zeus and Demeter's daughter, Persephone. So naturally, he kidnaps her, because that's the way old dudes woo chicks. But of course, Persephone grows to love Hades because bitches love confidence, right? (Polytheism is full of toxic masculinity stories.) This particular skit (we also did *Narcissus* and *Orpheus and Eurydice*) remains some of my finest directorial work. We shot it in Mindy's attic bedroom, her mom filming it with a VHS camcorder. I borrowed a gorgeous baby-doll lace princess dress from the Fine Arts costume department. The myth of Hades and Persephone has a vaguely sexual undertone, so there was a lot of giggling that we were unable to edit out. In the version

---

1. Although obviously he was not immune to my incessant boy-crushing.

of the myth our class read, which I am unable to back up with modern Internet searching, Hades disguised himself when he went to bang Persephone so she would be attracted to him. (This is the earliest known instance of catfishing.)

Theater kids made the best projects. But back to camp.

When lunchtime came on that first day, new friends flocked to my table. At my junior high, I had a modestly clique-y nerd lunch table. At theater camp, however, the Barbie-esque girls from private schools flocked around me *immediately* as their Regina George. I didn't understand it but sure as hell didn't question it. I embraced my new identity as theater queen bee. My new minions had *money* and honey-colored *highlights* in their trendy layered haircuts. They inched their plastic chairs closer to me when I whispered sarcastic digs out of the side of my mouth during singing class. My cynical dweeb persona was somehow cool. Theater camp was like Opposite Day! An older girl named Doreen befriended me immediately and took me under her wing—not as a subordinate, but as an equal. We sat in the back of the auditorium watching rehearsals and passing a Walkman back and forth. It was through Doreen that I discovered Violent Femmes, my anthem band all through adolescence.

Why can't I get just one kiss
Why can't I get just one kiss
Believe me there'd be somethings that I wouldn't miss
But I look at your pants and I need a kiss.

And it wasn't just the girls who gravitated to me. Wink wink.

For the first time in my life, THE BOY liked me. Mark Lorenz was the babeliest, coolest dude at theater camp. He was blond. He went to private school. He was even an athlete! I'm not sure how Mark ended up at theater camp. He wasn't the best performer—certainly not at *my* level. He went through the motions, but the stage never seemed like his thing. Perhaps his parents had forced him into theater to build culture, like the other private-school rich kids.

Mark went to Hawken, a cool, non-religious private school in the greater Cleveland area. Northeast Ohio had lots of private Catholic schools, of course, but in wealthy regions there were also several crunchy, liberal arts options. Hawken was one of those. A lot of theater camp kids came from cool private schools with *Rushmore*-esque names, like Hawken, Gilmour, and University. The closest private school to my district was Lake Catholic, and thus not cool. Nun schools are not cool. Hell, the Painesville Township Public Schools' Riverside Beavers were cooler than that.

Mom scoffed when I told her I had made new friends from these schools (disdain for family money is an inherited trait), but she was quietly pleased that I was now rubbing shoulders with Orange kids. Yes, Northeast Ohio has an Orange, just like Orange County, California. It has fewer frozen bananas but just as much privilege.

Mark and I shared a few intimate moments in the months following theater camp, namely, French fries at the mall food court and erotic hand-holding under the bleachers at my high school football game. He came all the way to public school to hold my hand! Did I mention he was an athlete?

In addition to landing THE HOTTEST GUY (athlete!) at theater camp—I also nailed my first villain role. To make everything more difficult on the camp staff, our director, Liza, decided that rather than performing an already existing musical, the staff would adapt the children's book *The Pushcart War,* creating "original" musical numbers to the tune of public domain classical songs. We sang a song about a search warrant to Mozart's *Eine Kleine Nachtmusik,* 1st Movement.

Could, there be, something illegal here?

Search the place, there's something here I fear.

We're here, for the benefit, of the people. We are looking for, something behind your chair inside your drawer or underneath your shirt!

We wonnnn't hurt you, we'll be gentle, please don't be alarmed. We just neeeed to ask you just a few questions.

It kind of worked. *The Pushcart War* has deeper political underpinnings, blah blah blah. But it was cool mainly because they taught us New York accents. I felt so bad for all the parents that week, having to suddenly house Midwest teens trying to sound like Rudy Giuliani. *Heeey, Mama, how's about you give me a slice of that pizza pie?*

I played the coveted role of Lucy Livergreen (adapted from Louie Livergreen), a macho trucker (and possible Men's Rights Activist) who wanted nothing more than to exterminate the underdog pushcart vendors. My costume was simple: a backwards cap, jeans, and yellow T-shirt. I relished an opportunity to showcase my young teen evil side, although (spoiler!) the pushcart vendors beat the truckers in the end. Commentary: Only in fiction does the underdog win.

That same time in my adolescence, I was obsessed with a street in Cleveland Heights called Coventry. It was *the only* hip place in all of Northeast Ohio. I dreamed of growing up and having a cool apartment above one of the storefronts. Kids from my school didn't really even go to Coventry, which made it more elusive and counterculture cool. Coventry Street had a coffee shop, a dope vintage toy store, miscellaneous head shops, and a pseudo-witchcraft boutique. Because a lot of the private-school girls lived in that general vicinity, we talked about Coventry often at theater camp. The last day of camp, one of my new super-cool private-school friends, Liv, who was 16 and had her own car, took me and another theater camp crush, Jeremy, to Coventry for a long lunch. It was clear that Jeremy had a crush on Liv, but I was still riding the Mark wave, so I allowed myself to lean into a platonic outing. For once.

Liv was stunningly gorgeous with long, messy ombre hair before ombre hair was cool and perfect eyebrows that looked like they had been painted on her face by an old master. She was slightly more hippie than the other private-school girls and smoked a cigarette out the window as we drove to Coventry. I had been well-trained that smokers are bad, so this made me a little bit nervous. But it also made her more appealing and made me feel all the more like a cool kid. Because Liv wasn't allowed to smoke in her car, we drove down Route 271 with the windows down, hot August wind whipping our faces and Screaming Trees blasting as loud as we could tolerate. It was glorious.

"We're breaking tradition, hardcore," Liv said, in between songs.

"We are?" I asked. "How?"

"The last day of camp everyone has a big group lunch together, it's kind of a thing," she said.

While I felt a twinge of FOMO, it was quickly replaced by the feeling of rebellion. I was doing the cool kid YET outsider thing, bucking the group norm and flying down the highway with a teen smoker to peruse vintage Whoopee cushions and bundles of witchy cleansing herbs. Even though we were certainly allowed to leave Fine Arts for lunch, it still felt like we were somehow breaking rules. The magical day ended with the three of use sharing a single order of mozzarella sticks at The Winking Lizard, Coventry's landmark pub grill, my cheeks flamed pink with the psychological drunkenness of acceptance.

The second year of theater camp was equally amazing and I was equally cool, but most of my core memories were formed in that first year. In year two we performed *Fame*, an on-the-nose fit. Since everyone paid for theater camp, they tried to rotate the most meaty roles around each year. Thus, in *Fame*, I was relegated to a minor role in the chorus. As a sage 14-year-old, I understood the complicated politics of community theater and was fine with it. The songs of *Fame* moved me. Such feeling! Such disco! I challenge anyone (besides maybe Boyz II Men) to improve on the harmonies of late-70s/early-80s show tunes. I *felt* myself in those songs, trying so hard to be the thing that everyone wanted, trying so hard to make it—just wanting to be recognized.

I'm gonna make it to heaven
Light up the sky like a flame, FAME!
I'm gonna live forever
Baby, remember my name.

Theater camp was a brief moment in time in when I felt like I could be myself. I could let my freak flag fly, as the kids say.[2] I felt accepted and even broadly idolized for the weird traits that often unnerved my usual school friends. I could sing my profane Violent Femmes songs out loud and wear dinosaur toys in my hair, and even the most vanilla folks at theater camp totally dug it. They *got* it. They got me. We were kindred artistes.

For two illustrious summers, I had *the* social circle I always wanted.

---

2. Do the kids still say this?

But then I had to get a summer job.

9

LIFE LESSONS OF THE DAIRY QUEEN SISTERHOOD

I sat on the stainless steel counter, examining my cherry-stained fingernails. Flimsy cold metal cooled the backs of my bare thighs beneath inappropriate-for-food-service black jean short-shorts. Rick the manager hated it when we sat on the counter, but he had gone out for bananas again. As the only fresh ingredient at Dairy Queen (pause to consider this), bananas were hard to keep in stock. Rick made an unreasonable amount of banana runs, which gave us time to kick back, gossip, and sample the merch. I sipped a sugary strawberry slushie, officially called a Mr. Misty Cooler, and examined my tan feet, highlighted nicely by faux-leather black Payless sandals. It was my first shift back after a family vacation to Sunset Beach, North Carolina.

"Oh my god," Kacey Cortez said, walking to the dusty boombox in the corner. "This song came out while you were on vacation." She turned it up. "It's *so* good."

A growling female voice hit me. The song was Alanis Morissette's "You Oughta Know." This was the first time I had heard it. When the chorus came around Kacey chimed in.

"And I'm hereeeee to remind youuuu of the MESSSS you left when you went awayyyy." She bobbed her curly bangs and aggressively wiped chocolate syrup from the milkshake blender.

Oh my god. Such angry rock. Such everything that we were all feeling! Beloved, relatable angst! I didn't know what Alanis Morissette looked like but imagined her as a small dirty-blonde hobbit type. She was obviously my spiritual twin.

BEEEEEEP. BEEEEEP.

The drive-thru alarm interrupted our wave of empowerment. I went to the microphone and growled, "Welcome to Dairy Queen, can I help you?" Emotions never had time to settle in those days. Angst turned to empowerment to glee to apathy within a matter of minutes.

There's a scene from *The Cosby Show* that has always felt akin to the honor of serving at Dairy Queen. In this scene, sassily side-ponytailed Vanessa Huxtable flirts with a guy who makes keys at a mall kiosk. The Key Boy, who completely rocks a 90s-era rugby shirt, gets all braggy like "Yah, sometimes I make two or three keys *at once*," while Vanessa gazes in awe at his alpha male dominance.

Try to imagine Key Boy's level of power times infinity.

For five years as a counter specialist, I controlled thousands and thousands of gallons of ice milk[1] and hundreds of pounds of Blizzard toppings. I was a regular Willy Wonka in a red polo, black shorts, and scrunchie. But the true essence of the DQ went beyond money, prestige, or even pure unadulterated sugar highs. DQ was the first community of women I joined and bonded with, and they taught me many valuable life lessons.

Life Lesson 1: There is a strict hierarchy to the DQ that is a metaphor for your life's failures.

I got the DQ job through Melissa D, not to be confused with Melissa P. Melissa D went to Riverside high school with me, while Melissa P went to Painesville *City* high school which we all thought was the hood because it was literally on the other side of the tracks. Melissa D was in color guard with me. Color guard is code for flag corps, aka one millimeter cooler than marching band, aka one millimeter nerdier than Dance Team, aka Those Girls Who Throw Flags Around At Football Halftime Shows. I do not know if high schools still have color

---

1. Dairy Queen's product couldn't legally be called "ice cream" because um, it wasn't legally ice cream.

guard, or if it's gone by the wayside like other adolescent treasures such as locker organizers and maxi pads. (I heard teenage girls now just take Plan B every day until they hit menopause.)

The Painesville DQ appealed to me because: 1) Melissa D said it was fun, and no kids I knew ever said their jobs were fun, and 2) Painesville DQ didn't serve any food-food, just ice milk. Unlike at the Mentor DQ, I would not need to slather shiny, metal coil-warmed pork products with chemical mustard. At 15, I consistently made the honor roll and didn't have any non-traditional piercings, so I was handily hired by a young-ish, relatively chill manager, Rick. I made a cool $4.25 an hour. This may not sound like much, but keep in mind that every season we came back to work at DQ, we earned a twenty-five-cent raise. By the time I finally left DQ, I was making well over five dollars an hour.

The unspoken DQ hierarchy was loosely guided by age, job-relevant skills, number of prior sexual partners, and hair awesomeness. My first year I was low on the totem pole: a child virgin with stringy hair. As new blood arrived, I began to slowly rise in status. However, I never acquired elite standing. The one key skill that led to the highest status was the ability to customize ice milk cakes.

Consider this situation, which is a hypothetical amalgam of experiences I had at Dairy Queen: A frazzled father, balding slightly and looking confused, comes to the DQ just hours before his son's sixth birthday party. Awkward Dad scans the freezer and a-ha! He spots an eight-inch round ice milk cake exhibiting an unlicensed-by-Disney Donald Duck holding a fistful of balloons. Awkward Dad brings the cake to the counter and asks for a relatively simple message, "Happy Birthday

Jimmy." I look around frantically for someone else to do it, like Darla.

A tall, athletic, college-aged blonde, Darla had particularly lovely cake penmanship and was our unofficial leader. She enjoyed hugging me because it required that I got up on my tiptoes. Darla's wrist would flick and glide gently, bending a tube of rubbery cake gel to her every whim. She created gorgeous cursive messages. (This was back when cursive was still a thing. And people ate real birthday cakes instead of just Snapchatting them at each other.) Darla tried repeatedly to teach me cake-writing, even holding my hand and guiding the formation of gel letters, to no avail.

Unfortunately, Darla does not happen to be working on the occasion that Awkward Dad comes in. It's an afternoon shift, and I am alone with the brand-new Laura, who still hasn't even mastered banana splits, for fuck's sake.

In this sort of scenario, I would gulp and reluctantly take the cake to the back. It would take a full 20 minutes for me to write "Happy Birthday Jimmy" (in kindergarten-like uppercase block letters). The cake would bear many visible scrape marks from attempts to correct errors. I would hand the cake around the corner and make Laura ring up Awkward Dad while I hid until he left.

Luckily, this situation was rare. I had support; I had teammates. When a customer handed me a cake and Darla saw my panic-stricken face, she was there for me. There was always someone at DQ who had my back. Even if it was the semi-useless Laura.

Life Lesson 2: Karma is a Bitch.

In general, we were good girls at the DQ. We would never dream of tainting the product. Blizzards were fucking sacred. However, with Rick's frequent banana-buying trips (which I now realize may or may not have been a euphemism for going to a strip club), we could be tempted into furtive wrongdoing.

There's this thing called group polarization[2] that happens often in group discussion. While it may seem like groups of people are better at discussing ideas and coming to rational, middle-of-the-road opinions, individuals in groups often egg each other on, slowly increasing extreme positions within a group. For example, imagine a group of women friends getting together to discuss the animated TV show *Rick & Morty*. One friend might say "It's OK, it's got some laughs I guess." Another will mention the fact that female writers on the show have been vilified by dudefans of the show. Yet another friend may mention that she really thought the whole McDonald's Szechuan Sauce craze was insane. This will continue and by the end of the conversation, the group of friends has decided that Rick and Morty is the downfall of feminist society and they must ritually assassinate all of its writers. That's how group polarization works. Loosely.

Within our tight-knit DQ girl fam, we easily succumbed to group polarization, especially in regards to our enemies. On one such occasion, an unsuspecting fellow teen girl came through the drive-thru. Her raspy voice and shitty-ass Pontiac Fiero were immediately recognized by Kelli, who identified her as "the giant whore who hooked up with my ex." Kelli had violently permed dirty-blonde hair and a tiny Madonna-esque

2. Check out Myers & Lamm (1976) for a full summary.

mole on her upper lip—physical characteristics that gave her a strict "don't fuck with me" appearance. She was a year my senior and a softball star.

This raspy-voiced tart, whose sole crime was to put her mouth on the genitals of Kelli's former lover, had fatefully come through the drive-thru during one of Rick's banana runs. We were dangerously unsupervised. In the length of time it took this girl to get up to the drive-thru window, we had convicted her to hell and DQ-style justice. The unsuspecting harlot's large Reese's Cup Blizzard was judged (A *large*?), blended poorly (leaving vast areas of plain vanilla ice milk, un-woven with delectable peanut butter chocolate chunks), and taken to the back of the store to be christened with a substantial amount of our saliva. Kelli ducked away when the target arrived at the drive-thru window, and my colleagues handed out her spit-laden Blizzard, smiling sweetly.

Do not provide fellatio to the current or ex-lovers of anyone who serves your food.

Life Lesson 3: Masturbation is COOL.

In the 90s, Midwest teens were particularly repressed about the art of self-love. (We did it, obviously, but would never ever admit to it.) Girls fiercely hid any hint of our own masturbation to the point of lying to the gross dudes in gym class that inevitably taunted us about it. The following exchange might have occurred:

Gross Teenage Dude: "Girls totally masturbate!"

Us: "NEVER THAT'S HOW YOU GET SHINGLES!"[3]

Jami, one of my favorite coworkers over the years, was about

3. Our public school health education was not maybe the best.

five years older and so committed to the DQ life that she continued to take a weekly shift each summer even after securing her master's degree. Jami was highest in the DQ hierarchy—she could even make sexual jokes with Rick. She'd flip her yard-long straight blonde hair over to one side of her head and then the other, filling our heads with erotica. At one point Jami was dating a man who purportedly tore her underwear off with his teeth. "I mean, like, I only have so many pairs of underwear," Jami said, rolling her eyes dramatically.

I tried to envision this but didn't understand how a human mouth could ever tear the robust, machine-stitched Hanes that rode around on my own pelvis. Jami was also the first woman I ever met who openly talked about masturbating. We younger girls would sit on the steel counter, awkwardly fingering the neckline of our red polos, a wide-eyed captive audience as Jami drawled, "I loooove masturbating." It was from Jami that I learned about the clitoris and manual stimulation, and thank god because I had been masturbating unsuccessfully with a Conair curling iron for about two years. Learning to masturbate was a slow process, particularly for those of us raised in Protestant houses. According to Sunday School teachers and other miscellaneous nutjobs, masturbation was a deadly sin.

This is one of my biggest beefs with organized religion: teaching children vague archaic principles that violate biological evidence and can lead to long-term psychological damage, be it masturbation, sex, or eating shellfish. (Please do not take away my vibrators or oyster po-boys, God.) When I first began to masturbate, it was tentative, guilt-ridden, and followed by hour-long apologies to Jesus. It was also confusing: There are just so many holes and flaps down there. When you're trying to get off by squeezing your eyes tight and methodically humping a stuffed elephant, you know something isn't quite correct but aren't sure what. Thank God for Jami, who not only took away the shame of masturbating but also provided clear-cut instructions on where to stick what.

Life Lesson 4: It's not stealing if you can ingest it.

Again, we were good girls. However, if you put five teen girls in a room full of candy unsupervised, they're going to eat the damn candy. It would take willpower far greater than our teen brains possessed to ignore the buckets and buckets of Reese's Cups AND Pieces, brownie chunks, M&M's, tiny squares of cheesecake, caramels, and Twix—all within an arm's reach. We had four taps that dispensed ice milk with the quick turn of a knob! We agreed that snacking on the merch was a fair addition to our minimum wage. DQ was a Candyland dream for any pubescent mammal; our hormones raged so hard that we never seemed to gain weight despite taking in approximately 5,000 calories of refined sugar each shift.

When Rick would leave, we would each take the opportunity to put together a mini-version of our favorite snack. Mine was compact strawberry shortcake: I placed the cake-like substance (sort of like a round, un-creamed Twinkie) at the bottom of a waxed cup, added a small amount of vanilla ice milk, some strawberries in syrup and a huge pile of whipped cream. My other favorite was to mix chunks of brownie with cold fudge. (The cold fudge, used for Blizzards, is far superior to the hot fudge – if anybody asks.) The only thing we never ate was the coconut because we all thought it smelled distinctly like ass. At the end of the night, no one wanted to refill the Ass Coconut.

Life Lesson 5: Getting dirty means you did it right.

Working at the DQ was sweet but filthy manual labor. In 1995, food service employees were still allowed to wear shorts and sandals, so by the end of each nightly shift our bare arms and legs were covered with the sticky film of a hundred milk-shakes. On busy nights, the ice milk needed to be changed frequently. Ice milk, stored in liquid form, was kept in the walk-in cooler in multi-gallon plastic bags. It only turns into soft serve through the magical dispensing machine. To change the ice milk when a bag ran out, one needed to go back and wrestle with a new bag and hose. Then we waited. The process of turning liquid ice milk into soft serve usually took five or ten minutes. If we tried to dispense before the ice milk had time to solidify, it burst out of the machine like a wild boar with food poisoning. Ice milk would splatter across the room. Really, everything at DQ splattered: Blizzards, milkshakes, fruit syrup, and artificial slushie flavoring. Overzealously dipping a ladle into waxy chocolate cone dip would leave our hair greasy yet crunchy to the touch.

For me, being short created another hazard, particularly when refilling the fruit syrup. Cherry syrup stained us the worst. I frequently lost control of the big jug, sending a cherry river cascading toward my abdomen. We always ended shifts looking like stigmata victims.

Electrical hazards abounded as well. Several times when wiping down the hot fudge warmer with a wet rag, I'd shock myself. Because teenagers are stupid,[4] it took at least 10 shocks before I finally learned to just unplug the damn thing. Or make a newbie do it.

---

4. The prefrontal cortex isn't fully developed until about age 26.

I proudly wore my gooey DQ outfit out to after-work parties, and by after-work parties I mean meeting theater kids at the coffee shop to listen to bad jazz. The chocolate skid marks and pineapple syrup stains smeared across my forearms were a badge of honor, a symbol of elite, vigorous summer work.

Life Lesson 6: Put your head down, work hard, and you'll make it to the end of the night.

Sunday nights at DQ were a complete shitshow. Lines were out the door and the drive-thru wait stretched all the way around the store and out to the street. When things got really crazy, small hiccups became large problems. As previously mentioned, the metaphorical thermal exhaust port to the DQ Death Star occurred when an ice milk bag was switched out, with a five-to-ten-minute wait for the liquid ice milk to solidify. It was a horrible, panic-inducing time when someone needed to go back and change the vanilla. We would all just sit there shrugging at the masses of customers as if to say, "Sorry bro, keep waiting." I could never understand how *angry* customers got. You're at an ice cream (milk) shop! Be happy! So you have to wait 10 minutes. In olden days you would've had to milk the fucking cow and then mix warm milk with mint chocolate chips because ICE WASN'T A THING YET. We live in a magical modern world where we can buy beautiful soft serve cones that look like piles of pillows with a delicate curlicue at the top. Be happy!

And then, at the most frantic moment, a T-ball team would show up for game-winning cones. We had a special side window for teams, and the worst was when their coach gave them no limit on their orders. Because they just won a T-ball game, not the fucking Tour de France, an appropriate treat was a small cone. But sometimes we'd get one of those rich coaches from Concord Township who would allow every child on the team to order complex blizzards and parfaits, and then get pissed off when they had to wait for it.

Sunday nights were wonderful and horrible in this way, like a long winter. They were extremely stressful and felt endless, but there was something about doing it together that was satisfying. Kacey would take the t-ball team, Hannah would change out the vanilla, and Darla would cake-write for the one idiot that needed an ice milk cake in the middle of a rush. The rest of it became a beautiful, coordinated group dance. We flowed gracefully between each other, navigating the tight space to churn shakes, snag a pump of hot fudge, or ladle chocolate cone dip over a semi-firm ice milk cone. All the while listening to Madonna on the radio, singing loudly in unison to transcend the angry throngs of customers who were very agitated that a large Blizzard cost almost four dollars.

When we finally got to turn off the drive-thru speaker at 10 pm, there was a freeing "We survived!" group solidarity that I think only comes from working in food service.[5] The endorphin release carried us through cleanup. For such a small place, cleaning took forever—about ninety minutes on a busy night. We had to refill everything and ensure every centimeter of stainless steel was sparkling, but it was a time filled with happy hormones, laughing, and general rowdy jokes. We had done it.

Life Lesson 7: DQ is forever.

I'm still friends with several of my former DQ coworkers, and

---

5. Or maybe from being in the Army. Or possibly being on any given sports team.

how could I not be? We sang Alanis Morissette songs together, looked the other way when someone gave a cute high school quarterback a free Peanut Buster Parfait, and shared the bragging rights of having made thousands of perfect soft-serve twirls at the top of a DQ-stamped wafer cone. When I meet someone as an adult and learn that she (it's always she) was also a DQ employee, I feel a strong affinity toward her. I know we share a similar coming-of-age. We are sisters of the DQ.

10

THE EVOLUTION OF MASTURBATION FOR VULVA-OWNERS

(This is true for every single vulva owner with zero deviation, obviously.)

1. Discover that rubbing pubic area on soft yet firm surfaces (couch arms, gripped pillows, rolled-up yoga mats, a bagful of guinea pig bedding) feels good.
2. Get weird, pleasant "stomachache" from watching _____ (i.e., the opening credits to *Dirty Dancing*, Halle Berry as Catwoman, or Kermit the Frog dancing). Subsequently, go to town on said bag of guinea pig bedding.
3. Hear whispered stories about sex, make the connection that the wiener goes into the bigger pee-hole. Experiment with anything remotely phallic (curling irons, unripe bananas, tofu hot dogs), usually with disastrous results.
4. Discover that the clitoris is a thing. *This will be the best day of your life.*

5. Achieve first self-orgasm. Assume it was a brain aneurysm and wait for death.
6. Discover vibrating toothbrushes. Attempt using bristle side only once; never make that mistake again.
7. Discover free internet porn. Watch disappointing forced blow job videos, feel nothing, switch back to Kermit the Frog dancing.
8. Purchase first real vibrator, hide in underwear drawer. When roommate asks what that smell is, learn that you need to clean it.
9. Learn good keyword searches and find better porn. Paired with a vibrator, you seem to be set.
10. Best friend gives you Adderall to help you focus on your homework/sketch writing/dissertation/memoir. Instead, you watch Kermit the Frog videos, orgasm 12 times, assume brain aneurysm, wait for death, and subsequently miss your deadline.

11

BILLY GRAHAM

Being a feminist, contrary to memes, does not mean that I don't place intensive value on the collection and acquisition of dudes.[1] I firmly abide by the rule "Always go for the cutest guy in the room." This has caused me trouble on a few occasions as I got older and some of the boys actually started to like me back—i.e., with awkward dads, friends' boyfriends and, as of late, college-aged donut shop employees. Always going for the cutest guy in the room has its hazards. It also requires one critical caveat: Just because there's only one guy in the room doesn't mean you should go for him.

It's tempting to go after that sole member of the opposite sex,[2] because humans' innate evolutionary animalness wants us to rub bathing suit areas with whoever is available. But we must sometimes resist for the mere sake of our own pride and reputation.

In addition to all of the glorious girls at DQ, there was one solitary non-managerial male employee. His name was Paul.

1. I might build a trophy room for them. They're so pretty.
2. This principle is pretty hetero-normative, because I tend to be hetero-normative. However, the cutest-dude-in-the-room rule can apply to any gender or lack thereof. EQUAL OBJECTIFICATION FOR ALL.

Paul was 19, and Paul wasn't cute. He was pale and vaguely ginger, with a hint of a mustache. If I squinted, he looked a bit like the short-haired member of Color Me Badd. Paul also wasn't particularly bright. All of my sarcasm was either lost on him or so hilarious that he would chipmunk-laugh for five minutes. But he was the only guy, the only possible source of male attention at the DQ.

The rest of the DQ girls—my friends, my sisters in soft serve—thought Paul was weird, because he was, so I had to flirt with him in secret to avoid embarrassment. (I mean, I *had* to.) Paul lived alone with his mother and worked at DQ to supplement their household income. He planned to go to community college eventually and could mop a floor like a champ (a task so sacred that it obviously couldn't be trusted to any of us ladies). Paul seemed very responsible and was objectively nice.

Another bonus: Unlike me at the time, Paul could drive and had a car, a bitchin' 80s Firebird. My house was on Paul's way home. Occasionally, after I'd ensured that all the other girls had left and no one would see us, Paul would give me rides home. These rides were full of awkward silences, punctuated occasionally by Paul's brief splashes of insight and philosophy, which tended to leave me wishing he had remained silent.

"You're wearing your seat belt," Paul said, giving me the side-eye through his middle-parted bowl cut.

"Yes," I said. Because I was in fact wearing a seat belt, in the front passenger seat of the car, as one does.

"I don't wear a seat belt."

I took the bait, because I knew that's what Paul wanted. "Why not?"

A pause for effect. "Seat belts will kill you."

"OK." (Trying not to engage further.)

"My buddy got into a car accident two years ago, and he wasn't wearing his seat belt," Paul said dramatically. "Head-on collision, crushed the car like an accordion. If he hadn't flown out the windshield, he'd have been crushed. He'd be dead."

"Yeah but, that's a pretty unique situa—"

"He'd be dead," he said solemnly.

Despite Paul's flawed critical thinking skills, he was my only prospect in the summer of 1994. And there was something endearing about the way Paul spat slightly when he talked about race cars. So I managed to keep it up for a couple weeks.

We went on one real date. In 1994, I was still semi-under the guise that I was a Christian. I occasionally attended Wednesday night teen youth group sessions, mostly out of guilt—these were usually held in our pastor's dining room but occasionally we would schedule outings such as anti-masturbation retreats or proselytizing missions to North Tonawanda, NY.

In the summer of 1994, my church youth group planned a local outing to a Billy Graham "Crusade" at Cleveland Municipal Stadium. In a massive reasoning failure, I decided to take Paul.

As my date.

To a Christian rock crusade.

Desperate for any boy to like me, I had lost all logic re: Paul in the summer months leading up to this evening. God may work in mysterious ways, because I had an out-of-body experience while barreling down I-90 in Paul's old Firebird toward a six-hour sermon held at a crumbling Rust Belt stadium. A faint, angelic shadow of myself hovered in the windshield like a Hawaiian dancer bobble toy.

Out-of-Body Melanie: What the fuck are you doing?

Bodied Melanie: I'm on a date! A date, a real date!

Out-of-Body Melanie: Girl, you're not on any date. You're going to church with a man you don't want any of your real friends to see you with.

Bodied Melanie: (*averts eyes, hopes Out-of-Body Melanie forgets she is there*)

Out-of-Body Melanie: You can't ignore me! I'm your (kind of) soul!

It finally sunk in that Paul had terrible skin and I was wholly uninterested in him. But it was too late. I was stuck with Paul and a bunch of Jesus People at a sports venue.

A mind-blowing 65,000 people attended this Billy Graham event. Popular Christian rappers DC Talk opened the show before the main event, Mr. Billy Graham. The man himself was a spry 76, clutching his podium with calm intensity. A cathartic moment came during Graham's sermon where he invited all those who didn't yet have Christ in their heart down onto the field. (Because they alllllways get to that part. For those of you unfamiliar with Protestant events, just know that it's impossible for a heathen to get away without accepting Christ into their heart, goddammit.)

At this point I was sitting four seats away from Paul, trying to forget that he existed. Someone from my youth group took my hand and suggested we go down to the field. I didn't want to, it felt weird and fake, but I also didn't want to be stuck with Paul. Standing on that field, amongst hundreds of teenagers and Billy Graham employees holding hands in prayer, looking up at the masses of white Cleveland suburbanites looking back at me, I realized that I just wasn't buying into any of it. I was ready to give up on God and Paul – they had about the same level of futility to me at that moment, and I just wanted to be anywhere else but the 40-yard line of Cleveland Municipal Stadium.

Things with Paul rapidly tapered off after that. We rode back from Billy Graham in relative silence, and I stopped accepting rides home from work with him. Like any reasonable teen girl, I went ahead and joined my friends in mocking him behind his back.

12

THE STORY OF PHINEAS GAGE

Senior year, in a last-ditch effort for high school popularity, I quit every extracurricular activity that led me down the traditional nerd pathway. I quit flag corps, I quit band, I quit yearbook. After trying out for the fall play and securing the lead role (obviously), I quit that, too. The only non-required activity I participated in during my senior year was volunteering as a "gym leader," which took place during school hours. This meant I was an assistant to the Phys Ed teachers during my free period, bringing out volleyballs and setting up Presidential Physical Fitness tests. Gym was only required for ninth and tenth-grade students, giving me an air of authority. (It was also counted as vaguely athletic and a lot of cute boys were gym leaders.)

The best part of my senior year was that I was no longer required to take math. The only math option open to me would've been AP Calculus with Ms. Dylan, i.e., hellish damnation in a bottomless abyss of despair. I abstained, certain that my future would not require calculus.[1] While my sucker

---

1. I ended up taking three semesters of calculus in college and getting easy As, although to this day I couldn't even define calculus if my life depended on it.

nerd herd took Calculus and burned in the flames of equa-
tional agony, I threw dodgeballs around the gym sexily whilst
attempting to get the star of the soccer team to notice me.[2]

Academic freedom also allowed me to take AP Psychology
with Mr. Sear. Mr. Sear had been a medic in the Coast Guard.
He was super worldly because he had studied in *England.*
Eventually, Mr. Sear had made his way back to the USA, where
he taught AP Psychology at Riverside High School. He had a
calming presence—he was over six feet tall and burly, with a
bald head and fantastically generous broom mustache. I never
saw Mr. Sear get angry at a student, ever; his voice was always
low and even.

Sometimes in AP Psych we watched videos starring Philip
Zimbardo—a pale, undead-looking social psychologist who I
would later count as inspiration toward my own doctorate.
Zimbardo is best known for his work in the 1971 Stanford
Prison Experiment as well as for producing fantastically educational but highly cheesy-ass videos. Think PBS but hosted by
a vampire.

The Stanford Prison Experiment[3] deserves a quick sidebar,
because it is widely known as one of the most important social
psychology studies of all time—as well as being the human ethical equivalent of basement cockfighting. In this study, Zimbardo and his fellow researchers randomly assigned male college student volunteers to act as either prisoners or guards in
a multi-week observational study. (The volunteers' role was
decided by a coin flip.) The newly minted "guards" and
"inmates" lived in a faux prison constructed in the basement
of a Stanford psychology building. It sounds like how 90% of

2. He did not.
3. (Zimbardo, 2007)

my sex fantasies begin, but unfortunately, the experiment took a cruel turn (also not unlike my sex fantasies).

Ultimately, the Stanford Prison Experiment "guards" became so authoritarian and brutal, and the "inmates" so powerless and humiliated, that the experiment had to be stopped. Guards belittled and shamed the inmates to the point of legitimate emotional damage. The experiment was intended to last for several weeks. Two participants quit after only days, and the entire experiment was called off after six days.[4] Despite methodology concerns, the study highlighted just how powerful conformity and perceived authority can be i.e., how social context can turn people from "good" to "evil." The study documented how human empathy can break down in group settings, as well as how careful researchers must be in preventing harm to their subjects.

The ethical fallout from the Stanford Prison Experiment is one of the key reasons why it's difficult nowadays for social psychologists to do any fun research, like guilting people, or lying to them, or waterboarding infants. The Stanford Prison Experiment has been replayed many times in current events (e.g. the terrors of Abu Ghraib) as well as pop culture. Even *Bob's Burgers* did a Stanford Prison Experiment-based episode, where Bob and Linda won a *Downton Abbey*-esque LARP contest. (Participants were randomly assigned to be either lords and ladies or servants—it played out in a similar fashion.)

AP Psych class made me fall in love with psychology. I loved understanding human behavior, especially what caused people to do bad things. Midway through the year, Mr. Sear introduced us to physiological psychology, or the biological causes

---

4. Thanks to pressure from Zimbardo's graduate student, Christina Maslach, because women.

and correlates of human behavior. I found the workings of the human brain and body fascinating and was TOTALLY feeling it. As with many units, Mr. Sear introduced us to the topic of physiological psychology with a Zimbardo video:

"OK, so today we are going to hear a story about the brain, and in particular, the limbic system. After the video we'll talk about the implications for psychology today."

I sat upright in my chair as Mr. Sear pulled the shades of the classroom, blocking out the unseasonably bright late fall sun. He steered the TV cart to the front of his desk and muttered briefly as he struggled to get the VCR to connect. Finally, the blue screen faded into the familiar image of a brain and the characteristic introductory music of the "Discovering Psychology" series.[5] In the video, Zimbardo introduced Phineas Gage.

(Hey—if you're super squeamish, you may want to skip down a bit.)

In the 1840's, Phineas Gage worked on a railroad gang in Vermont, blasting rock to put through a new line. One day, an accidental blast propelled a long iron spike clear through Gage's head, chin to scalp. This was some real-life gory *Game of Thrones* shit. Shockingly, Gage not only survived *being impaled through the entire head by a giant iron rod* but seemed generally OK and didn't even lose consciousness. Despite my fascination, as Zimbardo narrated Gage's injury I began to feel slightly queasy. Looking around uneasily at my classmates, I could see they were paying attention to the video. Kacey Cortez glanced at me with widened eyes as if to say, "This shit's fucked up."

5. You can still find these videos online. They remain great AND THEY SHOULD PROBABLY PAY ME FOR WRITING A WHOLE BIG THING ABOUT THEM.

*In 2009, historians identified Phineas
Gage in a newly discovered daguerreo-
type. From this new artifact, we learned
that even with a hole in his head, Gage
was, in fact, a stone-cold fox.*

I looked down at the laminate top of my desk. The moment I
became conscious of my mild nausea, the sensation accelerated
like the *Fast and Furious* franchise. Awareness of my discomfort triggered social fear. *Oh god,* I thought. *What if I puke/piss
myself/faint?*

Quickly determining that puking was the most probable scenario, my heart pounded harder and harder. I tried to block out
the sound of the video, but fucking Zimbardo rambled con-
tinuously about chunks of brain, pushing chunks of my lunch
up to my throat. I looked around frantically. *How can I puke
nonchalantly so that no one notices? Maybe into my textbook?*

Would anyone notice if I slipped casually to the doorway, swept up the steel garbage can, and walked out of the room confidently, as though I had some terrific plan that was NOT PUKING into that garbage can?

I need to get out of here, I decided. I was now in full on-panic attack: my vision tunneled, my breathing went shallow. But my body felt frozen. Panic attacks trigger fight-or-flight response, which made me want to flee but also terrified me of what would happen if I tried to, god forbid, stand up. I wanted to shoot out of a room like a bat outta calculus, but fear also rooted me to my chair. I couldn't make a scene by leaving class in the middle of the video. What if boys looked at my butt as I fled, and what if I pooped explosively on the way out? If I stood up, I would *certainly* puke/faint/piss/shit/trip. Irrational fears tumbled back and forth in my mind. I closed my eyes and tried to think about someplace safe, like my bedroom or a cozy bomb shelter, but I couldn't tune out the dialogue. Underpaid educational video actors continued to reenact Gage's trauma. The fake 1848 doctor examining the fake Phineas Gage, saying, "I'm putting my fingers through the bottom of his head, and through the top of his head, and I can touch my fingers together."

That was the last thing that I heard. The panic and vividness of the brain injury sent me over the edge. The dimmed room went completely black.

Then I was awake, slumped in my chair awkwardly, gazing up at Mr. Sear's mustache. Soft, fuzzy, and white, it reminded me of Falcor from *Neverending Story*.

"Hey there," he said calmly. "How ya doing?"

My classmates looked at me anxiously. The air felt tight and smelled funny, like sulphury eggs. I prayed to God that I hadn't faint-farted.

"That was a pretty crazy video," Kacey said comfortingly, and my classmates nodded. These were, largely, the same jerks that had pranked my anxiety back in 8th grade by faking an algebra quiz. But now their faces showed recognition and warmth. After spending so many years in the same classes, we knew each other. I knew that Tom Arkin's dad hit him, and he tried desperately to hide it. I knew that Heather and Anne, best friends for the past eight years, recently had a falling out due to dramatic infighting between their mothers. I knew that Charla's parents often couldn't afford to send her to school with lunch. The worst-case scenario had happened that day. Panic had won. I had tried so hard to block out the terror, but terror had overwhelmed me, turning me into nothing more than a smelly public-school faint-farter. But it didn't faze my classmates, my friends. It was just another layer of Melanie, the Melanie they had known since elementary school. Maybe the nerd crew wasn't such a bad group to align with after all. Looking around at the wonderful Mr. Sear and my classmates, I felt surprisingly safe.

Doctors later told me that I had a "sensitive vagus nerve." The vagus nerve is the biggest asshole of all the nerves and my least favorite part of the nervous system.[6] Sure, the vagus nerve does some nice stuff like regulate the heart and control the salpingopharyngeus muscle,[7] but overstimulation of the vagus nerve due to stress can result in "vasovagal syncope" or "blacking out and crashing your face on your desk in front

---

6. In case you are wondering, my favorite part of the nervous system is the parietal lobe, which is instrumental in imagination, i.e., vivid daydreams about (bearded, shirtless) Chris Evans washing his car.

7. Donate to Wikipedia, kids.

of your entire social circle." Strong vagus nerve reactions run in my family. When I had my wisdom teeth removed, my mom also had to lie down post-surgery. (The bloody gauze and my anesthesia-hangover sobbing made her swoon.) After my Phineas Gage episode, Dad told me about the time he fainted in the Marines when they had been getting a first aid lecture about...fainting.

I've fainted a lot since then. I fainted in AP Biology during a lecture about veins. I fainted when my brother had deviated-septum surgery and his eyes bled like a church oil painting. I fainted when I got stung by a bee on the El in Chicago. Being an easy fainter gnashes terribly with social anxiety; for me, it culminated in diagnosable panic disorder. Sure, I can't do one goddamn pull-up, but my body is readily able to panic itself into fainting. Not my favorite physiological skill set.

Panic disorder undulates. During some periods of my life, fear of fainting made it difficult to be anywhere that fainting could be embarrassing or dangerous. This included typically benign places like meetings, driving on the highway, crowded restaurants, and ironic puppet shows. Nowhere felt safe! But any blood or injury-related scenario was (is) the absolute worst. I've had panic attacks while working as an education researcher, observing fourth-grade classes learning about different types of bone joints. It felt so debilitating. The fucking ten-year-olds could handle learning about the difference between ball-and-socket and hinge joints, but I had to leave the classroom.

More recently, I had a panic attack at a Simon's, a classic Chicago bar. With a day off work, I headed out for some good old-fashioned Christmas *gluhwein* day-drinking. They were playing *Bones* on the TV over the bar. Even the slightly sedating effect of the *gluhwein* couldn't help me that day. It had been a stressful couple of weeks, and that, coupled with David Boreanaz vividly describing yet another badly decomposed prostitute—it was all too much and I had to leave. Situations like this dominated much of my twenties.

A big piece of my recovery was learning to stop giving so much of a fuck. I certainly still have attacks (why are medical examiner dramas so popular??) but can often work through them with a mental reminder that it *doesn't matter* if I faint. I don't give a shit anymore if I pass out in front of cute dudes or even a prestigious panel of government policy makers.[8] What's the worst that would happen? The absolute worst possible scene would be that I pass out, shit myself, give myself a nasty bump on the head, and it all ends up on YouTube. I can survive that. Hell, if it went viral, I'd probably get to be on *Ellen*. In many situations, I know that if I do faint, there will probably be a group of friendly nerds around to take care of me, just like in high school. The people who love me will still love me even if the worst thing happens.

In case you're wondering how Phineas Gage ended up: Gage appeared to (slowly) recover well, considering that his head was gutted like a chunk of French bread at an 80s fondue party. The iron spike severed parts of his brain's limbic system, which controls emotion and response. Prior to his injury, Gage had been a pretty chill dude; post-incident, he became erratic and prone to violent mood swings. He managed to be functional enough to hold a job and engage in many normal activities of the mid-1800s, such as shoeing horses, emptying chamber pots, and snorting absinthe. He died 12 years later at age 36 from seizures likely stemming from his brain damage.

8. I'd rather talk to the former, but sometimes my JOB requires me to talk to the latter.

Researchers continue to study Gage's injury. Thanks to trail-blazing freak situations such as Phineas Gage and the Stanford Prison Experiment, we are always learning new lessons about human behavior and the brain. Thanks to *psychology*, the legacy of Phineas Gage can still make innocent high school students pass right the fuck out in front of all their friends. His story made a positive and negative impact on my life. He taught me that my Nerd Orb was more protective and famil-ial than I had realized. He taught me that the human brain is as fascinating and mysterious as faraway galaxies, and maybe I should learn more about it. But mostly, he taught me the criti-cal lesson of avoiding *Bones* in public spaces.

13

ZEN & THE ART OF UNDERAGE DRINKING

The Riverside High School graduating class of 1996 had careful clothing choreography: girls in bright yellow graduation gowns and all the boys in black. The choir sang Boyz II Men's "It's So Hard To Say Goodbye To Yesterday." The principal read us Dr. Seuss's *Oh the Places You'll Go!* A lot of girls cried. (Which was fair; many of them knew their peak was now behind them.)

I had zero sadness. While not, say, *bitter* about high school, it certainly wasn't the *Fast Times at Ridgemont High* or *House Party* that I had spent my pre-teen years expecting. There was no climactic kissing of Jake Ryan outside of a church. I never got invited to parties where Martin Lawrence DJ'd and people danced in unison. No boy stalked my bedroom window with a boombox playing Peter Gabriel. I didn't even get a teen boyfriend that occasionally turned into a wolf and kicked ass at basketball. And I was too much of a goody two-shoes for the catharsis of Saturday detention.

Goodbye, suckers. Maybe you had your high school dream, but my dream was coming for me in college.

From a young age, I wanted nothing more than to go to college. High school was merely purgatory between a shitty childhood and the heaven that awaited me in Southeast Ohio. My parents had both gone to Ohio University as undergraduates, and I grew up enchanted by stories of their college antics.

OU had a bagel buggy! There was a bar on Court Street where you could DANCE in a LOFT! Girls and boys lived in the same dorm! The dining halls were basically an all-you-can-eat buffet! There was a place called "Bong Hill" where kids would hike and camp and (furtive glance to the side) *smoke weed*. OU even had a "beach" that consisted of a rocky sand patch next to a dirty river.

Mom had the best dorm stories. Her freshman year room was a 12×6 coffin with a triple bunk bed. All the roommates took turns taking the top bunk, which teetered at a precarious and possibly illegal height. Once, during one of the many middle-of-the-night fire drills, Mom's roommate Rose forgot she was on the top bunk and attempted to walk right off, breaking her ankle. They had another crazy roommate, Faith, who was *promiscuous* and constantly picking up STDs. Mom listened to her rub medicinal cream into her vulva from the top bunk and then drop the tube to the floor like an atom bomb. When Mom moved out of the dorm and into a house "uptown" with her roommates, the fun continued. Their house had a *toilet* on the basement stairwell! It was that year when my dad visited, fresh from a stint in Cuba as a Marine, and Mom talked him into giving OU a try. My parents remain good friends with their OU roommates. These people are as close, if not sometimes closer, than my aunts and uncles. Their children are like my cousins, or even little brothers and sisters.

Lifelong friends! Crazy party times! Screw high school, *college* would be the 80s teen movie I'd worked for. Despite that

OU was not the most prestigious of even the state schools, it was the sole university I applied to. I didn't want to go anywhere else. OU or die. I wanted the same miracle that my parents had. I wanted to find my husband and the bestest goddamn friends in the universe.

Whenever you set your expectations sky-high, be it college, or prom, or *Inception,* you are bound to be a little let down. Don't get me wrong—college was delightful. The traditional college experience is a charmed life, post-high-school angst and pre-adult-responsibility. It's like Disneyland, but with more nudity. However, I don't remain close with my college friends. They are lovely people, but for the most part, we have drifted apart save for the occasional social media comment. Sadly, I didn't have nearly the romantic-comedy-esque adventures my parents experienced.

I did, however, discover one incredible new friend. And her name was Alcohol.

———

Arriving on campus the first day, breathing the sweet college town bouquet of tanning beds and cigarettes, I felt uneasy. Once my parents left, I sat on the steps of a Civil War memorial in the heart of campus, chewing on a Wendy's Greek Pita. An overwhelming sense of aloneness hit me. I was on my own. If something earth-shattering happened, my closest relatives were four hours away. I experienced an immediate 30 seconds of heart-gripping orientation distress.

And then someone handed me a beer.

The real magic of freshman year can be boiled down to the adventures of binge-drinking. If anyone tells you that discovering alcohol is not all it's cracked up to be, they are lying to you. I'm not saying that alcohol *isn't* a legitimate poison. It's completely toxic and can potentially lead to addiction, illness, and death. BUT IT'S ALSO SO FUN.

College wasn't my first time drinking—but almost. I only had one other drinking experience: New Year's Eve my senior year of high school, Mindy Quinn and I rang in the New Year on her couch with her mom and two kiwi-strawberry Bartles & Jaymes each. I wore sweatpants, an RHS Beavers Colorguard T-shirt, and requisite scrunchie. The wine coolers tasted like generic popsicles, but we thought they were pretty great. We laughed maniacally and bounced around the couch through our Adam Sandler marathon. It was what the cool kids these days might call "a rager." I always felt, even as a teen, that drinking was really for college. Having seen a lot of National Lampoon movies, I was excited to do a keg stand with all the boys holding my legs. My parents didn't want me drinking in high school but acknowledged that once I was away at college, all bets were off.

My freshman roommates turned out to also be former good girls who came to college to party. There was Alexis, from the western suburbs of Cleveland, a former cheerleader in a graduating class of 40 kids. Lindsey, from the suburbs of Pittsburgh, who clearly came from wealth and pronounced aunt as "ont" instead of "ant." Christina, our fourth roommate from Strongsville, was perpetually trying too hard.

We had a quad room, which was the best dorm setup because one room had two sets of bunk beds and closets, and a WHOLE SECOND room had desks, our flip 'n' fucks, and a tiny tube TV. The flip 'n' fuck is another miracle of modern engineering—maybe even better than travel mini hair brushes.

It's a foamcore cushion with a slight lip on the back as lumbar support, and it unfolds to a "bed." And by bed, I mean that it will easily fit at least one underweight toddler. Common in undergraduate dorm rooms, flip 'n' fucks earned their worthwhile name. Also, I don't recommend a Google image search for flip 'n' fuck, which now also means a type of disembodied sex doll. Google instead "foam chair bed" to avoid nightmares.

Late weekend nights, the four of us would wobble back to our Brown Hall quad, most likely coming from a boys' dorm party that had just run out of Bud Ice. We were full-effect drunk. Alexis, Lindsey, and Christina faded into their bunks to pass out, still wearing spaghetti-strap dresses like respectable freshmen.

My biggest concern upon consciously deciding to become a "drinker" at age 18 was avoiding hangovers. Another gene I inherited from Mom is severe vomit-phobia. When deciding to take drinking under my pleather belt, hangovers were a definite known threat to my puke-free existence. My logical solution was never go to bed drunk. Passing out would surely lead to unconscious puking, possible choking death, and even worse, potential *bedwetting*.

Determined not to fall asleep intoxicated, I would remain in our quad's second room after my roommates went to bed. I curled up on the flip 'n' fuck with my knees to my chest and a space heater aimed at my face, sipping water out of a giant plastic Sigma Alpha Epsilon date party cup.[1] I then spent several hours punching my own torso, trying desperately to stay awake for as long as possible. These were the night vigils for my

---

1. That someone left behind at the dining hall and I pounced on; I wasn't actually invited to said date party.

malt-liquor-addled brain. Sometimes I would sing Mary Poppins songs.

The best help came at 2 am, when MTV started playing trance videos. Occasionally I could find something amazing on the late-night campus movie channel, like *My Girl 2*, but trance videos were usually the best option. Music videos might be too strong of a phrase for what these were…they were more like kaleidoscope soundscapes, or what I imagine the My Little Ponies experience when they dream. I forced myself to sit upright on the flip 'n' fuck, five feet from the tiny TV, eyes dry from forced wakefulness, watching blobs of color sway to thumping synth for three hours, punching away at my midsection. Believe it or not, this strategy successfully fended off severe hangovers for most of fall quarter. What I somehow didn't realize was that it was really the water sipping and not forced wakefulness that helped me feel semi-normal in the morning.

The system started to fail me when I discovered my signature drink. I wasn't able to get a job until my sophomore year, so for a while I had little spending money—whatever I had saved over the summer, and then whatever came mid-quarter from my student loan overage check. Thus, I had to maximize the delivery of alcohol to my bloodstream. I needed to involve hard liquor.

Hard liquor was (and still is) trickier to get your hands on in Ohio. Special laws prohibit it from being sold at grocery stores or out of grocery store workers' car trunks. Hard liquor can only be sold at state-licensed liquor stores, and these were rare around OU. There was only one liquor store at the top of a hill just outside of the heart of campus. To procure liquor, you had to find a brave over-ager, a car, and bribe money for the

RAs. When someone's brother's roommate's overage friend was willing to make a trip to the liquor store, word spread through the corner of our dorm like wildfire. It usually went like this (and this is also how I learned that dorm social hierarchy is not unlike prison):

1. Girl with Totally Legit Booze Connection (GTLBC) learns from her current hookup that Current Hookup's older cousin Ted is visiting for the weekend and is willing to make a liquor run.

2. GTLBC strategically and over-casually tells a select few (socially valuable) dorm neighbors of impending liquor run.

> **a.** First, she tells her roommates, as is required by the laws of the dorm. To leave one's roommates out of a liquor run would lead to passive-aggressive animosity and the potential for rumor-victimization.

> **b.** She also tells the pretty girls. Pretty girls have better access to a variety of penises, which can then be passed on to less-pretty girls. On the 4th floor of Brown Hall, the main room of pretty girls was a triple of former cheerleaders from Columbus. One was actually a cheerleader *at OU* as well, which was like…whoaaaa. Girls with blonde hair, seemingly permanent black eyeliner, and persistent vocal creak were the highest in the pecking order.

3. Rumors emerge (usually started by the pretty girls who have zero concern for anyone else's careful management of the situation, because why should they?) that a liquor run is happening. Dorm frenemies come out of the woodwork and jockey for the opportunity to get a bottle. Their strategies may include promising an in for future liquor runs, sharing excess meal card value, or good old-fashioned sexual favors.

4. On the day of the impending liquor run, GTLBC collects cash and carefully writes a specific, dummy-proof list of required goods. WE ONLY HAVE ONE SHOT AT THIS, PEOPLE. (List inevitably includes at least 18 bottles of triple sec.)

5. Current Hookup's cousin Ted never shows. This was pre-cell phone era, so GTLBC waits all day for this choad, missing stir-fry night at the dining hall. GTLBC finds out later that Ted started drinking too early and passed out by the time the liquor store opened at 12 pm. She is, however, forgiven without equivocation by all, because that's just how shit goes down sometimes in the trenches of underage drinking.

Though our hopes were often dashed, inevitably someone would come through and we would get our hard booze a few times each year. I would always purchase an $8 bottle of 100-proof Paramount vodka. With its stalwart Russian-esque eagle sigil, it was guaranteed to get the job done. I also purchased packets of cherry Kool-Aid (acquired much more easily at Kroger). *This* became my drink of choice: a shot of cheap 100-proof vodka with a half-packet of cherry Kool-Aid dissolved into it—followed by a chaser sip of Bud Ice or Natty Light. (Note that I also used this same recipe, sans chaser, to add pink highlights to my hair.) While this drink has an unparalleled alcohol-content-to-dollars-spent ratio, it led to several unfortunate crawling blackouts.

My roommates not only put me to bed regularly but took my contacts right out of my eyes for me. That's just what we learned to do for each other. Everyone had a night here and there when they killed off several weeks' worth of learned calculus knowledge. When the Paramount and Kool-Aid started, my late-night trance vigils fell by the wayside. I was unable to self-mutilate into continued consciousness for such a long period of time. I tried, certainly, but instead passed out within minutes, usually face-down on the flip 'n' fuck. The next morning, I'd wake in a pool of sweaty drool, my red Calvin Klein T-shirt clinging to my clammy arms. Puking, luckily, didn't happen often anyway. And I maintain a nostalgic affinity for shitty trance music.

It would be nice to end this reflection by articulating a moment of catharsis. But there just wasn't one. College kids are often spoiled and dumb, living a seemingly immortal life. We overdid it because our young bodies tolerated it. We were able to shake off hangovers, metabolize a breakfast of cheese fries and clam chowder, and be ready to drink again before noon. I eventually outgrew binge-drinking. Alcohol became a less important friend slowly over time. We still hang out, but only in smaller doses because she can be crazy abrasive. Now that I'm older and have lost most of my critical alcohol-metabolizing brain proteins, my booze nights are primarily *Broad City* reruns and a glass of moderately priced Sauvignon blanc. (Although I often still seek out cheese fries for breakfast.) And I definitely remember and use those early strategies I cultivated in Brown Hall to avoid hangovers. It's not rocket science: Just drink water, dummy.

14

THAT I MAY WALK TRULY IN THE LIGHT OF THE FLAME

Headed into sophomore year of college, popularity still eluded me, and quite frankly it pissed me off. Had my high school reputation somehow followed me to college? How did they know I was secretly a nerd? It was time for *me* to be the cool kid now, Universe.

I recalled the first few weeks of my freshman year when some women in my dorm did this thing called "rush." Rush was, in a word, bizarre. The young women doing rush had to dress up in matching clothes (i.e., one night they all had to wear black pants and solid jewel-toned blouses, another night they were required to wear black dresses). Once they were all dressed as clones, they attended carefully orchestrated parties, drinking tea, eating wafer cookies, and talking to strategically cycled active sorority members. Then, when the women in my dorm became pledges of a given sorority, their sisters celebrated them by decorating their dorm door and bestowing them with stuffed animals in the form of respective sorority symbols (i.e., squirrels, owls, and other adorable woodland creatures). And *then* their sororities started having EXCLU-SIVE parties with fraternities.

Maggie, a sweet redhead down the hall, pledged Alpha Gamma Delta. Her sisters decorated her dorm door with red and green and gifted her bottles of Tequila Rose and Boone's Wild Strawberry. Alpha Gams were tight with the Delts (Delta Tau Delta), a fraternity known on campus for their rippled pecs, aggressive hazing techniques, and sexual stamina. Hot, nouveau Nazi-looking dudes were constantly coming around looking for Maggie.

I WANTED THAT. I wanted those pecs looking for me in my dorm room. I wanted new friends so excited about me that they spent their hard-earned trust-fund dollars on children's toys to gift me. Rolling into sophomore year and *still* not get-ting invited to the date-rapiest parties, I figured maybe I should give sororities a try.

The night I signed up for rush, I fell asleep teased by visions of monogrammed forest animals and shirtless boys with mil-itary haircuts and Bud Ice breath. I told Mom and Dad I was going to rush, and they were skeptical. My mom in particular always thinks I make weird decisions, but this one was so tra-ditional that it felt like the weirdest thing I could possibly do.

Sororities offered an opportunity to maximize my college years with rich white wieners. While I don't think that many, possibly even most, women joined sororities for the dudes, I do think that many were seeking affiliation and objectively defined acceptance. Affiliation[1] fulfills a critical need for humans, and has obviously been a theme throughout my own life (in case you somehow missed me hitting you over the

1. (McClelland, 1961)

head with it). People are driven to feel a sense of belonging, and their affiliation with a group helps individuals feel protected, loved, and helps inform their identity. Sororities and street gangs are not dramatically unlike in this specific respect. Their existence is based primarily on the human need for affiliation, and thus, psychological and physical safety. Young men and women without a lot of social capital, and/or with a strong drive to feel accepted, may be particularly driven to seek out affiliation with organized groups.

Rush was both painful and awe-inspiring. Each sorority house was beautiful, with grand sitting rooms and coordinated window treatments. The houses themselves oozed privilege. I sat in the football-field-sized dining rooms of sorority houses, paired with an active sister for light conversation and fruit punch. Something about the sorority houses reminded me of horse stables—for the most beautiful, Triple Crown-winning champions.[2]

Sororities eliminated potential pledges after each night of rush. Those they didn't cut were invited back for the next night of rush. Ultimately, the process was intended to familiarize women with each sorority and match them to the best lady-house and respective woodland creature for their entire college career. IN. FUCKING. THEORY.

I was out of my league. Rush was the perfect storm of all my anxiety triggers: being openly judged, beautiful and confident women, and precise definitions of conformity. Insecure, hesitantly sarcastic, and sporting an unflattering pixie cut – I was rapidly ousted from the majority of houses. I struggled in particular with the insincere small talk that powered rush; I would sit across from these women each night, wanting so much to

2. It's totally feminist to allegorize women to horses, right?

be one of them, but feeling distinctly, innately outside. When my favorite sorority, Alpha Gamma Delta, cut me, I shed tears. Why wasn't I good enough for them? I watched unintelligent but classically hot girls struggle to whittle down their many sorority invitations, whereas I didn't have sufficient invites to fill my rush schedule. I was one of few women who had gaps in her schedule by the end of the week. It hurt. I was rejected by seven out of ten sororities solely based on looks and first impressions.

All of the sororities had distinct reputations. The Chi Omegas, for example, held the highest position in the Greek sorority pecking order. They were not only hot, but wealthy and intelligent. They regularly had the highest average GPA on campus of all sororities. Of the remaining three sororities that *didn't* cut me, one was "slutty," one was "nerdy," and one was, most unfortunately, the "fat sorority." These ridiculous reputations drove the entire social calendar for each house. Many fraternities flat-out refused to have parties with the "lesser" sororities.

(I am getting angry again as I recall this.)

I chose the slutty sorority, Delta Zeta. If I was going to affiliate, this felt like the best of the three stereotypes to align with, and I recognized that I was certainly boy-crazy enough to make it work. Plus, they had the best woodland creature mascot of my remaining options: the turtle.

Many of the active sisters fought back against their reputations with a vengeance. In retrospect, it's no surprise that I was slut-shamed my first night as a pledge to Delta Zeta. The first night was called "Bid Night," in reference to the "bid" I had received for my membership. It was common for a sorority to pair with a fraternity for the Bid Night celebration, to introduce the new sisters to their future with socially contracted men. That night we had a party with Sigma Alpha Mu, or "The Sammies."

I arrived early to the party because I didn't know any better or have anything else to do. It was held at a fraternity annex, an informally designated house on campus that was not the official fraternity house. This allowed more flexibility to the already flexible drinking rules for campus fraternities. (Official fraternity houses were allowed to have alcohol. Official sorority houses were absolutely not allowed to have alcohol.) My social jitters were dependably suppressed by the two Natty Ice bottles I had chugged while applying glitter makeup in my dorm room. Upon arrival, a couple of women I vaguely recognized pointed me to the pile of hard liquor bottles in the corner, and I poured myself a blue plastic cup full of vodka with a splash of 7 Up. Although there weren't many people yet at the party, I began the standard process of rubbing my butt into an arbitrary backwards-hat-wearing dude's abdomen, to the tune of Biggie Smalls's "Hypnotize." It was enjoyable. Who doesn't enjoy a good ass in the abdomen?

A woman I didn't recognize suddenly appeared at my side. I noticed her sorority uniform of black Express pants and cross-body leather snap purse. A sister, coming to introduce herself! My mouth melted into a sloppy smile and I "Heeeyyy"-ed at my new friend with vodka eyes.

Her eyes were not vodka. Her eyes were critical.

"Just, like, tone it down OK?" she said to me. "Like, I don't mean to be rude, but just like, calm down."

And then she walked away.

Montell Jordan rang in my ears. The booze and hip-hop

couldn't prevent shame from flushing through my body. I walked to a corner and sat in a chair.

Welcome to the Madonna-whore complex! I never had my behavior judged and monitored by "friends," only by parents and teachers. It hit me that I was no longer just Melanie. I was a Delta Zeta. Because these women had let me be part of their group, I had to follow both their written and unwritten rules of behavior. I represented them now.

Hooking up, a critical part of my college experience, suddenly came under much more scrutiny. There a strong culture of sexual expectation between fraternity members and sorority members, yet it was artificially hidden. Hooking up was only acceptable to a point. There were women in various sororities known for bouncing around the rooms of fraternities. These girls were often mercilessly mocked behind their backs by the very men that welcomed them into the houses and beds in the first place. I learned that one girl in my sorority, whose name was Sunspring, was known as "Bed Spring" to the entire Phi Theta Beta house. Due to the Greek system's intrinsic cliquiness, slut-shaming suddenly loomed bigger, more threatening. Word spread quickly within the Greek community. The slut-shaming contrasted starkly with the simultaneous physical expectations and undercurrent of sexuality so pervasive in the Greek community and college as a whole.

Sororities left a bad taste in my mouth since that first week of rush. Looking back, I am frustrated that, starting with that very first week, I let myself feel so shitty about being rejected by a bunch of Vaseline-toothed clones. A more self-aware woman would've peaced out right then and there, but my dumb 19-year-old brain was still clouded by the glistening possibility of boyfriends and organized binge-drinking. I had committed

to the idea that I would be a "sorority girl" and I let that affiliation guide me for the next three years. It's difficult to start
from scratch when you've committed yourself so wholly to one
group, to one identity. I'm grateful that I learned that from
being in a sorority and learned to pick my affiliates more carefully in the future.

For decades, I felt cynical and angry at the superficial conformity inherent in the Greek system. However, in the past
year, so many of my sisters, even those who were not very close
with me during college, reached out to support me when my
dad got cancer. It blew me away. Their selfless support and true
concern gave me more positive feelings about Delta Zeta than
I had since the first week I joined. One woman religiously followed my dad's online cancer journal and provided me extensive support, even while balancing her own life struggles.

In truth, I blame myself far more than the Greek system
for my experience. I got out of my sorority exactly what I
thought I wanted: A bunch of over-priced Greek letter T-shirts
and plenty of check marks in my blowjob book.[3] I thought
that by joining a sorority, I would finally have an identity that
made me popular. It wasn't really Delta Zeta's fault. If I had
been stronger and more confident, I could've been a sister that
embraced the friendship and rolled her eyes at the silly conformist elements. Being in a sorority taught me how critical
acceptance was to me—and that led to a lot of reflection and
growth. And because I was (am!) a Delta Zeta, I have women
in my life who truly love me—which is far more important
than cunnilingus in a former funeral-home-turned-fraternity-
house basement.

---

3. What, you didn't have a blowjob book?

15

THE NAKED MOLE RAT

If it wasn't for joining a sorority, I probably never would've started shaving my pussy.

Before that fateful day, I was only vaguely aware that genitalia grooming was a thing—and in particular, that some women shaved their vulva[1] completely. Well before the advent of The Internet, the only commercial female nudity I'd really seen as a child was in *National Geographic* or in the 1981 *Playboy* that my dad kept hidden alongside my mom's Wurlitzer organ sheet music. I had learned about sex from good old hardback textbooks where discussions of pubic hair grooming were remarkably scant. However, I did spend a fair amount of adolescent time squinting at Spice, the scrambled cable porn channel that everyone peeped during the 90s. Through the squiggly black-and-white analog lines, I could decipher that some adult women (often engaging in sex with EACH OTHER, can you imagine?) had a bare mons pubis.

Awareness of fashion trends tends to come late to us in the

---

1. Incidentally, to the disappointment of feminist America, "vulva" is a word I still can't say with a straight face. It sounds like a sorority woodland creature mascot! I can just hear David Attenborough reciting the care and feeding strategies for the Common Midwestern Vulva.

Midwest. Pubic hair styles were no exception. I estimate that women in California and New York have probably been shaving their pussy since the late 1800s, and thus it trickled down to Ohio by about 1998. My decision wasn't based on a preference for this particular look, or curiosity, or even a desire to please some idiot Broseph—I decided to shave because my Delta Zeta sorority sisters did it.

The challenge was first posed to me by my sorority "little sis" and roommate Lydia. All active sisters in any given sorority have a big and little sister—sort of an apprenticeship program in the craft of Basic Bitchery. I had taken on Lydia as a little sis in spring of my sophomore year, and she moved in with me and two other sisters the fall of our junior year. Despite being my sorority subordinate, Lydia was wise in the art of the razor.

"You have to do it a lot, as often as you can, so your skin gets used to it," she said.

Gets used to what? I wondered. I had shaved my legs and armpits, and it had never seemed to violate my skin in any way. Lydia then announced that she shaved *her entire body* every single day. Arms, armpits, stomach, pussy, legs, butt, feet. I suddenly felt uncomfortable and Sasquatch-esque.

The next day, armed with a pastel teal razor, I locked myself into the second stall of the Delta Zeta house shower. About 90 minutes later, I emerged, and eyed the naked mole rat staring back at me in the mirror. And this was not just your average naked mole rat. This was a naked mole rat that appeared to have (just barely) survived The French Revolution. Battered and puffy, with a few errant rodent-like hairs I had missed despite elaborate razor aerobics, my genitals looked back at me wearily, as if to say "This better be worth it."

This is a rather unfortunate public-domain photo of a naked mole rat eating a sandwich. This is exactly what my vulva looked like post-shave, minus the sandwich. And teeth.

Fall of my senior year, my pseudo-boyfriend (i.e., a fraternity dude that I would semi-regularly find stoned at an underage bar and then take home) complained about my prickly labia. My genitals, unlike Lydia's, had failed over the previous year to "toughen up." Initially, I did try (for about a week) to shave daily, like Lydia advocated, with disastrous results. Hundreds of angry red bumps emerged, only to have their heads repeatedly chopped off by my teal razor. My pubes had become less "Sexy Coed" and more "Trampled Raw Chicken" so I subsided and reduced shaving to once a week—the maximum frequency I could maintain to keep my genitals looking reasonably like genitals. This meant that after a day or two, stubble happened. (I won't begin to describe the nightmare of an attempt at pubic waxing. But regardless, despite what pop culture would have you believe, bare labia always has to experience a period of regrowth.) Because of this, I always shaved on Fridays for maximum weekend hook-up potential. However, occasionally I would finish my homework early on a Wednesday and get drunk like a good public college sorority girl should. Inevitably, some men were thus exposed to my less-than-perfect-mid-week vulval lips. And then one bastard had the gall to complain about it.

What the hell was the point of all this conformity? I couldn't even do it right. I started to feel like a shell of myself, a shadow of the former teen who had written angry zines and ruled the roost at theater camp. So desperate for popularity, I had become a woman who IRONED HER JEANS, for fuck's sake. I'm not knocking shaved pussy, or even sororities for that matter. Many women engage in these practices and truly find joy in them. But it wasn't me. The mixed sexual messages, the gossip, the forced social activism[2]—all of it was garbage.

Slowly, I tried to salvage the Melanie I used to be. I started with a landing strip, allowing a small patch of my junk to reclaim itself, like those feral houses covered with ivy that you see in Detroit. I contemplated deactivation from my sorority, which would formally extract me from the Greek system. However, by my senior year, I feared losing the only social circle I had attained. So, I stayed. But dammit, I resisted to the extent I could socially manage. I went to the minimum creepy formal ritual ceremonies, where we were required to wear all white and weren't allowed to put on makeup—how cult-like is that? I even skipped a bunch of the fraternity parties, my for-

---

2. In the name of Delta Zeta, I got roped into picking up trash on the side of a highway. You really haven't lived until you've picked up bloody moonshine bottles with your bare hands next to certainly drunk drivers flying down an Appalachian highway.

mer lifeblood. I had outgrown the naked-mole-rat race. The decreased lack of social pressure that year was freeing.

This year, 2018, marks the 20th anniversary of my pussy-shaving inauguration. I'm unlikely to reattempt a nostalgic naked mole rat. However, some aspects of my sorority years do maintain. I still keep things trimmed, and I still enjoy looking at college boys. I've retired my black Express pants, but I do wear Victoria's Secret Pink in the privacy of my own home. Every once in a great while, I'll even order a Long Island Iced Tea and bum a Virginia Slim. That's about it.

16

THE SHIRE TO THE CITY OF BIG SHOULDERS

My life in The Shire was ending, and now it was time to move on to Mordor. The Shire was a place where the darkness of Mordor failed to break through the seemingly endless sunshine…

Hold on. Let me back up for those of you who are not fantasy nerds.

The Shire is the realm of hobbits in J.R.R. Tolkien's immortal Middle Earth series. (I feel comfortable affiliating with the Hobbit race for many reasons including their sturdy squat body types, deep love for eating, and affinity for hallucinogenic smoke.) The Shire is arguably the most idyllic land in Tolkien's world. It is pastoral as fuck, full of miniature carriage horses, cherubic toddlers, and monthly pop-up smorgasbords. This magical Never-Never Land is essentially what a traditional college-going experience is for many students.

In the traditional college-going experience, the burdens of adulthood are not yet present, but the independence is. It is a magical place between childhood and adulthood where one can ingest the best of both worlds. Even amidst my homework, part-time job, and sorority-related drama, college was a pretty goddamn charmed existence. There were no graduate school-induced panic attacks, no fear of the disappearing middle class, and no student-loan repayment plan. For most of my time in college, I didn't even have to plan my meals. I just ate fettuccine alfredo or red-sauce spaghetti every night at the dining hall. (Vegetarian options were limited. Yes, my blood became 30% wheat gluten and I gained weight like Christian Bale playing Dick Cheney.) In college, we spent the majority of our waking hours drinking disgustingly cheap alcohol and engaging in promiscuity. For me, college in Athens, Ohio was like Amsterdam's Red Light District. (Minus the sex trafficking.)

I.e., it was The Shire. It was easy, pleasant, and magic.

And then I moved to Chicago.

I liken Chicago to Mordor with the utmost love in my heart. There are plenty of reasons I have stayed in Chicago for 18 years. But after several years in the small, rolling Appalachian foothills of the Shire (we didn't even have a Walmart yet!), Chicago loomed like Minas Morgul. (This is where the most evil people in Mordor live. I promise I'll stop with the Tolkien references soon. Maybe.)

As wonderful as Chicago citizens are, we are also total garbage people. Big American cities have a tendency to break down wide-eyed, sincere humans and turn them into jaded, careless ogres.

This became particularly obvious when I started visiting other cities of the world—especially European cities. In many other cities, citizens can be trusted. Public transportation often works on an honors system. In Munich, you purchase a train ticket and then just hop on. There are *no turnstiles.* You are trusted to have honorably bought your fare. This could never happen in Chicago. People would exploit the system constantly. I sure would.

Similarly, I was recently at a bar in Copenhagen and needed to pee. I had to walk outside of the bar into the cold to get to the restroom. Anyone off the street could access the restroom, which was a large, multi-stall unisex[1] bathroom, covered in playful graffiti. I thought *ugh* and prepared myself for the impending grossness and lack of toilet paper that was sure to greet me in the stall. But no. It was perfectly clean, even late in the night, and contained a completely adequate amount of toilet paper. I have yet to urinate in a public restroom in Chicago that does not have: a) a sticky bodily-fluid-covered toilet seat b) feces smears on the (empty) toilet paper dispenser and/or c) the hot water faucet handle torn out of the wall.

The most appropriate metaphor for Chicago, more so than even Mordor, resides in its signature liqueur, Jeppson's Malört. Made from wormwood, Malört is like absinthe, but if absinthe had been bullied in high school and grew up to be De Niro in *Taxi Driver.* Malört is like building your vacation home on Garbage Island. Malört: Popular amongst masochists and comic-book villains alike! Malört is...Santorum. (I could do this all day.)

Malort is so shockingly offensive that its makers have had no choice but to capitalize on its awfulness in the name of street cred. Jeppson's proudly boasts that Malört is not for the faint of heart. I've had Ohio friends ask me to purchase and ship

1. Full support for unisex bathrooms as the norm. I just wish penis-owners could aim a bit better.

Malört to them as gag gifts. There are many online videos of unsuspecting humans ingesting Malört for the first time and subsequently gagging until they expel a spleen. Its flavor has been likened to hairspray, gasoline, and most articulately, asshole.

It's bad. Yet surprisingly beloved. Chicago is Malört and Malört is Chicago. Both are fierce, disgusting, yet somehow all your friends want to try it. And keep coming back for more.

When you are a dumb white kid fresh out of The Shire and the internet doesn't really exist yet, there is only one neighborhood in Chicago. It is called Wrigleyville, and you hear about it from a sorority sister's cousin's girlfriend who just moved there. That's just where you go. When I was accepted into my doctoral program in Chicago, I was only aware of this neighborhood.

I can easily say now, with zero qualms, that Wrigleyville is the absolute worst neighborhood in Chicago. It is truly everything that is wrong with America. The biggest problem with Wrigleyville is that it tries, like college, to be The Shire. Wrigleyville is full of bars and mediocre restaurants and America's lovable underdog, the Cubs. But it fails because adulthood *isn't* Never-Never Land. Adulthood is Mordor, just like Chicago. Or at best, adulthood might be Gondor, land of humans, where there are plenty of good-looking men but you still have to piss in a chamber pot and stay up all night manning the goddamn watchtower.

The lure of Wrigleyville's faux-Shireness pulls in astronomic crowds of assholes. There are SO MANY people in

Wrigleyville. And they are SO AWFUL. These are a people somehow permanently drunk, tanned, and wearing backwards baseball caps. I didn't know that dudes still wore pleated khaki shorts *anywhere*. They do in Wrigleyville.

Despite it being the only neighborhood I had heard of, I wasn't able to live in Wrigleyville, much to my dismay at the time. Wrigleyville is so coveted by idiots that it's become incredibly expensive. There was no way for me to afford Wrigleyville on my $11,000/year graduate student stipend—even with a roommate. The apartment I finally found was in a "less desirable" neighborhood, i.e., no one without a trust fund can afford to buy property there, but you *might* be able to afford to rent. My first place was eight blocks north of Wrigleyville, at the north corner of Graceland Cemetery. The rent was $825 a month for a two-bedroom, so cheap for Chicago's north side that I can't even fathom it now. My apartment was above a Filipino restaurant, so it constantly smelled of spicy pork, which made it difficult to maintain stoic vegetarianism. Our front window overlooked a divey gay karaoke bar and a Family Video. My bedroom window faced the alley, which smelled like a combination of rotting Filipino seafood, rat feces, and sun-baked garbage juice.

I didn't think of myself as sheltered or privileged when I moved to Chicago. There's a thing called self-serving bias[2] that everyone (yes—you and also your mom) is affected by. Self-serving bias comes into play when individuals make a judgment or any kind of evaluation about something. Whether the judgment is about yourself, or others, or media—YOU are biased to view things in a manner that is favorable to you. (It's a

---

2. See Campbell & Sedikides (1999) for a comprehensive look at self-serving bias.

fact. It's not just you. We're all terrible!) For example, it is much easier for you to recall instances where you were woke than when you were not-woke. It's easier for you to justify or at least semi-excuse your own bad behavior (if you even see that it was bad), but much harder for you to consider the context and circumstances that contribute to with others' bad behaviors.

I had grown up in a lower-middle-income Democratic household. Plus, I had a gay family member! I thought I was pretty pre-woke. But moving to Chicago, getting a graduate degree in human behavior, and eventually working with Chicago Public Schools opened my eyes to how utterly shitty things could be. How Mordor-iffic the world really is. The transition to Chicago was rough.

First, I quickly acclimated to fear of strange men. While there is certainly no shortage of gross men in Ohio, Chicago sexual harassment was a whole new horrifying world. In my hometown, most people drove. Out and about in Ohio, I was safe and hidden in my Lake Erie-blue Chevy wagon. In Chicago, all of my transportation became public and vulnerable.

The first of many Chicago street harassment incidents happened at the bus stop across the street from that apartment—a prime location for sexual harassment. Dudes *constantly* tried to talk to me while I waited for the bus. Once, a rusty brown pickup truck pulled up at the stoplight next to me and a slimy maggot of man leaned across to hold up a photo of his pasty erect penis.

"This is a picture of my dick," he announced, as though I needed the clarification.

I had not yet learned the vital city skill of ignoring creepy people. When someone talked to me, my instinct was to pay attention. I turned to look at this human invertebrate before the words were completely out of his mouth. I felt my face flush as I unavoidably caught a glance of the photo. It looked like a small capybara fetus.

"You want to put it in your mouth, don't you?" And then a series of sucking sounds. If Chicago was Mordor, this dude was definitely a cave troll.

Someone in my graduate program told me about the sexual predator online repository, and I was dismayed to learn that a child sex offender lived in the apartment below me. I never saw the offender in question in real life. I did, however, frequently see his roommate, who resembled a hillbilly version of Sirius Black. He had stringy black hair, a glass eye, and a mangy black German Shepherd that growled at me every time I passed him on the sidewalk. A few months before the end of my one-year lease, the entire apartment complex became infested with mice. I constantly caught mice running around the living room, in and out of the radiators. It turned out that when Pedophile McGee and Hillbilly Sirius Black moved out, the landlords found their apartment so filthy it had become a mouse commune. Dozens of mice lived there comfortably; it was the perfect wall-to-wall carpeted location for rodent-style scavenging and free-love mentality.

I had a new set of post-idyllic life experiences. There was the ongoing sexual harassment, frigid, whipping winds from Lake Michigan, rodent-infested living conditions, and an alley garbage juice stench so pungent it could probably be used as chemical warfare. But it wasn't all bad. I discovered two other very important things in Chicago that first year. 1) MAC Lipstick. 2) A new posse of nerds.

I walked into Damen Hall at Loyola University of Chicago for orientation, armed with a pocketful o' Xanax and my mom's voice echoing in my ears.

"Everyone's in the same boat," she had said. She invoked this phrase often when I was afraid of a situation. It comforted me to know that everyone was going into this new chapter as uncertain as me.

Orientation began with a brief tour of the 6th floor of Damen Hall. I was given an "office," which was actually a cinder block hole in a wall behind an elevator. It had no windows, fit only a small desk and shelf, and was painted the color of hangover urine. But it was mine! I met other students in my cohort—Renee, Kelly, Fred, and Janet. After our brief introduction, the psychology department held a seminar as a "special treat" for the new graduate students, possibly the raddest academic seminar I've ever attended. Sex researchers came in from Northwestern University and detailed their arousal research, which involved extensive use of penile erection instruments and vaginal wetness monitors. I jealously imagined all their graduate research assistants getting to hook up genital probes. I had picked the wrong path! I could've been a sex researcher handling people's junk all day!

A main finding from the Northwestern researchers' study was that cis-hetero men became the most aroused while watching female-on-female porn. Cis-hetero women, however, got turned on by everything the researchers put in front of them: female-female, male-female, male-male. The researchers suggested at the time that this might be an evolutionary benefit;

that it is in a vagina owner's best interest to become easily wet so that injury was less likely.[3]

I was eased into comfort by this new world of academic appropriateness. In a psychology department, there is no need for phony prudishness, so long as the sex talk can be backed up with requisite statistical rigor. I kept looking around the room, waiting for someone to burst into giggles after the umpteenth mention of "erection." No one did. Strange.

After the seminar, we were led by our new professors/bosses to an informal reception. *With alcohol.* At 22, I was barely used to the fact that it was legal for me to drink alcohol, much less in the company of people who would be giving me homework next week. They also had incredibly fancy cheeses that blew my mind—*Boursin* and *brie.* (I now know that these are pretty common—one can get brie or Boursin at any grocery store in the city. Painesville even has brie now. Come to Painesville, Ohio! We have brie!) But that year, since Boursin and brie were not yet found in either Painesville or Athens, Ohio, my gustatory horizons were greatly expanded by this alien ivory, soft, spreadable cheese.

I slowly warmed to my cohort as a new set of forced friends. In this way, grad school reminded me more of high school than college. I had the same peer group taking all of the same classes. We could work on statistics problems together and weigh the merits of political psychology paper topics. My new nerds were SO INFORMED. They listened to NPR constantly and voluntarily went to hear *jazz music.* These were not the rural northeast Ohio nerds of my past. These were cultured and socially just nerds. Graduate school is also flush with anx-

3. (Chivers, Rieger, Latty & Bailey, 2004).

iety disorders, so much so that we sometimes traded sedatives over lunch.

"I'll give you one Xanax for two Ativan."

"No deal. Those are only .25 milligrams, not .5."

"Oooh, you have Xanax BARS? God, you have the best shrink."

In order to "beat" (or at least, temporarily suppress) self-serving bias, you truly have to put yourself in other people's shoes. It sounds easy, right? It's not. It takes a level of constant awareness and cognitive work, and the human brain just doesn't do this without major effort. You have to drag your brain into the perspective of others, kicking and screaming. And do it repeatedly. (The "good guys" AND the "bad guys.") If you think just because you're woke that you're not subject to self-serving bias, you are sorely mistaken.

My best friend in graduate school was black. Her name is Kelly. When we became friends, I didn't think much about our race differences other than that they existed. She was my first close black friend. She was patient with me in a way that she didn't need to be, because it wasn't her job to educate me. But she was anyway. Because Kelly and I spent so much time together, I began to see some of the differences between Kelly's and my life experiences.

One day we were looking at MAC lipsticks to charge to our already heavily indebted credit cards. Kelly and I shopped together a lot. She had recently lived in Oklahoma City, which had more commerce than Athens, Ohio, but we still both felt a surge of giddiness by the mass amounts of shopping opportunities in Chicago. Forever 21 was the height of affordable glam for us. ($20 pleather pants! Four pairs of on-trend socks for only $3! Thank you, sweatshops!) And the lipsticks. Lord, there were so many lipsticks in the Magnificent Mile area.

Unfortunately, however, most of our livelihood was funded by a meager assistantship and student loans. It took a decade for me to pay off the debt I incurred during the first year of graduate school. By the end of our first year, shopping trips dramatically decreased in frequency as our dinners of canned beans increased. In the fall, however, it was a fucking MAC lipstick free-for-all whenever we could manage it.

"Should we go to this party on Friday?" I asked her while scanning Marshall Field's fall collection of earth-toned lipsticks. One of the clinical psych second years was having a party Friday. We didn't know him that well, but we didn't know anyone in Chicago that well.

Kelly made a barfing noise. (I felt very cool that Kelly liked me, because she showed disdain for most people.)

"That neighborhood is kind of ghetto anyway," I said, absentmindedly fingering a Viva Glam lipstick.

Kelly stopped browsing and turned to me.

"What's *ghetto?*" she asked.

I frowned, realizing for the first time the potential implication of that term. "Just like, it has more crime," I said. My heart caught in my throat. She and I both knew that it was in a lower income part of the neighborhood with a higher proportion of black people.

"Mmhmm," she murmured, and turned back to the lipsticks. She could sense my sudden revelation of the years of oppression linked to that single word, and left it at that—generously.

Without her subtle challenge, I would never have considered the ramifications of tossing the word "ghetto" around like a MAC lipstick at an Orc rave.

We opted to go to the party Friday. The building was a high-rise overlooking Lake Michigan. Kelly and I met at the train station and we walked into the lobby together. Kelly approached the security desk.

"We're going to Shawn Turner's," Kelly told the security guard, a thin, balding white man who appeared to be in his late 60s.

The security guard didn't respond. He kept his eyes down. Kelly coughed, and he continued to ignore her. I walked to the desk and spoke up.

"Excuse me?" I said. "We would like to go up to Shawn Turner's apartment."

His eyes flickered up and he asked us both to sign the clipboard on the granite desktop.

Walking to the elevator, it hit me that the security guard had deliberately ignored Kelly because she was black. I was appalled. I had never witnessed anything like it before. I had lived a suburban rural majority white existence for 22 years. I couldn't believe that someone would act so openly racist in this day and age. I was ashamed, disgusted, so shocked that I didn't know what to say. Kelly calmly pressed the elevator button for the 12th floor. I realized that this was not a new experience for her. She was used to it.

In my third year, I had to start teaching my own class—Lab

in Social Psychology. It was a requirement for psychology majors; few students were excited to take it. I was 24 when I first started teaching this course to upper class (junior and senior) students, making me a mere two or three years older than them. My need for approval still raged hard. I tried desperately to maintain an air of youth and coolness in my teaching experience. I wasn't completely alone in this; many graduate students cared too much about what their undergraduate students thought. This was exacerbated by the recent release of an internet tool called "Rate My Professors." (I am beyond disappointed that this website still exists in 2018 and has not gone down in virtual internet flames like the popular Ask Jeeves and AOL chat of the late 90s/early 2000s.) Rate My Professors is just what it sounds like. It's a forum where college students can rate their instructors on a scale from 1-5 and even acknowledge whether or not they are physically attractive by awarding them a red chili pepper emoticon. My graduate student cohort talked about Rate My Professors *constantly*. We stalked each other's reviews, our advisors' reviews, and our own reviews almost daily. I desperately prayed for a new chili pepper each time I logged in.

I maintain that Loyola University Chicago undergraduate students are monsters. They may as well have been from fucking Wrigleyville. Many of LUC's undergrads grew up in affluent North Shore suburbs of Chicago, and matriculated to Loyola as a backup when they couldn't get into Northwestern or the University of Chicago. (This was, at least, what grad students told ourselves to feel better about their acute awfulness.) Many of my students were entitled as all hell and viciously cranky when they had to actually work for a good grade.

"I'm not reading Rate My Professors anymore," I said nonchalantly to my friends Renee and Fred. We were sitting together in the psychology department lobby, our bagged sandwich lunches spread out over the coffee table atop old academic journals. Several weeks into the semester, I had forced myself to stop checking the website.

"Oh?" Renee said, giving Fred a side-eye.

"What?" I asked. My heart thumped. "Is there something new on it?"

"It's stupid," Renee said, rolling her eyes. "We reported it."

I dropped my sandwich and rushed to the rickety desktop PC in the corner of the lobby. I started to sit in front of it, then changed my mind. I didn't want to open up that website in front of anyone else.

"I'll be right back," I said to Renee and Fred, bolting.

In the privacy of my office, I read the new review:

"This class sucks. She thinks she's cool, but she's not. You can see her butt crack all the time."

Mortification. I mean, could I help it that low-rise jeans were in style? I had been unwittingly showcasing my tramp stamp and coin slot to my students all year long. Those ungrateful fuckers.

But my nerd posse had my back. If I didn't bring up Rate My Professors to Renee and Fred that day, I may never have known about the nasty comment. They had already both written up the comment to moderators, asking that it be taken down as irrelevant and inappropriate. (It went away within a few weeks.) We watched out for each other's fragile egos.

My grad-school friends helped make a life transition palatable. Chicago isn't really Mordor, but she certainly can be brutal. The beautiful asshole people are what makes Chicago such a wonderful city. Sure, we need to be tracked with transit cards, and sometimes leave poop smears in public restrooms. Sure, you can't leave a half-drunk beer on your porch without it getting stolen. But that's how things go. Chicago ain't gonna sugar-coat anything for you, and for that you have to respect her. Like any well-rounded character, Chicago's challenges come with its beauty and diversity. The people of Chicago, like my graduate school cohort, are united by our shared experiences. If I had gone to grad-school anywhere else, I would not be the woman I am today. Chicago has opened my eyes, finally. At least until I take my next nap.

17

NON-BREEDING FOR ROCK STARS

As mentioned, I typically follow (often subconsciously) the rule of going for the cutest boy in the room. Most notably and successfully, the cutest-boy-in-the-room rule is how I ended up with my husband Dave. In 1997, we were both sophomores in college and everyone called him by his last name, Abbott. He was a houseboy at the Delta Zeta house, which meant that he had the elite job of washing dishes. He spent one two-hour shift a week cleaning up after the forty women living in the house. In exchange, he got to eat two meals a day with a bunch of ovulating repressed sluts in their pajamas. (I mean this in a good way.) Abbott was about 10 pounds overweight (hey—it was a Midwest college town, we all had a beer and corn syrup spare tire) and was rarely seen without a dirty baseball cap and mischievous grin.

When I first met Dave, he was dating another woman in Delta Zeta. Her name was Laura, and she was the raddest, most atypical sorority girl I had met. Jewish and bitterly sarcastic, Laura was a well-respected elder in the sorority. She was one of my favorites. Laura introduced me to Dave at party with his fraternity. I shook his hand and awkwardly said "Nice meet to you." He leaned forward and whispered in my ear "I know who you are." My heart shivered gleefully.

As with most college relationships, Laura and Dave eventually faded. Laura is now married to a woman and they live in Park Slope. We get to see her every few years and she continues to be the raddest sorority girl I know, a solid holdover from Delta Zeta. (I never said it was ALL bad.) So, I got to move in on Dave by 1999. I was living in the sorority house, trying as often as possible to fight off other needy girls and sit by him, as we dined decadently on mashed potatoes with cheese sauce.

At any given time, there were about six houseboys "employed" at the sorority house, selected carefully from neighboring fraternity houses for their abilities to withstand hot dishwashing water and hide their boners. While we ladies weren't allowed in the kitchen, ever, the houseboys were not allowed anywhere *but* the kitchen and dining room. No men whatsoever were allowed in the bedrooms at the house. (This rule was frequently broken.)

Like most fraternity boys, the houseboys were generally a safely attractive, bland group. I had mild crushes on most of them, with their uniform hemp necklaces and cargo pants. Most of the women living in the Delta Zeta house had crushes on multiple houseboys. With six dudes to forty women, you had to maximize your odds. But Dave was always my favorite. Not only was he the cutest, but he had a spark that the other houseboys didn't. He was clever while remaining completely sincere.

And then he totally played me, that rat bastard.

Dave lived in his fraternity house, which can only be described as a nest of intoxicated, unshaved vipers. I remember the horror of first urinating in the bathroom at the Phi Tau house, drunkenly trying to avoid what looked like solidified piss smears and spilled cocaine on the toilet seat. Dave shared a room with two other guys. When you walked into his room, you wouldn't know there were any beds in the room at all. One was tucked into a nook in the wall. (Dave eventually moved up to senior status and acquired the nook.) The other two beds were lofted so high that they were unnoticeable to the naked, inebriated eye. There were thin privacy curtains around each bed, but it was college, and you just accepted that your sexual encounters would be overheard and possibly viewed by at least a dozen people. Our heads inches from the ceiling, Dave and I spent our first night together in the spring of 1999. The next day he informed me that he had a girlfriend already. She was his high school sweetheart, lived in Indianapolis, and was conveniently absent from his life 95% of the time. I stormed out of that dank frat house, vowing never to return.

But we became friends anyway. It's *really hard* for me to hold a grudge against cute guys for an extended period of time. Dave apologized for being a horrible skeevy man, and I, of course, forgave him. He was just so damn likable. And then one day he offered to teach me to smoke pot.

I had never "hit the hippie lettuce" before. I was afraid of weed primarily because it was illegal. But it was fucking college, and by my senior year, it was past time for me to learn how to smoke pot. Dave came to my apartment, sat next to me on my shitty twin mattress, and proceeded to pack four bowls over the course of two hours. Nothing whatsoever happened to me. (I later learned that it was normal for it to take several attempts to first feel the effects of marijuana.) We ended up snuggling until Dave got so stupid high that he wigged out and had to leave. But the tide had turned, and we were back to romance.

We got married relatively young, as was relatively common for sheltered Midwest kids. It's interesting what matters to you when you're 24; today I can't believe we got married as young as we did. We lived together for not quite three years in tiny Wicker Park apartments before we got engaged, which felt like *eternity*. Dave's sister Susie called him one night in 2002 to tell him she got engaged. I cried all night. I was so jealous that Susie would get all the wedding attention before us.

If Dave and I met today, I wonder if we'd even bother to get married, mostly out of laziness. Or maybe we would have an outsider wedding, like at a petting zoo, or an ironic landfill wedding. In our early 20s, however, we did a wedding like we thought we were supposed to, complete with matching bridesmaids and tiered cake and sloppy-drunk groomsmen.

My parents had gotten married at Ohio University in the 1970s, so we went full Kool-Aid and also had our wedding at the same tiny chapel on College Green. The alumni newspaper even did a feature on our wedding. It was a very traditional ceremony and reception that we spent $10,000 of my student loans on. (Again, we are still paying it off in $60/month increments. Use your student loans wisely, folks.)

About eight seconds after we were married, people started asking me why I wasn't pregnant yet. My aunts got together to make a scrapbook as a wedding gift with many pages dedicated to Dave's and my future children.

Reasons to not have children came fast and furious. First, there was grad school, an easy excuse to delay making a deci-

Mom and Dad rocked the 70s OU wedding.

sion about kids. There was no chance I could juggle the stresses of my dissertation while toting a second human inside of me.

Then I got a job working as a researcher for Chicago Public Schools. I do not understand how parents work full-time and have kids. We could never imagine having the time. But mostly—kids are fucking expensive. My own Dad's anxiety and depression often made steady work difficult for him, and I knew from a young age that my family struggled with money. It was a visible stressor for all of us, particularly Mom, and I dreaded that lifestyle in my own adult home. All too vivid were the days when Mom couldn't pay the bills. She would put her head in her hands and quietly place the electric bill back into our blue and white ceramic bill bowl, hoping she could pay it in the next month before service was shut off. Financial fear was the same reason I picked psychology and graduate school over pursuing theater and writing. I wanted stable finances. I didn't want any excuse to be afraid of becoming homeless. Babies are a huge threat to financial stability: A cheap daycare in Chicago for two kids costs *the same as my mortgage.* And that's just daycare! Apparently, you also have to feed children.

Her clock is ticking

Time to move from the front of the line to the back of the line!

The baby-forward scrapbook

Then there's the whole pregnancy thing, which many women find magical.

Pregnancy is alien-level creepy, and birth is essentially a *Walking Dead* battle. First, there is a tiny Cthulhu growing in your gut. (I personally had enough hypochondriasis, blood-related fainting, panic attacks, and body insecurity to fill two lifetimes *without* a Cthulhu rooting around in my gynecological regions.) Then the Cthulhu has to come out in a blaze of gore and pain and literal shit.

Vanity also played a role in my pregnancy fears. I didn't want to have my body stretched out and pieced back together like taxidermy. I wanted my perky boobs to remain perky and my ankles to remain un-canked. (Spoiler alert: You'll grow up to have a Mom butt even if you don't become a Mom. Embrace it.) While it mystified many of my hometown friends and family, there was just never a good enough reason to get my tin roof rusted.

Over time, Dave and I have grown to be rather pretentious about our lack of ankle-biters. Together we are a force to be reckoned with; if we weren't so lazy, we'd probably clean up at couples competitions—like Warrior Dashes and cosplay and Cheetos-eating contests.[1] We aren't jealous people, so we rarely have romantic drama. And because we don't have our own children, we readily acknowledge that we have a bit of adult arrested development. We can enjoy the luxury of getting too drunk on any given Saturday afternoon without having to worry about, like, forgetting to water our toddlers. We have a plethora of needy rescue animals, but we can easily toss a dog bone into the living room and leave them alone in the house for up to six hours at a time. Try THAT with your baby. (Although I bet dog bones are great for teething infants!) We can travel alone without guilt, we can die poor, and we can make lots of stupid decisions without worrying that it will impact some tiny human. It's pretty great.

I adore my friends' children. They are so fun, such delightful little cherubs. I have enjoyed seeing my loved ones blossom into fantastic parents. It's truly beautiful—but I don't need it for myself. Dave and my dumb dogs are my pack. He is the cutest boy and my dogs are the cutest offspring. I can't ever imagine

---

1. I know this isn't a real thing, but a girl can dream.

needing more in my life than those I already have. A life without parasitic progeny has truly made us blessed.

18

LITTLE BOYS

I was sitting on the floor outside of my bathroom recently, staring at the ceiling tiles, which have one of those weird coffee-looking stains. I was thinking about making a New Year's resolution. Emma the dog lay next to me on the circa-1892 pine floorboards. All of the wood floors in our house have intricate maps of dog scratches and give you splinters if you walk around in your bare feet.

Emma's one of our three rescue dogs mentioned in this book. Currently the eldest at age 16, she's a forty-pound black supermutt whose shedding is on par with with a wooly mammoth on Propecia. While she's always been deaf, she is now also mostly blind. In her younger years, she had terrible separation anxiety, as well as odd, seizure-like mannerisms. Specifically, she bit the air at invisible flies repeatedly until the invisible flies overcame her and she hid under a chair. Elsie was my husband's and my first dog, a wiry thirty-pound golden shepherd mix with expressive black eyeliner. She was excellent at biting small children and hunting city rats, though sadly her long, happy, rat-hunting life ended in 2016. Sumo is the third dog, a gray eighty-pound gorilla-eyed pit bull who only wants to be everyone's friend.

I was told that dog photos sell more books.

I stroked Emma's fur and considered my New Year's resolution options. In general, my past New Year's resolutions have tended to be a smidge on the unattainable side. For example, in 1998 my resolution was to be a hot girl in an Usher video. So, I decided this year to try a resolution that was a little less…objectively fail-able. Something more nebulous so that in 12 months I could convince myself that I'd been moderately successful.

"IN 2018," I shouted.

"What?" yelled my husband from inside the bathroom.

"I'M NOT TALKING TO YOU, I'M MAKING A NEW YEAR'S RESOLUTION" I shouted back.

Emma seemed to feel the vibrations of my shouting and abruptly stopped licking her butthole to look at me, wondering if she was in trouble.

"IN 2018 I WILL BE LESS COMPETITIVE WITH WOMEN," I shouted.

My husband laughed from the toilet. Emma went back to licking her butthole.

What a gross, unlikable trait. Not the butthole-licking—Emma's gotta keep her anal sac area clean, can't blame her for that—but the fact that I so often see women as a threat. This is a key reason why it's been difficult to find an adult community I can really be absorbed into. I have particular trouble with the writing and comedy communities. If a woman can be perceived in any way as a competitor or someone attempting to succeed at the same thing I'm attempting, she becomes my enemy. Or at the very least, my frenemy. I see the world as having a finite amount of resources that *only one* of us can have. These resources could be anything from monetary success to laughs at a group dinner to the last remaining pretzel in the communal office pretzel jar.

This attitude is *terrible.* Despicable. It's an instinct that I loathe, and work to constantly untrain, with little avail. Why can't my brain rationally see women as a resource, a collaborative, a group of persons who can make me whole? Women power, right? Unite or die!

Fuck that. Every bitch for her goddamnself.

No, sorry! NO, Melanie. God, shit. I am Bette Davis and the rest of the vagina-toting world is my Joan Collins.

I mean, I *want* the ladylove. I LOVE IT IN THEORY. I want to *collaborate* and *work together* and *share the spotlight.* I really do. I want to extol successes of other women, *even when I am unable to ride their coattails.* Why does it elude me? Often I'll read these great quotes on Instagram like, "Her Success Does Not Mean Your Failure," written in a curvy femme lipstick font and placed atop graphics of tropical plants, and when I do—I literally pound my iPhone into my head. Perhaps through osmosis I can push a message of ladyunity deep into my cerebral cortex.

When my girlfriends tout their improv and stand-up shows and personal essays on social media, I find myself making excuses for why I can't attend/read. When a friend's web series won an Emmy for one of its actors, I threw a tantrum and shouted off a list of all the reasons I was too busy to write my own goddamn web series already. Successful ladies are the WORST. Like, just who the fuck does Amal Clooney think she is? Plus—don't even get me started on the unreasonable bar that Beyoncé has set for women. NO MOTHER OF TWINS CAN PULL OFF THAT WORK SCHEDULE IN A CROP TOP, YOU SATAN'S HELPER.[1]

I am gross. So immature. One of the worst parts of this irritating competitiveness is that it's really relegated solely to people who identify as women. We live in a world where gender continues to be a defining trait. I dream of someday living in a world where I can be equally as blindly, childishly jealous of men, but we're not there yet. (Or maybe I'm just not.)

I can begrudgingly admit that a big reason for this nasty trait is that I thrive on competition (at least temporarily, before learned helplessness settles in). I recognize that this is how other women help me—by giving me enough hellfire to get off my dog-anus-juice floor and actually do something. At work,

---

1. I'm sorry, Bey. You are queen. I am weak. Please forgive me. I shall burn a KALE sweatshirt in your honor.

competition is the only thing that gets me to try hard. If I didn't have to BEAT somebody, I'd probably still be working at Dairy Queen.[2] There's this woman who works at a different university than me but holds a similar position. She's a decade or two older but has made concrete steps to compete with me. We'll call her Mariah Carey.[3] Mariah Carey publishes journal articles on the same topics as my team but never cites us. When we wrote a large grant proposal, she complained that it sounded too much like her study. It wasn't until Mariah Carey started openly competing that I started to give a shit about publishing journal articles—which is like *the thing* that academics are supposed to do. If it wasn't for Mariah Carey, I'd be an even shittier scholar than I already am.

My competitive streak with women is probably inherited from my mother. If you get my mother and I together to watch *House Hunters*, there is no end to over-rationalized jealous anger. Why do people so stupid get to buy houses so nice? How are idiots richer than me? You don't deserve a beach house on Mustang Island, Texas, Mr. and Mrs. Brathton-Smythe of Houston! I DO. I DESERVE THE FUCKING BEACH HOUSE ON THIS TERRIBLE ISLAND WHERE EVERYONE LOOKS LIKE A DRIED APRICOT. GIVE IT HERE.

And it's not just me. Despite the recent uptick in women bonding together, there are still plenty of women pretending to love on each other who then go home and rage-cry into their quinoa pasta. This is rooted in the widespread phenomenon of social comparison. Social comparison posits that we determine our own self-worth by comparing ourselves to others.[4] Other people are a source of information about the world and our

---

2. Wait. Wait. I'VE MADE A HUGE MISTAKE.
3. *Author's Note: For legal reasons, we must clarify that it is not Mariah Carey.*
4. (Festinger, 1954).

place in it, and provide us with some frame of reference for our own successes and failures. This is why you feel so much better about yourself when you deactivate social media for a month. You get to stop comparing yourself to everyone else 24-7.

Strangely, I've done well with communities of women where competition is the innate part of our relationship—namely, sports. It's like once we get it out of the way that we're competing, we can take that as a given, and move on to super-fun girly things like sharing clothes, having photo shoots, and arm-wrestling. However, given my druthers, I tend to gravitate to men for friendship, especially in environments where competition is less overt. I know, I sound like a Judd Apatow-created Manic Pixie Dream Girl character. I just don't want to deal with my tendency to constantly compare myself. I mean, let's face it, once you figure out that cis-men are too simple to be a threat, they are pretty innocuous. You can just sit back and relax and not worry about them taking any of the shared resources because they are too busy making fart jokes. As well as actually farting.

In particular, I find myself drawn to friendships with younger men.[5] I occasionally take classes and perform at The Second City, and my best friend there is Seth. Seth is 12 years my junior. We both frequently work from home; thus we text stupid jokes to each other constantly. I was recently referencing Erma Bombeck and Dave Barry, and Seth, the ripe grape to my moldy raisin, had no idea who they were. He sent a gif of Jason Segel[6] shrugging to highlight his apathy. This followed:

5. I've also typically found myself physically attracted to younger men, which is maybe a horse of a different color, and why I'm not allowed at high school basketball games anymore.
6. Some of Segel's best work involves him eating a watermelon and making Scooby Doo noises in the 1990s movie *Can't Hardly Wait*.

There, now you have a flock of Segels

Flock of Segels. A+. This is the simple brilliance of younger men that I want in my everyday conversations. I'm much more comfortable around younger dudes, because I don't find them remotely threatening. One of the key reasons for this, I think, was that I spent an unreasonable amount of formative time around little boys.

In addition to my own little brother, Dusty, who is three years younger than me, I have two little pseudo-brothers. Mom's best friend and former college roommate, Rose, birthed one son, Brad, a mere month before my brother was born, then another son, Brett, several years later. We spent so much time with this family that Brad and Brett were like my own siblings. They are wonderful human beings, but they were the absolute *worst* when I was a kid. I was the oldest, and as the only girl, I had limited entertainment options when our families hung out. I was relegated to sitting quietly on the sofa alongside my mom and Rose, listening to awkward gynecologist visit stories, or holding my nose and watching the little boys play Masters of the Universe in the basement. Neither option was particularly appealing.

Brad and my brother Dusty have called me out on misremembering our childhood times together. *I feel like I spent an inordinate amount of time watching them play with Micro Machines in basements.* According to them, they spent most of our time together acting out my various schemes—such as the aforementioned day camps and talent shows. They feel that they were wonderfully obedient little minions and that I was their oppressive She-Leader. This debate resurfaced years ago in Chicago. Brad, Dusty, and I were sitting on the fire escape outside of my bedroom window on North Avenue, drinking shitty beer, watching the neighborhood sex workers, and kicking back old times, as you do. I complained about how hard it was for me to be the only girl growing up.

"What the hell are you talking about?" Brad asked. "We did everything you wanted us to. Don't you remember that one time where you got us to sing 'Kokomo' and record it on a tape? You were so sneaky. We didn't want to do it, because we didn't trust you to not share it with all the parents. So you recorded yourself singing first. And then you recorded us."

"So what's wrong with tha—" I started.

"But you *rewound the tape* so that when we sang 'Kokomo,' it recorded over your voice. And then of course you played it for all the parents."

I can see how this incident might be upsetting to a child, although I personally think it was outweighed by broadening their cultural palate. How else would they get exposed to the soundtrack from the iconic Tom Cruise beach bartender movie *Cocktail*? If it wasn't for me, those boys would've had nothing but fake sword fights and *G.I. Joe* cartoons. I gave them opportunities for imaginative play, like Pretend Day Camp and Pretend Zoo and Pretend New York City Apartment. (The latter was my version of playing House, because I'm a tastemaker.)

But Brad brought up a relevant point. I am infinitely more comfortable bossing around men than women. In addition to wrangling my real and pseudo-brothers, I babysat a lot as a young teen—and almost all of my charges were little boys.

———————

I would've liked to have been a babysitter in the early 1960s, when television was relatively novel in the suburban Midwest and kids were allowed to smorgasbord it. Unfortunately, I grew up in the super square Reagan-era 1980s, when parents of small children began to realize that these light-up metal boxes emitted enough microwave rays to bake a potato. By the 90s, parents were limiting kids to a maximum of one hour of TV time a day.

That's when I started babysitting; in the sour spot between post-TV craze and pre-iPad craze, when babysitters actually had to do shit. This was a common scene for me:

I rolled onto to my side, panting.

"OK guys. How about you just play nice by yourselves?"

A chorus of three small boys spewed screeches of protest.

"NOOOO, more!"

I struggled to catch my breath. *Maybe if I am just quiet, they'll walk away and do something else.*

"Mel-knee?" one of the twins leaned down, his blond bowl cut hiding his eyes. He slapped my face. "More airplane."

I swallowed a bit of the residual vomit threatening to ooze out of the side of my mouth.

"Mel-knee needs one more minute," I chortled.

The other twin plopped his skinny legs astride my hip and began to ride, a lengthy booger dancing dangerously from his right nostril.

"AIRPLANE! AIRPLANE! AIRPLANE!" he cried.

My body was exhausted. I'd been giving them airplane rides for the past two hours.

A proper airplane occurs when a naïve adult human lies down on her back and places her feet in the air, not unlike the position she assumes when getting a Pap smear. Instead of receiving a speculum, she balances a small child on her feet, grasps their hands, and raises them horizontally in the air, jerking uncontrollably and making artificial turbulence sounds. Good airplane turbulence sounds are guttural, somewhat Germanic—projecting from the back of the throat.

Airplane rides were a constant when I babysat the Fischer boys. The Fischer boys were Alex and James, four-year-old twins, and Toby, age six, and they were a particular challenge. I could manage two little boys at once—like the Smith boys, who were children from church. With two boys, I could keep them from drawing wieners on the wall and still be on my game enough to accurately diagnose their tongue lesions. But three little boys is just unreasonable.[7]

The Fischer boys' father, Frank Fischer, was a young and

---

7. This is why there are SO MANY mid-level managers in corporate America.

attractive colleague of my father—they worked together in the prosecutor's office. Frank's wife Denise was the first Jewish person I ever knew in my life. She was several years older than Frank, and the kids celebrated both Hanukkah and Christmas—a novelty in early 1990s Northeast Ohio. I found both of these facts pretty badass. Babysitting the Fischers was a mixed bag. While Mr. and Mrs. Fischer paid quite well ($2.50 an hour!), they had spawned three young boys, and for that, I could never forgive them. Like most of my charges, the Fischer boys were limited to a half-hour of television, which usually left me with another six hours to figure out how to entertain them and keep them from turning my body into ground beef.

This was a far cry from how things went down with babysitters when I was a kid. At age five I remember wandering the house alone for an hour until I finally walked in on my babysitter having sex. She said she was lying down because she didn't feel good, so I assumed that her boyfriend needed to take her temperature with a butt thermometer because why else would she be pantsless? Another babysitter threatened that if I didn't eat the Welsh rarebit she had made for supper, I would have to sit outside in the dog house until my parents came to pick me up.

Compared to these situations, I was a goddamn *saint*. I channeled Claudia Kishi to be the best babysitter those little boys ever saw. I powered through hundreds of airplane rides, toy truck wheel-burns on my forearms, direct farting into my mouth, urine-stained He-Man pajama pants, and bedtime refusal temper tantrums.

And the boogers. Lord almighty, the boogers.

The Booger Champions, however, were not actually my babysitting charges, but my best friend Mindy's little brothers.

Dean, Mike, Jim, and Tyler were constantly covered in a thin layer of snot. They were basically just screaming human snot rockets.

Mindy was the only friend I felt truly comfortable enough with to spend the night regularly. I remember one particular sleepover at Mindy's, possibly late high school or even early college on a break, and awakening to the sound of Jim Carrey talking from his asshole.

"Excuse me, I'd like to ASS you a few questions."

The sound from the television was interrupted by cackling howls. Then a fart.

I sat up straight and felt around for my glasses on the side table next to the couch. My eyes were dry and my knees stiff from sleeping on the overly plush floral sectional in the Quinns' living room. The sunlight felt unreasonably bright. I shivered. The blanket had fallen off me sometime in the middle of the night.

Mindy's three youngest brothers, Mike, Jim, and Tyler, sat on the floor in front of me, passing a bag of generic cereal back and forth. They looked like three little elves.

"What time is it?" I asked them.

Deeply zoned into Jim Carrey, they appeared to not hear me. I squinted into the kitchen, where the digital stove clock read 7:09am. Given the point in the movie, those little fuckers must have put *Ace Ventura* on at top volume sometime around 6:30am. The Quinns were heavy sleepers, but the youngest were irritatingly early risers. Mindy continued to sleep, her face buried deep into the other half of the couch sectional across the room. I pulled myself off the couch and threw my sweatshirt on over my tank top because the last thing I felt like at 7am on a Saturday was to have Jim or Mike point out my nipples again. I walked through the dining room, sidestepping the table piled high with four boys' worth of laundry, to the far bathroom, because I also didn't feel like having the boys shout at me, asking me if I was pooping.

At this point, Mindy's brothers ranged in age from 13 to 6. Dean, the oldest, was actually quite mild-mannered and tolerable and generally slept, like Mindy, until the sun was ready to set. This left me awake and alone with the younger boys. I was a light sleeper and they had the energy of rabid chipmunks. Most weekends that I slept there, I awoke to gross-out comedies. Over the years, the sheer level of subconscious exposure to 90s comedies in this manner has made me able to quote every line from *Billy Madison, Tommy Boy, Happy Gilmore,* and *Ace Ventura, Pet Detective.* I cannot remember my social security number, but thanks to the Quinn boys, I have this unnecessary but slightly great wealth of knowledge. Waking to Adam Sandler or Chris Farley was definitely preferable to being roused by a Quinn boy straight-up hurling himself onto me like a cannonball, usually a result of a 6am inter-brother wrestling match.

Between my babysitting career and my own little brother and pseudo-brothers, I grew accustomed to the mildly irritating but wholly easy presence of little boys. Eight-year-old boys may truly be Buddha's most enlightened beings. It took me until my 30s to achieve the peak lifestyle that all the little boys in my life led. All they did was pass body gas and talk about wieners. They chugged grape soda and slurped raw hot dogs—with their hands, directly out of the packaging. They amazed me with their efficiency and lack of concern for social norms.

Ultimately, a constantly replenished buffet of younger males likely contributed to my preference for them. Boys are socialized to give less of a fuck—hence all of the fart trains. With younger boys, I can just stop trying so goddamn hard all the time. I never worry about them judging me, and even if they do, I am clearly superior. I'm the leader. I'm older, wiser, and more sensitive. My confidence with younger men translates to my interactions with them. Like Brad reminded me, I got away with being bossy as fuck. Not just a boss, but downright *bossy* for no real good reason other than getting someone else to do my bidding. It's rare in today's society that women can get away with being the bully (in their relationships with men). It's a lovely way to flip the patriarchy right on its ass. For fun!

Despite how much I relish bossing around little dudes, I need to work out my jealousy issues with women. There are certainly moments when the presence of women comforts me more than any little boy ever could: the warm smile of a strange woman who can see me on the edge of panic in the airport security line, the hug of a female friend after oversharing during a boozy brunch. Until we can figure out how to break down an unhealthy level of masculinity, women remain much better during emotional crises. Women trump men when it comes to empathy and social support. This is, to me, is the beauty of womanhood.

These are all generalizations, of course. As our social climate changes, old stereotypes of masculinity and femininity break down. Typically, however, there's just something about ladies when it comes to *getting it,* emotionally. This year, I am going to work on remembering this. I will remember the unparalleled benefit that women bring to my life. So watch out, ladyfriend, I'm about to spend a lot more time crying in your lap. By sharing our vulnerabilities, I might just stop wanting you to get hit by a truck.

My other New Year's resolution is learning to poop outdoors.

It just seems like a good skill to have.

19

CHRISTMAS IS SACRED

Every holiday season, my brother Dusty tries to get the family to watch Christmas horror movies. He knows this will reliably get my goat. Few things are morally sacred in this world, but Santa Claus is one of them. It is *never OK* to mix Yuletide with gore. If I have to tell you this, you are what's wrong with America. Yet Dusty will always capitalize on our family's indecisiveness to throw in his vote for campy violence.

"What should we watch?" I whined again last year.

"*Black Christmas,*" Dustin suggested (again), widening his eyes.

Sigh.

"CHRISTMAS IS NOT THE PLACE FOR HORROR," I told him, again. I then began my monologue, which was punctuated with annoyed pauses:

"Christmas is for artificially scented pine candles and plastic Santas."

(pause)

"Christmas is for getting gifts for your dogs and posting at least a half-dozen videos on social media of them unwrapping organic Milk-Bones."

(pause)

"Christmas is for buying fresh chestnuts in November and throwing them away in January after you find them rotten in the fridge because you have no idea how to roast chestnuts."

(pause)

"Christmas is for getting drunk and sending ellipses-laden texts to your male coworkers."

(pause)

"Christmas is not for slasher films."

"*Black Christmas* is one of the best horror movies ever," he persisted. "Plus, you've picked three of the movies we've watched so far. OK. How about *Silent Night, Deadly Night?*"

"I picked two," I said. "The first was *Bad Santa,* and you like *Bad Santa*. And the second movie you were asleep for," I added, referring to the iconic *Muppet Christmas Carol.*

"Plus," my husband said helpfully, "*her* movie picks don't give *you* nightmares." MY LIFE TEAMMATE.

"YOU DON'T KNOW THAT," Dustin said.

I attempted to ignore my brother and went back to rereading December back issues of *Country Living.*[1]

"But you like *Die Hard,*" he pointed out, unwilling to let the bit drop. "Let's compromise and watch *Christmas Evil,*" he added with a grin.

"*Die Hard* is different," I said. I know that Dusty is just giving me shit, and he would never actually want to watch a Christmas horror movie with my mother and I. Regardless, I form a snobby academic rebuttal.

"Modern pop culture likes to identify *Die Hard* as a Christmas movie, but it's really just an action movie that happens to

---

1. I love *Country Living.* You never know when you'll need a molasses cookie recipe or a guide to successfully winterizing your chicken coop.

take place at an office Christmas party. Plus, it's not *horror*. *Die Hard* is just Alan Rickman and some nameless blond German villains. And what's more Christmas-y than Germans?"

"Mmmhmm," Mom murmured her agreement, without lifting her eyes from her Candy Crush game.

Secular Christmas is more than my favorite time of year, it is my favorite thing ever. If I had to choose between Christmas and world peace (or immortality, or unlimited puppies), Christmas would win every time. Many people, especially in Chicago, find it necessary to divorce themselves from the holiday season. The endless parties, pressure, and frantic shopping are just stressful and commercial—and frankly, not "cool." I mean, yeah, OK. They are all of that. But they are also a time for *flying fat men and magic reindeer*.

Christmas was the one time of year that Dad was dependably in a good mood. Dad's depression and anxiety remained undiagnosed until he was almost 50. While we always knew how much Dad loved us, his emotions could occasionally send him into a rage over literal spilled milk. The most explosive outbursts came with autumn. Nothing made Dad angrier than the Cleveland Browns. The LaForces (Dad's relatives) often use the word "holler" as a synonym for "yell." Holler was the perfect word for Dad's football outbursts; it's a word that means "shout" but somehow gives shouting more resonance, more passion and dynamism.

Despite the seemingly eternal, raw hollering inspired by the Browns, Dad religiously watched them each week. I could never understand this. He *knew* it would put him in a bad mood, even on the rare occasions when the Browns came out on top. But without fail, on Sunday afternoons, Dad fired up the game while my mother, brother, and I slid quietly down to the basement. There we could read or play games, and the echoes of disbelieving anger were muffled slightly to us below ground.

"YOU HAVE NO FUCKING PLACE BEING A REF-EREE!!!"

"Let's play my old 45s!" Mom suggested brightly as my brother and I quaked.

"ROT IN HELL, YOU PIECE OF SHIT QUARTERBACK!"

"What…shall we play…?" Mom asked in a sing-songy voice, as she flipped through an orange-and-white case of late-1960s bubblegum pop.

"YOU LOUSY *SON OF A BITCH!* YOU CALL THAT A PASS!? HOOO HOOO HOOO!"

Maniacal, jaded laughter accompanied the climax of Dad's frustration. The hallowed cackles of a psychopath usually indicated he was only minutes from turning off the TV with the force of a small earthquake and driving off angrily to a bar.

By this time, Mom had managed to semi-suppress Dusty's and my stress by taking our hands and leading us in vigorous dancing to the tinny, spinning albums of Tommy Roe and The Monkees. She excelled at distraction.

But Christmas. Christmas was different. We could count on Dad to be nice. We loved Christmas, and Dad loved us being happy. And mercifully, the Browns rarely played on Christmas Day. Dad would smile and pretend to enjoy the gifts we painstakingly picked out. He was incredibly difficult to shop for; over the years, we relied on lots of Chaps aftershave and

Looney Tunes DVDs. Christmas had the power to subdue all of our anxiety, not just Dad's. For this reason, I continue to hold Christmas and its happy magic sacred.

Anything sacred must have rituals.

Christmas Eve, 8pm: Eat a big dinner. This was *the* splurge night of the year, which meant putting crab legs on the credit card. Mom hovered over the boiling pot of water, threatening the crab legs. "You better be good," she warned them, "at that price." In addition to crab legs, Dad required a pan-fried steak. Between the smoke from the steak and the steam from the crab legs, our house felt like a foggy moor next to an active volcano. Lack of proper ventilation also ensured that we spent at least a half-hour taking turns flapping a dish towel at the smoke alarm. We typically ate dinner in pajamas, due to the inevitable butter stain splatters across our chests and laps. It is the most *glorious* meal of the year.

11pm: Go to midnight church service smelling of shellfish. Christmas Eve was the one time church didn't stress me out. I loved the hymns and candles. Toward the end of the service, a volunteer church family, sometimes ours, passed out small stick white candles with a flimsy cardboard tutu—a poor shield from wax drippings. (All the children in our church grew up with hot wax scars on our thumbs and forefingers. Never forget that religion is about suffering, kids.)

12:00am: Sit in freezing car while Mom dutifully said hi to all of her church friends. Wait impatiently and give a half-hearted wave to passing parishioners. The sooner we got home, the sooner there would be snacks and a fire and general pre-Santa excitement. Dad put on Christmas music as we waited for the old Buick Skylark to warm up, which felt like it took about the same amount of time that it took Emperor Hadrian to build his great wall. Our impatience finally burned out and Dusty and I would fall asleep before we got out of the church parking lot. Dad took turns carrying us into the house.

12:15am: Rally. Create elaborate tray of snacks for Santa, because he always leaves a nice note. Include a variety of cookies (yell at Mom if there aren't enough different kinds, because that is just bullshit and a failure on her part as a mother) and carrots for the reindeer. Even after we found out that Santa was maaaybe Mom and Dad, I insisted on a tray of snacks just in case, and because I loved getting Santa's notes the next morning. I asked Mom recently when she knew I found out the truth about Santa Claus. "The year you started putting out beer for him," she replied.

1:00am: Pass out, drool on Dad as he carries us to bed. (Christmas was a great workout for Dad. Perhaps it's all of those post-sweat endorphins that kept him in a good mood.)

6:00am: Wake up, gleefully. Open door and tiptoe into the hallway. "IT'S TOO EAR-LY," Mom called. The upstairs area of our house, where the bedrooms are, is at most 600 square feet for three bedrooms and a full bathroom. The walls between the bedrooms are about the width of a noodle. It is an intimate space.

6:02am: Crawl into Dusty's bedroom to wake him up as silently as possible. Tiptoe downstairs together to look at presents. I remember each year I would feel a wave of disbelief that some of the packages wrapped in glossy reindeer paper could really be for ME.

6:03am – 7:00am: Sit with Dusty on one of our beds, staring at the ceiling, occasionally dozing off.

7:00am: Parents start to rustle. Run to the basement for stockings and wait FOREVERRR as Dad made coffee.

The rest of the day was an unimportant blur. My gifts were always adequate, though mildly disappointing. In the mid-80s, I started asking my parents for something called Omnibot 2000. Omnibot 2000 was a life-size (well, life-size for me at 25 inches) Japanese robot, always prominently displayed behind protective Plexiglas in the most baller section of Toys "R" Us—alongside military-grade remote control tanks and miniature CHiPs mopeds. It didn't hurt that Omnibot was adorably humanoid: a rough version of Wall-E or a slight predecessor to *Short Circuit*'s Johnny #5. In addition, Omnibot had basically every accessory a growing girl could want. First, he[2] had a cassette player on his chest. If you're going to arm a robot with tunes, slap that shit squarely on the pecs. Omnibot could also be programmed to do things at certain times, like act as a mobile alarm clock. Instead of being awakened by my stupid family every morning, I could've had an adorable E.T.-esque machine roll into my bedroom carrying a cup of Carnation Instant Breakfast.

I had literal fantasies about Omnibot and how cool I would be if he came to elementary school with me. What's up, Chris Ferrari? You like my robot? Sure I'll kiss you behind the bleachers. Why yes, Omnibot and I will be happy to join you onstage, New Kids on the Block. What's that, PBS executive? You want to give Omnibot and me a feature Saturday morning show? We accept.

Alas, Omnibot cost multiple hundreds of dollars, so while I put him as #1 on my Christmas list every year, I had no real expectation of receiving him. My parents dependably ignored it each year, and by a certain age I was old enough to know

---

2. I'm not sure why I decided Omnibot was a "he," but I'll go ahead and blame the patriarchy.

that Santa had a finite spending limit. My parents still went out of their way to get us as many thoughtful gifts as they could, although God bless my mother, she cannot pick out clothes that I like to save her life.[3] Still, I always enjoyed the *Baby-Sitters Club* books and boxes of nonpareils. Each year Mom surveyed the tree with gifts, shook her head frowning, reiterating how *many* there were and how *lucky* we were: a constant reminder to be sufficiently guilty for the money spent. We were, I think, adequately grateful/guilty. The best part of Christmas had nothing to do with gifts, or even Christmas Day itself. The magic of Christmas was rooted in the weeks leading up to it when everything sparkled and every adult and child had a twinkle in their eye.

In addition to the traditional Christmas time frame as a child, there were a few other rigid Christmas rules. I still follow these in my own home.

1) The tree must be real. What is the fucking point of having a fake tree? At worst, an admissible tree can be stolen from the remnants of dry white pines at the Home Depot parking lot late night on Christmas Eve (as long as you can climb a fence and run fast). At best, I'll fake a sick day and drag my husband all the way out to Wisconsin to cut down a fresh Concolor Fir.[4]

2) Tree-trimming requires a few ingredients. First, you must have decades of ugly ornaments, preferably handmade by nieces and nephews, as well as the naked demon ornament purchased from the back of a bodega in Mexico. If you don't have your own collection, some of the best ornaments can be found in the alley the week after Christmas. Next, to properly

3. Dear Mom: I will admit to you now that I wear that polyester T-shirt, patterned with the beach umbrellas and slit-up across the back, as ironic.
4. Concolor Firs are the absolute Rihanna of Christmas trees. Soft, fragrant, and decidedly erotic.

trim a tree, you must imbibe. If I'm prepared, I make mulled wine from scratch. This is much easier than it sounds (about as complicated as packaged ramen), yet super impressive. Usually, I'm not prepared, so the backup bev is whatever liquor happens to be lying around, mixed in packaged hot chocolate. If neither is possible, I've relied on just tossing some nutmeg in a shot of bourbon. One year I tried to make Malört eggnog. I do not recommend.

3) Everyone was must have a stocking. In our house, each dog plus our foster turtle has a meager stocking (sometimes a literal sock). Stockings always had some of my favorite gifts: Dad threw in a few scratch-offs for everyone, and Mom always included a jar of pickles for Dusty and olives for me.

Going to Painesville for Christmas is a delight for a lot of reasons, not the least of which being that I am considered attractive in Northeast Ohio merely because I have reasonable posture. However, given the fact that my brother lives in L.A. and my parents in Painesville, Chicago often makes a better meeting point.

My rigid Christmas authoritarianism requires many of the same childhood traditions upheld as adults. There will always be Christmas eve crab legs, cookies, and Miller Lite for Santa, and I will always climb into my little brother's bed at 6 am on Christmas morning, no matter much he absolutely despises it.

My parents' house echoes into our house in Chicago. Technically we have two full bathrooms, but the downstairs shower is used solely for bathing dogs…thus, try as we might, we can't convince my family to use it when they are in town (even though the wet dog odor has permanently mellowed to a faint background smell). So, the five of us share a bathroom, as we would in Painesville. It wouldn't feel like a Christmas tradition if I didn't break a bottle of my dad's Chaps because he has stationed it irritatingly in front of my special juniper-scented holiday body lotion on the bathroom sink. And although I assure my family each year that Dave and I own sufficient towels and toiletries for everyone, they insist on bringing their own, so the bathroom is cluttered with years-old travel-size shampoo bottles from the Las Vegas Holiday Inn and my parents' faded floral beach towels from 1987.

I have never seen humans as able to spread out and claim turf as my parents. When they show up on our doorstep for a 72-hour visit, they have enough luggage to transverse the Silk Road. It would take Dave and Dad a half-dozen trips to get all of the luggage into the house.

"What's in there?" I asked Dad, as he struggled with a Great Dane-sized suitcase.

"My CPAP machine and four gallons of distilled water," he growled.

"You know they sell distilled water in Chicago, right?" I asked.

"Well, I just didn't want it to be difficult!" he retorted, essentially having a stroke as he tried to get the bag up the stairs to the guest room.

I turned around and Dave was breathing heavily, laden down with old gift bags my mom[5] has filled with god knows what.

"What's in that bag?" I asked Mom, as a large gift bag dec-

---

5. My mom is less excited about actual gifts than the reusable containers they come in. For her birthday once, I had a florist carefully organize a bouquet in tissue paper and a brown twine-handled paper bag for the six-hour drive from Chicago to Painesville. The bouquet was beautiful—white irises intermingled with delicate mossy greens. "Ooh, look at this bag I can use for recycling!" was what my mother exclaimed.

orated with "Happy Mother's Day!" marched past in my husband's hands.

"That one has Kleenex and glow necklaces," Mom said.

And so it goes. Within 24 hours of their arrival, our dining table was covered in at least two dozen medicine bottles, Dad's laptop, numerous books of crossword puzzles, Mom's back issues of the *Nutrition Action Newsletter*, and about 20 balled-up napkins that Dad somehow has never learned to throw away. At our house around Christmas, it always smelled like hot-dogs and fries from the nearby bodega-meets-greasy-spoon, Ziggy's. (No matter where I've lived across my life, my father always managed to hone in on the cheap hot-dog joint within two blocks. It did not mesh well with his colitis.) He goes to buy a hot-dog *while* my husband is cooking dinner. This really wasn't a problem because Dave tends to kick everyone out of the kitchen for his *process*. Mom would be constantly shooed away from her desperate attempts to contribute to prep cooking.

"Please, just let me cut some carrots," she begged.

"Out," Dave pointed. My mom and rescue pit bull both hung their heads and exited the kitchen.

It's smart of Dave, because LaForces tend to get dangerously underfoot in the kitchen. While my mother and I are short enough to get trodden on, Dad's curiosity can take more perilous turns.

"What's this?" he asked one year, picking up a small aerosol cylinder from the back of the countertop. "Some kind of spray oil?"

He gave it a test spray. It was Mace. All of us were still coughing and rubbing our burnt eyes through Christmas dinner.

Dusty and I are skilled at avoiding the kitchen during Dave's meal prep tornado. For us, evenings started with Miller Lite (my brother) and Great Lakes Christmas Ale (me) and rapidly devolved into shouting about critical life topics such as holiday horror movies, various types of pickled vegetables, and strong female comedy leads. We also spent an inordinate amount of time laughing at our mother. In particular, we focused on Mom's various conspiracy theories, most of which center on whether or not the mainstream manufacturers of America are trying to squeeze a few more pennies out of her wallet. During the Great Avocado Shortage of 2016, she was particularly filled with spite for the Mafia-esque behaviors of avocado farmers.

"They all just started talking to each other and decided to rake up the prices," she said, her thumb emphatically jerking upwards on the word "rake."

Mom also believes that pump lotion is a conspiracy and was created so that no human can successfully get the final 5-10 pumps of lotion out of the bottom of the bottle. She really showed Big Lotion a thing or two when she began slicing the bottles open to dab out the remains.

My family was all I ever wanted at Christmastime. We may not be able to accomplish:

- Putting together a VCR
- Taking a road trip without getting lost at least 47 times
- Staying awake for an entire day without napping
- Selecting a movie to watch without a two-hour debate
- Selecting a dinner restaurant without a door-slamming fight

But we do Christmas perfectly. It is beautiful and holy. This past year was the first Christmas without Dad. We lost him just a few days before Thanksgiving. Once your pack loses its alpha, it's never the same. After Dad passed, Mom and Dusty came to Chicago a few days before Christmas. Mom predictably tried to help in the kitchen and drank too much wine with her pre-dinner grazing. Dusty and I fought over world politics and *30 Rock*. But it was hollow without the scent of Chaps aftershave or Dad's takeover of the television to stream endless British sitcoms. Dad being gone makes me want to hold all the LaForce Christmas traditions all the more dear. And that is why I will never, *ever* watch a Christmas horror movie.

20

7 LAYER BURRITO

Quitting all of my after-school groups back in my senior year of high school freed me up for my new favorite extracurricular activity: Eating 7 Layer Burritos at Taco Bell. My brother Dusty was a freshman when I was a senior. I drove us together every day, in my sky-blue hand-me-down 1986 Chevy Cavalier station wagon. (I loved that car. Before I went to college, my parents decided to sell it. I had to spend hours cleaning well-aged boogers from underneath the driver seat. What, like you didn't realize the staying power of boogers as a teenager? Give me a break. It's a lesson we all have to learn.)

Mindy and her little brother Mike also hitched rides home from school with me that year. They lived just on the other side of the creek from our house, although the thick woods made trekking between our houses impassable as the crow flies. Mindy and I would race out to the parking lot after school and wait for our much slower brothers. The key was to get out of the school parking lot before the buses started moving. Otherwise we'd be stuck for at least 15 minutes, eating away at our precious caloric gorge time. The four of us dined at the Taco Bell in downtown Painesville after school *at least* three times a week. Taco Bell was a fast food saving grace; it was one of very few cheap restaurants in the state of Ohio that had any vegetarian options. My favorite was the 7 Layer Burrito, vegetarian by design, although you can pretty much make anything vegetarian at Taco Bell without significantly impacting taste. (It may even improve it.) An unfortunate proportion of my DQ summer savings was blown on meatless Mexican pizzas within the first month of my senior year.

It was a charmed time. Instead of building my college application and advancing my social and cultural capital through extracurricular activities, I was stuffing my face with all the commercial TexMex food I could buy for under $1. I felt comfortable and happy with Dusty, Mindy, and Mike. We laughed, we told mean stories about other kids at school, and we still got home by 4 pm to watch reruns of *Get A Life* with Chris Elliott.

The day my dad died, November 18, 2017, I went back to that same Taco Bell.

We knew that we were in Dad's final days. In the prior month, pancreatic cancer had made him exponentially sicker day by day, and that final week, the cancer had begun to rip the insides of his body apart. I hadn't left my parents' house in six days; we spent day and night feeding Dad dozens of medications, trying desperately to keep him clean and comfortable. Finally, I decided that I should leave the house, just briefly, to pick up one of his prescriptions. I was afraid because he could very well be nearing the end, although he could have just as easily still been several days away. It was so hard to know. I hemmed and hawed all morning, but he needed the prescription at some point—and I needed a half-hour to clear my brain of the past week's terror, at least briefly. I drove to CVS in downtown Painesville, which happened to be right next to our old Taco Bell.

There was a mix-up at CVS. It turned out that Dad's hospice nurse had already picked up his prescription. My gut told me to hurry home. But something about the call of nostalgia from the old Taco Bell moved my gut as well.

"7 Layer Burritoooo," it whispered to me. I hadn't eaten much the past few days. I remembered happy times sitting in Taco Bell with Dusty, Mindy, and Mike, laughing loudly and surreptitiously stealing as many hot-sauce packets as we could. (It was the "baddest" thing I did as a teen.) Drool formed at the corner of my mouth as I considered the pleasing texture of guacamole, beans, sour cream, and rice wrapped in a giant warm shell. My heart lightened for a moment.

Unlike back in high school, I managed to get through the drive-thru without driving my mom's car over the curb. At the pick-up window, the cashier smiled warmly and briefly at me, reaching out a small paper bag and turning her attention immediately back to her headset. A 7 Layer Burrito cost almost three times as much as it did back in high school…but was still under $3. I tried not to think about the quality in the ingredients that allowed a full, 2017 restaurant meal to be cheaper than a 1996 pack of cigarettes. The poor factory-farmed dairy cows that had suffered to give me 10 cents worth of sour cream.

I drove towards home and pulled off into a new condo development about a mile from my parents' house. I didn't want to take the burrito home. Dad wasn't able to eat anymore, but he still felt the draw of food when he could smell it. The prior evening, he had randomly asked for spaghetti. It killed us to not be able to give him food, although the hospice nurses promised us that he wasn't really hungry, he was just "going through the files in his brain."

I cried heavily as I ate my 7 Layer Burrito in that cul-de-sac, in front of a new, split-level cookie cutter condo with ample landscaped lot. Crying was so familiar by that point that I barely noticed when tears were falling and when they weren't. The burrito didn't taste as good as I remembered; the sour cream and guacamole weren't spread evenly throughout the tortilla, giving several bites the sensation of biting into a gushy intestine. Or pancreas. The condo neighborhood was ugly and coldly sparse. It didn't feel like my hometown. Painesville was failing me on all fronts.

I couldn't finish the burrito. I wanted to throw it into the yard of one of the vacant condos, but I didn't.

At home, Dad was awake and in bad shape; I was immediately back in nurse mode. I crushed Dad's afternoon Xanax and Dilaudid, mixing the powder with a few drops of Lemon Lime Gatorade, then sucking it all up into a small syringe. I felt like I had done this a hundred times in the past few days. By that point, Dad was unable to swallow even this pasty liquid mixture, so I carefully inserted it near the back of his tongue. Close enough to the throat to dribble down, far enough so that I didn't gag him. He finally eased into a twitching sleep. I leaned over the hospital bed guardrail and put my head on his chest. The hospice nurses had said the prior day that it seemed like Dad was struggling to stay alive, holding on for something. I had been dreading what I knew I needed to say to him. But it couldn't wait.

"It's OK to let go now," I whispered. "Dusty and I will take care of Mom."

"You've been such a good dad, we love you so much. You've had an amazing life. It's OK to let go." I just repeated these sentiments over and over, hoping that some of it was getting through to him. My tears soaked into his flannel shirt.

I stroked his bony arm, 7 Layer Burrito churning in my stomach. Somehow each day, just when I thought it couldn't possibly get worse, it had. Now it was difficult to recognize my dad, not only from the weight loss, but the personality shift. Gone was the fearsome man from my early childhood who screamed at the Cleveland Browns, threw tantrums at car rental depots, and was known to whip a golf club into the air after a bad shot. Gone was the man who guffawed so loudly at *Monty Python* that the neighbors could hear him. Gone was the comforting, unwaveringly loyal father who loved seeing his kids succeed.

Dusty put Spotify's "Peaceful Piano" playlist on the stereo, and I sat on the couch, not sure what to do with myself. It was too hard to concentrate on anything. I pulled one of Mom's many photo albums out of the coffee table and flipped through it. We checked on Dad every few minutes. He jerked occasionally but remained asleep. I pulled out photos of Dad in the Marines, in Cuba during the 70s. Dad's buddy had found a litter of puppies on the base, and we had a photo of 19-year-old Dad holding two cherubic fuzzy little black-and-white puppies. Dad's own dog tags dangled around his neck.

I rose one final time to check on Dad. It had only been a couple of hours since I got back.

He was gone.

Adulthood is irritating in that many of your favorite childhood memories and associations become marred by the gory details of regular passing life events. When you grow up, all of your favorite old shows are racist and rape-y. When I pass by a city park, I think more about the dog feces and broken glass than how super fun it would be to swing until I puke. Trauma has a particularly efficient way of ruining nice things, so I will always associate Taco Bell with my damn dad dying. (It could be worse, I suppose. At least I don't have any negative associations with marijuana or string cheese or baby hippos.) Taco Bell certainly isn't the only thing I associate with Dad's illness and death. Gatorade, gentle piano music, *The Little Rascals* (Dad watched a lot of *Little Rascals* in the final months), to name just a few. But I'm weirdly grateful for the trigger memories, as painful as they are. I like keeping Dad close to me. Enjoyment of a 7 Layer Burrito is a small sacrifice to pay for remembering Dad's final hours. I've said it before and I'll say it again. There are other burritos in the sea.

21

THE HOUSE OF UGLY ART

At a recent housewarming party, I sat on an Ottoman-esque piece of furniture in my friend Erica's open-plan home, admiring the sheer adult-ness of her house. She's a tall, chatty Chief of Operations-type executive at a prestigious Midwest cookie company. This means that she makes enough actual money to afford high-class luxuries such as name-brand tortilla chips and hiring a designer to help decorate her house. Maturity and success oozed through calmly neutral Chevron wallpaper, delicately upholstered furniture, and unbleached linen tea towels. Granite countertops are apparently still the universal symbol for material success, by the way. They're the BMW of kitchen architecture. And Erica's kitchen cabinet handles, GOD. Buttery brushed silver, they were curved like God sculpted them. I never realized it was possible to have an emotional reaction to cabinet hardware. Every room in Erica's house was complete. It looked like the type of house that adult people should own: graceful and sophisticated. Quietly stylish without being over-done.

Now that you've imagined this lovely dwelling, I'd like to take you back to our house, where decorating did not happen in a comprehensive process. Very little decor in our house is properly thought out. We mostly pile crap on top of crap. It's sort of like when a dog pees on the floor, and you cover the pee with newspaper, and then try to add glitter paint to make the pee-newspaper look cool.

First, the fact that my husband Dave and I own a house at all is a small miracle for which we can begrudgingly thank the Bush Administration, but mostly a stroke of real estate luck. A great thing about living in a Midwest city like Chicago, unlike cities on the coasts, is that at some point you *might* actually be able to afford real estate. (Why is Boston so expensive? It's cold and small and is 90% comprised of old guys named Mickey, no?) In contrast to New York and L.A. and the pit of sin that is Miami, some folks in Chicago are occasionally able to purchase old, linoleum-clad, turn-of-the-(20th)-century homes.

We purchased our house in 2007, idiotically latching onto one of those "ARM" loans that have bankrupted plenty of good citizens. (Never trust any financial acronym named after a body part.) However, it was the only option for people without a 20-percent down payment. I remain mystified at how *anyone* can save 20 percent of a house sticker price. At any given time, Dave's and my savings account maintains enough cash to buy us each a one-way ticket to the Amazon to spend the remainder of our lives camping on a secret jungle river beach and drinking fresh coconut juice. (I think they have coconuts in the Amazon. Otherwise, this plan is complete shit.) Why would one ever need to stash any more dollars than that? It's not like people get to retire anymore.

I really wanted a *house*, not a condo. Condos are plentiful in Chicago. A "condo" is a living unit encased amongst many other living units, run by a strict condo association whose overlord is always a finance-lawyer-and-budding-amateur-beer-brewer named Bill. We didn't want to have to deal with Bill's inevitable strict condo rules, like no firecrackers on the roof or illegal bonfires in your bathtub. Plus, we had dogs, and Dave and I are lazy. We wanted a yard so we wouldn't need to walk their ungrateful asses four times a day in the winter. Thus, despite having no financial assets or foresight, we bought our house in the up-and-coming neighborhood of Logan Square. We chose the neighborhood because we wanted to stay on the Northwest side of Chicago, where it's much less crowded than the affluent neighborhoods of the Northeast. We also wanted to maximize proximity to both downtown and O'Hare Airport. Logan Square was in the perfect place and had a small number of houses we could afford. We moved to a street of mostly single-family homes in a mostly Latino neighborhood. Now Logan Square is less than half Latino. Guess who filled that gap? White idiots like Dave and me, with mustaches and vintage beer cozies.

Our house was built in 1892 and has therefore seen over a century of Chicago winters, shitty renovations, and owners who have died on the property. God willing, we'll die there next. However, if you're someone who can only afford to spend, say, less than a million fucking dollars on purchasing a house in a large city, you need to put up with drawbacks. We chose our house largely because:

1) It was available.

2) The inspector ensured us that despite everything that was wrong with the house, it had a solid foundation, and

3) It had an "in-law" apartment capable of generating rental income. I loved this house and saw it as a blank slate. There

were so many great DIY projects we could do to make it amaz-ing! It had so much *potential.*[1]

Eleven years later, our house seems pretty content in "poten-tial" state. The only things we've replaced or fixed are those things that we had to fix, lest we die. Like the time we had to replace our furnace because it was pumping out *three hundred* times the safe limit of carbon monoxide. Keep those CO detec-tor batteries FRESH!

Dave's little brother Steve, who we affectionately call Boo, was the first person to point out to us that our house was ugly. He was living with us for a month right out of college, and for someone just getting out of a period in his life when he deco-rated primarily with liquor bottles, he was awfully judgy about our interior design.

One afternoon, I sat with Boo on the couch, watching him mow down a quesadilla. He stared at the thrift-store-pur-chased paint-by-number kitten portraits hanging over the TV. Boo is six-foot-two and beanpole-skinny but then touted a slight post-college pot-belly just like his big brother had. He could put away twice the amount of food that Dave and I nor-mally eat as a couple, and while living with us, he supple-mented Dave's cooking with mass amounts of quesadillas and Aldi chips with hummus.

"You know," Boo said, pulling cheese out of his mustache, "This is the House of Ugly Art. You guys could probably mar-ket it as a museum and sell tickets."

Despite our house's flaws, we did try to make it our own and even saved up for a couple of pieces of Ikea furniture that didn't look "tooooo Ikea." We wanted our house to feel personal, not cookie cutter. I once read an article on household organization

---

1. If a realtor ever tells you a house has "potential," run. Run for your goddamn life.

(and by read an article, I mean I read the headline) that said you should only keep possessions that bring you joy. I totally agree with this principle and filled our house with objects that bring me joy. A lot of them. A borderline-fire-hazard number of objects that bring me joy.

My philosophy for decorating is essentially based on two principles:

1) Don't have stuff that other people have.

2) Anything you need, you can probably find in the alley.

Most items in our house were acquired under one or both of these principles. I like to call our style "eclectic crap." One of Boo's most hated pieces is a tapestry of mountain rams that hangs over the turtle tank. The tapestry features three identical rams sharing a nice moment atop a particularly desirable rock pile. In the background, there's a solitary ram, looking away into the abyss, clearly being ostracized. The sad ram adds emotional depth to the tapestry; this is not just another wolf howling at the moon piece-of-shit wall hanging.

We also have a large vintage taxidermy turkey,[2] posed in flight, in an upstairs guest room. (My friend Megan once said that the guest room looks like the place you'd put someone with tuberculosis to die.) I'm not sure what inspired some taxidermist, likely in the early stages of dementia, to pose a flightless bird in the throes of aerodynamic wonder. Was he trying to be ironic? Was he being compassionate, trying to give the hapless beast the gift of flight in the afterlife?

In addition to the turkey, the rams, and the paint-by-numbers kittens, I suppose there are other elements of "ugliness"

---

2. I feel the same way about vintage taxidermy as I do about second-hand leather. If it's used, I'm not contributing to dead animals by purchasing it. Judging by its dilapidation, our turkey was probably murdered by colonists in the early 1700s.

See the sad ram in the corner?

throughout, like cheap prints picked up roadside in Guatemala while we were drunk, a portrait of Gizmo from *Gremlins*, and a stack of costume-y spectacles that I decided could qualify as sculpture. And a lot of alley furniture.

You can find all your furniture in the alley. There's this guy in our neighborhood, Harvey, who has furnished his house entirely from alley finds: appliances, furniture, and flooring, you name it. Harvey is in his early 60s, tall, and nondescript other than being a tad effeminate and cartoonishly gregarious. He's completely lovable, although accidentally creepy. We went to Harvey's Easter brunch one year, and he was wearing an Easter Bunny costume that he had found in the alley. However, the costume was missing a critical piece—the bunny head. Harvey walked around all morning wearing what resembled dirty, fuzzy, one-piece pajamas, complete with poof tail and a gap below the tie in the back that revealed the moles between his shoulder blades.

He resembles a dragon, no? Slayed by a wooden stake to the heart.

In the winter, Harvey floods his yard and hosts a skating rink. In the summer, wildflowers and oddball yard art bloom where the ice melted. Inside his house, you might find things like an ancient kitchen stove brought back to life and turn-of-the-century dentist toolkits. The tiniest details of his house are alley finds. There is no Tupperware. Dinner leftovers are confined to decades-old Mike Sells potato-chip tins. Harvey lives a few blocks away, but at least once a month I'll see him in the alley looking for more goodness. He's also got this thing where he doesn't like hard angles, so over the years he's slowly been sanding down and rounding out every single one of his house's angular corners.

Dave and I also have a lot of alley furnishings. Our "entertainment center" is a metal-legged wood workbench that we spray-painted blue. My favorite chair is a neon orange upholstered wingback that was just sitting on the sidewalk. Just. Sitting. There. (And luckily, bed-bug free!)

It may very well be that I've been a hipster since I was a child and decorated my room with Mom's weird antique sewing tools. (They offset the mainstream but vital New Kids on the Block posters.)

I didn't realize all of the decor in our house was ugly until Boo told me. I thought I was being offbeat and cool with my design. But there's a fine line between edgy and queer (the kind of "queer" that my mom says). I'm sure next year I'll be into something else stupid, like art comprised of foreign condom wrappers or something.

We continue to evolve in the never-ending continuum of adult nesting. As I age, I'm starting to understand the brain of the hoarder. Why get rid of something when it's so much work to throw things away? Plus, you never know when you might need several faux-severed arms or stacks of 1996 hockey programs.

Despite our endless frustrations with the things that are wrong with our house (a recent appraiser benevolently called it a "project" house), it's certainly a step above places I've lived on my own before, like my first dorm room in college. There's an ecstatic freedom that comes when decorating your first adult space. Rather than merely unplanned, the overall decor in your dorm room is likely somewhat of a Jackson Pollock painting: clashing, nonsensical splatters. Because it doesn't matter! You can decorate your dorm room with anything short of hate-crime propaganda, and no one will give a shit.

I bought a *Playgirl* on Valentine's Day my freshman year. Using the RA's scissors, I cut out 10 naked male specimens and pasted them on the front door of our dorm room, because I COULD. I quickly learned that subversive decor gained me street cred in the jungle of the Southeast Ohio higher education system. Cheap, temporary decorating was always reasonable, because it was implausible to own anything at age 19 worth more than $11. And none of my decor was functional. My most functional piece of room decor was a hot pot that someone drew dicks on with a Sharpie.

In Chicago, I first lived in the aforementioned Sexual Predator Central, which I didn't even bother to decorate because it was so gross. When Dave moved to Chicago a year later, we rented a sunny one-bedroom above at tattoo shop in Wicker Park. After my previous apartment, this new place felt like Windsor Castle, albeit more realistically the size of the Queen's loo. We overlooked a machine shop that has long since been torn down and is now a pet nutrition boutique. This is what happens with gentrification: Factories that provide dozens of jobs are torn down for shops where you can buy mint-scented cat enemas. The most fantastic thing about our apartment was its large fire escape landing overlooking North Avenue. We could climb out our bedroom window on a clear night with a couple of lawn chairs for people-watching. Most weekend nights on the fire escape we drank cheap pinot grigio (which was cool in 2001!) and watched the sex workers. North Avenue was a well-known area for picking up prostitutes. We inadvertently witnessed many errant alley blowjobs. On weekends, herds of suburban Moms would get bussed in to protest the sex work on North Avenue. We didn't have cable, so we sat on our fire escape and watched the moms and prostitutes clash. It was the eternal Midwest struggle between passion and Puritan: Frustrated women in unfathomable high heels just trying to make a buck alongside equally cranky women with blunt haircuts and velour hoodies. Ultimately as the neighborhood gentrified, Puritan won.

After many years in "apartments that build character," we finally have our own place—for (mostly) better and (frequently) worse. Regardless of whether you rent or own, you will feel like you're constantly throwing money away and will twitch with annoyance at all the small idiosyncrasies of your space—like the toilet handle that needs to be held down for a full five minutes in order to flush completely, or the bathroom door that won't shut all the way, or the party of pigeons that happens on your roof every morning. I wake up to pigeon chatter at dawn and visualize the mass amounts of bird shit piling up on the thin sheet of asphalt separating pigeons from my head. When you rent, it annoys you that your landlord won't fix these things. When you own, it stresses you out that you can't afford to fix these things. Owning a house is in this way is very frustrating. Particularly our house. I do not recommend that you own our house. I find myself hating on it frequently like this until someone else starts ragging on it (read: my mother). Then I'll cheerlead for my house like it's an underdog sports team.

"It's got a lot of heart," I'll say. "Next season I think it will really hit a good stride."

22

SILENT G

Today, before I could even get through the front door of my house, I became annoyed at the never-ending piles of trash in our front yard. Every few days, Dave or I play rock-paper-scissors, and the loser unenthusiastically goes to the front yard to gather trash. Our parkway (the grassy space between the street and the sidewalk) is bordered by a small fence that opens toward the street. The fence has been bent and mangled multiple times by city construction workers and serves as an open invitation for all of the trash blowing around the block. Sometimes the pigeons go down from the roof to party with the parkway garbage. There's also a fire hydrant in our parkway. Since it's a no-parking zone, naturally people will pull their cars up to this spot and sit smoking cigarettes and eating Filet O' Fish for hours, mercilessly tossing their rubbish into our yard. I watch them and do nothing, stewing in my own conflict-averse frustration. One of these days, I'm gonna charge right out there, fists clenched, and politely ask them how their day is going.

Cigarette butts and rubber band-rolled pizza menus abound on our property, as well as decimated bags of Funyuns and

Flamin' Hot Cheetos.[1] Occasionally meth dime bags turn up, as well as empty liquor bottles. It's also common for me to find a damp box of grape- or apricot-flavored cigarillos. They probably sell them at toy stores.

The current front porch of our house is essentially a death trap. Each Halloween since we've lived here, small children in plastic superhero costumes totter precariously up the steps as Dave and I hold our breath and pray that none of them falls through. There are some deep holes in the porch floorboards where grown adults (Dave) have fallen through, but luckily these traps are far enough away from the front door that it's really only a danger when I'm refilling the squirrel feeder.

I feed squirrels constantly, to the disdain of the more responsible homeowners on our block. Chicago squirrels, as hardcore vegetable thieves, are particularly troublesome in the spring and summer. And since having an urban veggie garden is the new having granite countertops, everyone hates the squirrels. My neighbor Joanie recently complained to me about them. We were outside on our respective back porches and she squinted at her tomato pots, carefully plucking off dead leaves with one hand and stroking her long, blown-out ponytail with the other.

"Have you seen that big squirrel?" she asked.

"I think so," I said. "The one with the huge dick?"

"He keeps eating my cherry tomatoes."

"Oh, I'm sorry. I just fed that guy. He's probably hanging around more lately because he knows I'll give him peanuts," I replied, simultaneously guilty and proud of my squirrel-whispering.

---

1. Seriously though. Flaming Hot Cheetos are the best. I think Flaming Hot Cheetos are primarily comprised of opium and orange dye.

I've trained several neighborhood squirrels to eat out of my hand. My favorite (with the big dick and a penchant for cherry tomatoes) is Old Notchy Ear, the neighborhood alpha male. Over the years, Notchy's ears have become less notchy and more nonexistent from fights with competing squirrel dudes. He favors his left paw and has a noticeable scar down the right side of his torso. It is wholly possible that Notchy is a reincarnated pirate.

On hormonal days, I park myself on the front porch in pajamas with a bag of raw unsalted peanuts and wait patiently for my magical furry friends to come to me.[2] The front porch is a lovely place to hang out in the evenings, have some beers, and watch tweens engage in heavy petting between parked cars. The backyard, however, adjacent to the alley, is often much more colorful—literally.

So, Chicago has gangs. It turns out that when a city fosters systematic racism and class division for hundreds of years, organized crime happens. (Shocking!) Typically, Dave and I have not had any directly bad experiences with gangs and often talk to the junior gang member who patrols the alley. He's a nice kid and lets us know when we accidentally leave our garage door open.

The general gang information we've gleaned is that there are three gang territories overlapping on our block: these include The Imperial Gangsters, The Maniac Latin Disciples (MLDs), and the Spanish Cobras. The Latin Kings also have a presence, because no one wants the Latin Kings to feel left out. Gang-tagging is common in our alley. Dave and I thought we would be immune because we have a dark brown garage door. Those

2. This is also why I'm definitely a Snow White and not a Cinderella, no matter what those fucking BuzzFeed quizzes say.

with white garage doors are obviously much better targets. Soon after we bought our house, MLDs did scrawl a small pitchfork on our recycling bin in a badass attempt to sully a municipal conservation effort. (I guess?)

One sunny June day, I pulled our car down the alley and fired off a series of fucks. Yellow spray paint was scrawled all over our garage door. I'm fairly certain it was the Spanish Cobras tag: displayed prominently was a "C" enclosed in a diamond. Like a typical middle-class white lady, I get most of my gang-related information from other middle-class white lady forums on the Internet. However, this particular tag also included a crown of sorts, which I thought was an MLD symbol. The tag's diamonds and crowns seemed antiquated as popular gang crest symbology. Shouldn't gang symbols be more modern representations of excess and wealth? I would expect an AmEx Platinum card and a Vuitton clutch on my garage door. Our masterpiece was signed by Silent G, which I felt was kind of a pussy gang name. Shouldn't it be "Angry G" or "Screaming G" or at least "Outdoor Voice G?"

Silent G had helpfully left the bronze address numbers marking our house untouched. Clearly, he wanted to demonstrate metaphorical ownership over our property but still wanted Streets and Sanitation to be able to find us.

Chicago has gotten quick with the graffiti cleanup (in the wealthier neighborhoods), courtesy of former Mayor Daley's Graffiti Busters trucks. If you're fortunate to live in a neighborhood that the city actually services, tags repeatedly called in by agitated homeowners are usually gone within a couple of days. Dave and I could've waited for Graffiti Busters to take care of our garage or repainted it brown like normal homeowners. However, like a couple of cynical, superior pricks, we wanted to use this opportunity to make an ironic statement.

"Wouldn't it be funny," I asked Dave, both of us standing in the sunbaked alley, staring at Silent G's work, "if we painted rainbows and unicorns over the graffiti? Can you imagine that? You'd be going to show off your sweet tag to your gang buddies and then BAM. Unicorns."

It would be so punk rock to give the alley the Lisa Frank treatment. Then they'd see. Dave looked skeptical, as he consistently does with my decorating ideas.

"I guess. I wouldn't want to leave that up, though, it would look crazy."

"Oh no, of course," I said. "We can just leave it for a few days and paint over it in brown this weekend."

"OK," he agreed.

We headed to the suburbs (spray paint is illegal to sell in Chicago, which clearly makes it only more enticing) and loaded up on spray paint. Hot pinks, neon blues, and greens, even metallic silver.

"Do we need a faux stone finish?" I asked Dave, reading the label.

"No."

Barefoot in the alley that afternoon, we began painting a giant, sloppy rainbow across the middle of our garage door. We quickly realized that the final result would inevitably look like a five-year-old's art therapy project. And with only a deformed rainbow, it almost looked like LGBTQ-hate graffiti. Precise spray-painting is not an easy feat.

"What if I add a smiley-face sun?" I asked.

"Sure," Dave said.

Neighbors drove down the alley as we painted, inches from our dirty alley-juice feet, and gawked. Dave attempted to paint two hot-pink unicorns, which ended up resembling four-legged amoebas. The final product was less Lisa Frank and more Juggalo Birthday Party.

"Shit," Dave said. "We forgot to get brown paint to paint over this mess."

"That's OK," I said. "Pick some up tomorrow, and we'll paint over it on Saturday."

The acid-trip mural on our garage stayed up for over a year. We kept forgetting to buy brown paint, and then it got too cold to paint. And then spring came and we kept forgetting to buy

We are not talented.

brown paint again. We had become *that house* on the block. But thus far, we have not been tagged again.

23

THE BUTTER

"Can I turn the heat down?" Dave asked.

I looked at him. There was an irritating innocence to his voice, though he already knew the answer to his question. We were speeding up I-94 in our teal 1998 Honda Civic. In the passenger seat, I wore my winter coat, buttoned up, and had a blanket tucked around my legs. Dave had stripped down to a T-shirt.

"No," I said. "The dogs will get cold."

I glanced at the brown and the black lumps in the backseat, who couldn't give two shits about the temperature. We had fed each dog a peanut-butter-wrapped Benadryl this morning, and they were now fast asleep.

It was the Friday before Pulaski Day when I still worked as a researcher at Chicago Public Schools. CPS employees got a bounty of paid holidays over the course of the winter to honor various dudes. These holidays included Martin Luther King Jr. Day, Presidents' Day, Lincoln's Birthday, and Pulaski Day. Pulaski Day falls on the first Monday of March and celebrates the life and death of Polish-born general Casimir Pulaski, who trained patriot soldiers during the Revolutionary War. Chicago has one of the largest Polish diasporas in the world, so Pulaski Day is a relatively big deal.

Pulaski looked like a helluva kisser.

It was one of the years when I decided that Dave and I were too superior for the pedestrian Valentine's Day and must therefore skip it. I determined that we would instead celebrate our love on a non-traditional day, i.e., the birthday of an Eastern European mercenary. For Pulaski Day, we rented two nights in a tiny log cabin in Black River Falls, Wisconsin (population: 3,600). Wisconsin is a popular getaway destination for Chicagoans. It's close, has trees, and you can engage in fond

Midwestern activities such as grilling brats,[1] breathing smog-free air, and starting bar fights with Packers fans.

We were really looking forward to this weekend. Getaways for us were rare; I had only finished my dissertation the previous year so I was still getting used to this thing called "leisure time." The weekend promised winter hikes, snuggling under blankets, and cabin sex. But mostly, I was excited for Wisconsin's primary export: DAIRY.

For the life of me, I cannot empathize whatsoever with people who say that they "aren't into food." Food truly controls life—like gravity, but tastier. LaForces plan vacations around the promise of continuous eating. At Thanksgiving we sit down and plan our Christmas meals. Before a summer destination is chosen, a grocery list is drafted. And prior to visiting my parents, my mother will pepper me with meal planning texts:

Mom: Can you believe that April the Giraffe has not had her baby yet?

Me: I totally forgot! Wow.

Mom: You will be here at 7 tomorrow night, right? I am thinking about making quiche for that night. Also planning Catfish Cajun tacos, crab, and roast chicken.

Me: You know I'm coming alone, right? For like 24 hours?

It's genetic.

To be clear, loving food doesn't always mean that I eat like a bougie food critic, shucking fresh oysters in the sun and sipping on freshly squeezed grapefruit juice. No. One of my life's

---

1. "Brats" is short for "bratwursts." Grilling brats does not refer to the charcoal-fueled cooking of insubordinate rich children, which I would prefer.

biggest struggles is that I am a lazy foodie. (The word "foodie" is arguably the worst. I'm sorry.) Luckily, I got contractually bound to a man who loves to cook and is pretty great at it. Recently, while munching some stale tortilla chips *because he wouldn't make me dinner already*, I wondered out loud.

"I wonder," I said, holding a chip high, "how long a human being could last eating solely tortilla chips."

"I don't know," Dave replied. "But if we ever get divorced I'm sure you'll find out."

This is what Dave cooked us for dinner last night: A salad of parboiled curly kale with roasted beets, baked tofu, chickpeas, white onion, tomato, peanuts, toasted sesame seeds, basil, cilantro, and sesame dressing from scratch.

This is what I made myself for dinner the night prior, when Dave wasn't home to cook for me: Butter sandwiches with a side of stale Easter candy.

Butter is a staple.

All dairy is vital to the Midwest. Our top exports include John Stamos butter sculptures and jalapeño-spiked cheese curds. But butter is particularly special. Although raised during the era of margarine, I became a devout worshiper of the butter gods in my adult years. When I was young, butter was widely accepted as evil. Ingesting a tablespoon of butter would not only cause you to immediately gain 13 pounds, it would also clog your arteries faster than a tampon in the toilet. The norm was margarine. We actually *sprayed* chemically liquefied margarine out of a plastic pump bottle onto our food. The occasional spread of real butter became a guilty thrill, reserved for adults' birthdays and church potlucks. Nothing was more exhilarating than a sinful pat of butter spread sexily across a slice of church potluck bread.

Gradually, science showed us the danger of trans fats and the relative innocuity of dairy butter. (If you're still eating margarine, you are clearly a monster. The next major comic-book villain will be powered by margarine, no doubt.) Thankfully, by the late 90s we were able to hop once again onto the butter train.

The Honda's windows were steamy with dog breath. I rubbed my hands together and Dave shifted awkwardly in the driver's seat.

"OK, fine, turn down the goddamn heat," I said.

He compromisingly clicked the dial down a single notch. Snow thickened as the Honda trudged further north. We were almost to Black River Falls when I spotted a cute general store on the side of the road and insisted we stop for wine. Deep in the wilderness abyss of the Wisconsin northwoods, opportunities to purchase liquor are few.

Inside, Dave examined wine labels while I scanned the dairy cooler. Cheese curds, cheese curds, cheese curds, as far as the eye could see.

HELLO.

A two-pound brick of local, fresh, salted butter sat innocently in the corner of the cooler. Was it my imagination, or was it throbbing? Pulsating slightly, as though alive? My hands grasped it. I felt its pleasing weight, its firm yet permissive softness through the chilled wax paper.

It was mine. Dave pushed back on the purchase, given the sheer size of the butter, but I persisted.

"How often do we have the chance to buy fresh, local, happy

cow butter?" I asked. "It's worth any price. JUST LET ME HAVE IT."

Dave was mildly taken aback by my frantic begging, which was usually reserved for more rare delicacies, like the last weed brownie, or the sole remaining string cheese. He conceded.

Shortly afterwards, we arrived at our cabin. Our dog children burst from the Honda and ran circles through fresh snow. The log cabin was as adorably American Gothic as the vacation rental photos promised. Inside, moderately comfortable log furniture filled out the small space, and a narrow ladder led upstairs to the sleeping loft. The concrete floor was radiantly warmed by hot water pipes below. Dave and I placed The Butter on the wood-block kitchen counter to unwrap and examine.

Wisconsinning

Never had I laid eyes on such an amazing specimen of lactose. Like the sun just before it sets, The Butter's color was a deep, warm yellow, with a vague hint of orange. It smelled as clean and tangy as a newborn baby. Similes and metaphors continued to inundate my brain as I gazed, without words, at the finest product ever to come out of a cow's teat. Tenderly, Dave cut off a slim slice and smiled as he placed it on my tongue. (It was romantic as fuck.) The Butter was so rich and earthy, it had the mouthfeel of a delicate, fancy-person artisanal cheese.

It was late by the time we arrived, so we lovingly rewrapped The Butter and placed it in the fridge. Cabin sex and stress-free slumber ensued.

Upon rising the next morning, I immediately checked the fridge to ensure The Butter was still there and sliced off a small hunk to warm on the counter while we got ready. After donning snowpants and industrial winter boots, Dave and I spread The Butter and local blackberry jam on a baguette for late breakfast-slash-lunch.

The next several hours were spent chasing our insubordinate dogs through deep snow in the Black River Forest. Back at the cabin, The Butter quietly waited for us.

"Why don't we fucking own snowshoes?" I huffed at Dave, running as Elsie again disappeared from my sight.

"This is the first year I could even get you to wear a scarf," Dave said, running alongside me.

A loud echoey pop suddenly filled the air. I stopped running.

"Is it hunting season?" I asked, realizing that we were woefully unprepared. "Are we all going to get shot? Should we have dressed the dogs in little reflective coats? IS THIS THE DAY WE ALL DIE TOGETHER?"

"Maybe it's time to head back," Dave said calmly.

One of the many nice things about Dave is that it's *really* difficult to panic him. Even with a threat of possible maiming, he barely flinches. Once he and I were hiking deep in a Honduran forest and accidentally stumbled upon an illegal logging operation. Our homestay host had, of course, just finished telling us about the murders prevalent in the illegal logging industry. We had trapped ourselves, with no way around the logging site back to the homestay. The loggers hadn't yet spotted us, but I had panicked. I laid down on a rock, certain that we were about to die in a gory death-by-machete massacre. Dave calmly tucked his pants into his boots, then mine, and took my hand to lead me across a deep river, away from the loggers. The water was rough, up to our chests, and almost knocked us under several times. Dave just held the backpack high over his head and hummed a Talking Heads song while I sobbed, helplessly holding his shirt. That dude will be just fine when the zombie apocalypse comes.

While the panic of being fatally mistaken for a family of deer flowed through me, Dave tackled Emma, rolling her onto her back. Her stupid tongue lolled out of her mouth and he laughed. We finally lured Elsie back with the false promise of treats. We leashed up both assholes quickly and rushed out of the snowy woods before getting shot. I felt comfort in knowing that I would soon be away from the guns and in the presence of The Butter again.

Back at the cabin, my heart rate slowed to normal—I'd nibbled on The Butter and chugged a few glasses of panic wine. Dave and I changed out of snowpants for dinner. We drove around for an hour, realizing that all but one of the restaurants in Black River Falls was closed on Sunday night. The sole open restaurant was the Howard Johnson's Motel buffet. Starving and cranky from blaming each other about the lack of available establishments, we pulled the Honda into the HoJo parking lot. A giant, orange, fiberglass moose greeted us—in retrospect, a bad omen.

Dave and I seated ourselves at a faded maroon velvet booth. Fluorescent bulbs flickered. The only two other patrons, an elderly, flannel-clad couple, stared at us from several tables away. A despondent teen appeared out of nowhere and handed us laminated menus. The entire scene was not the romantic dinner I had hoped for, though vaguely Lynchian. Dave and I, as "mostly vegetarian,"[2] found little on the menu. There was, however, a 12-foot salad bar. The lettuce greens were wilted, but everything else looked edible—for a reasonable $8.95 per person. We ate an uneventful, dissatisfying dinner.

That night I had a series of bad dreams. You know how when you're sick, you have increasingly uncomfortable nightmares? The dream will start with something common like you're running late for work. Then you realize you can't get into the office because your legs have become mozzarella sticks. And then a gang of feral cats start eating your mozzarella stick legs. Finally, you collapse into a swimming pool full of Gatorade. Sick dreams are the worst. I woke abruptly with a stomach full of acid. Because of the narrow space in the sleeping loft, I was tucked tightly in corner of the mattress; Dave and the dogs had me hemmed in on all sides. Normally being surrounded by cuddly mammals would soothe me back to sleep, but I couldn't ignore my gut.

My stomach lurched again and again, more and more urgently. And then that dreaded moment when you have to

---

2. "Mostly vegetarians" are typically worse than vegans in their over-explaining of food preferences. I won't go into it. You're welcome.

decide if SOMETHING IS HAPPENING and if you need to get out of bed.

It was, and I did.

I barely made it down the ladder to the cabin's tiny bathroom before the eruption. I think I pooped myself slightly; it is difficult to remember the exact moment the deluge began. Seated on the icy toilet, I became violently ill, sickness and salad coming out of all orifices save my ears and peehole.

Food poisoning is very scary, almost like a panic attack. Death felt imminent, and the situation felt wholly unjust. *WHY ISN'T DAVE'S ASSHOLE ROCKETING LIQUID SHIT?* I thought, *THAT FUCKER MADE A DEAL WITH THE DEVIL.* He slept soundly all night.

After a painful hour in the cabin's bathroom, I limped to the rigid log sofa in the living room. The sleeping loft was out of the question, the ladder far too precarious and complicated for the certain additional urgent bathroom trips. I couldn't get comfortable. The log sofa was too small to fit my entire body. Finally, I took a wool, moose-printed blanket from the sofa and curled into a ball on the heated concrete floor. Every 20 minutes or so I was required to run and vomit in either the toilet or the adorably rustic wooden trash can next to the TV. I fell in and out of nightmares; a looming orange fiberglass moose with a sadistic clown smile appeared repeatedly in my subconscious.

"JUST TAKE ME, YOU GIANT ORANGE BASTARD," I cried.

The next morning, the inner storm slowed enough for me to speak to my husband.

"Do you think it was The Butter?" Dave asked, attempting a comforting stroke of my cheek.

I swatted his stupid hand away.

"No!" I snapped, on the verge of tears.

It was bad enough that I was violently ill. Could it be that The Butter Gods had served up some sort of wrathful karma? *What was my sin?* I wondered, thinking guiltily back to making eyes at a hot blond dad in the Black River Falls general store.

"It was probably the salad bar," Dave said soothingly but keeping his distance. He raised his hand in the air as if to pet me from afar. To prove his point, he cut off a large hunk of the butter and ate it plain.

"Now we'll see," he said matter-of-factly.

I was too weak to get upset about the size of butter he was basically wasting to prove his point. But the Butter Gods smiled on us that day. Dave didn't get sick, and the godforsaken HoJo bacteria evacuated itself fully from my body by evening. After one more day, I was finally again able to eat The Butter.

I viewed The Butter as a mythical gift; it had stayed with me through the Howard Johnson Disaster of 2008 – it was somehow both a harbinger and a savior. All through the rest of March, The Butter rooted itself in my consciousness. When I was away at work, I wondered if The Butter was lonely.

I woke up each morning for The Butter, spreading a tiny bit on a stale tortilla chip. I snapped viciously at Dave when I thought he was sneaking The Butter behind my back. I became like Kino in Steinbeck's *The Pearl*, waking up late at night to sneak down to the fridge and stroke The Butter tenderly.

We managed to make The Butter last until the final snow of early April, keeping it frozen in several small chunks to ensure not a single molecule spoiled and went to waste. (We gave it ample time to warm to room temperature because cold butter is Satan.)

A quiet weekend in March tuned me deeper into my Butter Religion. That Pulaski Day weekend, like Moses crossing the desert, I was comforted during my tumult by the presence of my Lord and Savior: the small-batch, sunset-hued, salty Butter of Wisconsin. In addition to The Butter, that weekend gave me a deeper appreciation for Dave. The worst situations make me realize how great he is. He and the dumb dogs are my team. (And by "team" I mean that Dave is the adult coach, I'm the sobbing five-year-old right fielder, and the dogs are the drunk dads in the bleachers.) Dave always sticks by my side. When I was younger, I imagined marriage and love differently than what it turned out to be. I was certain that my future husband and I would have endless romantic moments. And really, we do. The romance is just a little different than I expected. Romance is not necessarily candles and flowers, or even cabin sex. Romance isn't showering together[3] or long walks on the beach. Romance isn't even Netflix and cold pizza together. The most romantic gesture possible is getting a hug and a kiss even when you smell like diarrhea and are throwing a tantrum over a brick of butter.

Like The Butter, I hope Dave sticks around.

---

3. I don't know who started that lie. Showering with another person sucks. It's cold and awkward and your nose fills with water and then you have to kick the other person out so you can shave your armpits already.

24

COMPLETELY VALID MEALS

1. Buttered noodles[1]

   a. The best kinds of noodles to hold butter (in descending order):

- Wagon wheels
- Small or medium shells
- Elbows
- End of list.

2. Buttered rice

3. Butter quesadilla (Instead of cheese, substitute butter.)

4. Buttered tortilla chips

5. Buttered potato chips (bonus points for adding hot sauce)

6. Butter sandwiches (Two pieces of hot bread, buttered; DO NOT SUBSTITUTE RICE CAKES.)

7. AlterEco Dark Salted Brown Butter Bar chocolate[2]

8. Buttered quinoa, if you're feeling like health food

---

1. Salted butter, obviously, unless you're a demogorgon.
2. I do not receive promotional moneys from this company. The Brown Butter bar is simply chocolate MDMA. You will want to touch people.

9. Buttered (non-factory-farmed) eggs

(I'm so hungry now.)

10. I haven't tried them but a friend swears that buttered saltines are IT.

11. And also another friend swears that buttered matzo is IT.

25

SURVIVING MIDWEST WINTERS

It's fucking snowing again.

It's what the Midwest does in February. It snows. And snows. Chicagoans forgive brutal winters for beautiful, briefly mild springs, and hazy, debaucherous summers. One might think that I choose to live in Chicago because I love the snow. This is false. There is no such thing as loving snow; it is a liberal conspiracy theory created to keep Northerners from flooding to more temperate climates like Key West, Los Angeles, or Branson, Missouri. Midwesterners hate a long winter just as much as any given Miami native. We're just too frozen solid to go elsewhere.

February is a particularly tough month, sandwiched in between the downward spiral that is January and the learned helplessness of March.[1] In January, the snow and cold are still novel enough that we maintain sanity and occasionally enjoy the fluffy, glittery snowbanks. (Yes, snow actually glitters sometimes! It is a gift from the mythical Midwest Unicorn God.) In January, we're still basking in the holiday afterglow. February, however, is winter's Ironman: pure unadulterated frigidity. There's no holiday afterglow, no remote hint of spring yet. It's just bitter.

Over the years, I've become savvier in my survival. If you're going to make it through a long winter, you need to follow the rules. New transplants to the Midwest typically attempt a strategy of resilience against winter. Despite the high of eight degrees today, I saw multiple commuters on bicycles, decked out in wind goggles and scarves. I even saw one *jogger* deftly avoiding ice patches on the sidewalk. Riding the bus past Humboldt Park, I spotted a mom attempting to frolic in the snowdrifts with two young children.

I hate all of these people and I curse them under my breath.

---

1. In a series of tragic 1960s experiments, Martin Seligman (a psychologist well known for, of all things, happiness psychology) put dogs in harnesses and then shocked them repeatedly. For dogs who had no way of escaping the shocks, they gave up and just cried. They stopped trying to escape and mentally threw in the towel. This is essentially how March in Chicago feels.

Screw them, these people who still maintain the will to live. They will soon learn.

Try as you might, you naive lambs, winter will end you. It's best to learn that the only true way to "beat" winter in Chicago is to submit. Roll over on your back and just let it wear you down, because February will fucking win every time. Seasoned Midwesterners know that the only successful strategy for surviving the vilest month of winter is to let it vanquish you thoroughly and hibernate.

On Winter Socialization

Once you have succumbed to the fact that winter is better than you and can beat you at arm-wrestling, your life becomes easier. The winter laziness factor is actually highly rewarding.

Consider the following two Friday nights in Chicago. One in February and one in July.

Friday night, July

5:00-6:30 pm: I spend 90 minutes throwing clothes onto the floor in search of the right outfit. Is this the kind of bar where cut-off jeans will be perceived as laid-back-cool or laid-back-dirty? Should I showcase cleavage or sideboob? Will the combination of cutoffs and sideboob make me look like I'm trying too hard? Am I too old for sideboob? Will these ankle boots be comfortable all night? Who let me buy ankle boots?

7:00-8:00 pm: I ride the bus to meet a friend at yet another outdoor fried chicken/craft cocktail restaurant with throwback bocce ball and horseshoes. I spot my reflection in the window across the aisle and notice that mascara has melted off my eyelashes into an undereye cesspool. I arrive at my stop and pry my sticky legs from the bus seat, transporting the prior sweat of 100 commuters with me on my inner thighs.

9:00-10:00 pm: Stifling a yawn, I readjust my cut-off jeans to pull them out of my ass crack. I sip a $14 tarragon huckleberry whiskey cocktail named after an obscure insider reference to the movie *Weird Science*. It is served in a tiny glass bottle with an old-timey striped paper straw. In the corner of the bar, a sullen, mustachioed food worker serves Frito pies and tamales from a faux food truck. My stomach growls but I know that if I ingest a Frito pie, my precariously tucked abdomen will burgeon ungracefully out of my cut-off jeans. Said unreasonably tight cut-offs result in accidentally butt-dialing my mother-in-law repeatedly.

10:00 pm-12:00 am: Having spent too much money on cocktails in cute containers, I'm finally drunk enough to not care about the layer of sweat crust that's formed between my breasts. I give into a Frito pie and spill half on my T-shirt. Next, I drunk-text Dave, asking him to give "The Fat Dog" (Sumo) a kiss for me and to send me a video of it. Unable to find a cab or Lyft driver, I run 20 minutes in ankle boots down Fullerton Avenue to get home and avoid would-be late-night murderers.

Friday night, February

5:00-6:30pm: I transition from elastic-waist jeans to velvet butt-flap onesie pajamas. While picking my onesie pajamas off the floor, I recall that Emma the deaf dog had wiped her impacted anal glands on the left leg of my pajamas last night. I gently sniff the pajamas. Since the smell of dog anus has somewhat dissipated, I put them on.

7:00-8:00 pm: Aww, shit ... *Naked Guns* 1, 2 1/2, AND 33 1/3 on Netflix. And I HAVE FOUND AN UNOPENED JAR OF SALSA VERDE!

9:00-10:00 pm: I engage Dave in an animated discussion about how we should form our own two-person book club because everyone else's opinion sucks. And we won't read stupid shit like *The Alchemist*. Wedged in between dog butts, I attempt to reach for potato chips and crush them into my lap. Dogs readily dispose of said potato chip crumbs. (You absolutely do not need to own a vacuum cleaner if you have rescue dogs.)

10:00 pm-12:00 am: I try to talk Dave into getting stoned and watching *Mary Poppins* again. We compromise with *Lord of the Rings* instead.

February Fridays are the clear winner here.

In addition to the bouquet of rewards for the truly lazy, winter in the Midwest is also amazing for socially anxious people. Some snazzy marketers should get on this: vacations for introverts! Escape all social interaction and visit Chicago in February! Chicago in February is the most anonymous that one can get in a big city. When you walk down the street in February, you'll notice that everyone looks like a coal miner. Grime-covered black coats, head down, eyes squinting bitterly against the elements. I rarely have socially induced panic attacks in the winter, because I become a blobby, Thinsulate-laden clone. Winter garb is an invisibility cloak.

On Staying Warm

A nice thing about growing up is that you age out of caring when you resemble a blobby, Thinsulate-laden clone. By the time you hit your 30s, your winter wardrobe will finally represent function over style. Back in college in Southeast Ohio, winters were milder but still cold, and because we were vain morons, women at my college wore zero outerwear on most weekend nights. We went out in stretchy Limited-era black pants and embellished tank tops, sprinting frantically from bar to bar. Losing a pinkie finger to frostbite was worth it as long as your ass looked good, right? If the temperature dipped below 20 degrees, we *might* throw on a cardigan.

The legitimate problem with coats in a college town bar atmosphere was that there was just no physical room for them. A Friday night at The Crystal bar on Court Street, always densely packed with fraternity boys, looked just like those YouTube videos of Tokyo subways. Plus, the mass amounts of booze ensured that if you *did* find a nook in a bar to stash your coat temporarily, you would leave with someone else's coat (if you were lucky enough to leave with a coat at all). So you might as well just leave the outerwear at home and use it on the days when you were just going to sociology class. (There were no attractive people in the social sciences anyway.)[2] And don't forget, when you're in your 20s, you're more resilient against physical threats like cold weather and alcohol poisoning. So ignore those goosebumps and drink up, kids.

Once you hit your 30s, your skin will thin and your stomach will begin to react to alcohol in the same way that it would if you ingested topsoil. You'll need to start bundling up (and cut back on malt liquor). Remember: I grew up on the east side of Cleveland and made my adult home in Chicago. Other than the brief hiatus in my college dumb era, I've been wearing unreasonably ugly winter hats since 1977. There's no shortage

2. I can say this because I am a social scientist.

of photos of me as a toddler, wearing an adult's winter cap with the "Caterpillar" farm machinery logo across it. When dressing my brother and me, Mom was more about practical than aesthetic.

Another satisfying part of winter is that the likelihood of sexual harassment drops significantly. Since we've already established that everyone is a blob clone and no blobs are inherently sexier than others, people leave you alone. Creepy men are too busy trying to conserve valuable heat for their internal organs to let it drift downwards into their man-junk. The downside of this, of course, is that when temperatures rise just enough for me to lose the puffy Michelin coat for something dramatically more sexy, like cargo pants and a high school marching band hoodie, it's like dudes have never seen a lady before. Early spring is the peak sexual harassment time, as blood begins to flow back to the penile areas and away from the brain.

On Germs

Despite the blissful lazy anonymity, winter also comes with germs. Unlike the male penis, germs thrive on chafing Midwestern winds. This is particularly bad for someone like me whose immune system is about as functional as a Pontiac Aztek.[3] My job involves a lot of travel, and it's 100% guaranteed that merely by setting foot on a plane, I will end up catching some disgusting bug.

My coworker Lila, with whom I often travel, suggests that I get sick so easily because I wash my hands too often. She says that my body can't handle germs because I'm too clean. She

---

3. This was a car made by GM in the early 2000s. You probably forgot it existed.

said this over drinks in her hotel room on the second day of a work trip to Houston. After she mentioned this, I went into her bathroom and found that the soap was still wrapped and appeared untouched.

"Do you not wash your hands after you go to the bathroom?" I asked her.

"Not really," she said.

I considered this.

"What about when you poop?" I asked.

"Not always," she responded.

"But like, what if you got poop on your hand a little?"

'Well, yeah, if I saw that I got poop on my hands I would wash them."

"But what if you didn't see the poop?"

"If I got poop on my hand I would see it."

"BUT WHAT if you DIDN'T?"

Growing up with a preschool teacher mom, this disturbed me to no end. LaForces wash hands with an almost OCD-like frequency. (To be fair, we also touch dogs and boogers and put our hands in our mouths a lot.) I couldn't imagine someone *pooping*, and then just walking away. But Lila never gets sick. She has the immune fortitude of a pioneer woman. I think she used two sick days in her six years of working with me. I, however, know that my own hand-eye coordination is not reliable enough to skip a hand wash after using the bathroom.

On Street Cred

Despite how much Chicagoans hate winter, there's still a disturbed sense of martyr satisfaction that comes with Hoth-style living. The amount of snow we get here is less than I saw growing up on Lake Erie. But it's much more difficult to navigate winter in a big city because people actually walk. In Ohio, I might have walked from my front door to a garage and then from a parking lot to a heated building. At most, I spent a maximum of one minute outside at any given time. This morning in Chicago (temperature: nine degrees), I walked 20 minutes from the northeast side of downtown to the southwest side of downtown. My eyes were the only part of my body exposed. No big deal. Chicagoans are fiercely proud of our winter toughness. We imagine ourselves as hot-dog-eating Vikings of the 21st century. (Vikings, I am told, were also fiercely anti-ketchup.)

We become particularly enraged when New Yorkers try to talk a big game about *their* obviously inferior winter storms. NYC has objectively milder winters than us Windy City folk, so we scoff and laugh at their weakness. Every year, there's a national news story about a large NYC snowstorm, and every year, Chicagoans brag amongst ourselves about how much worse *we* got it. They only got five inches of snow! WE GOT 19, BABY! When I worked for Chicago Public Schools under Arne Duncan, that dude never closed the schools. It added to our city's toughness. We laughed at schools in Virginia Beach that closed if they got a half-inch. In 2011, the city finally closed the schools when Chicago got 24 inches of snow, along with 60 MPH winds. It had been over 10 years since the district closed schools for winter weather.

Even at an individual level, we become competitive about how much worse winter sucks for each of us. There's a *Monty Python* sketch, beloved by Dad, called "The Four Yorkshiremen" that serves as a nice metaphor for Chicago's winter one-upmanship. If you're not familiar, the premise of the sketch is four upper-crust Englishmen enjoying a smoke and cocktail after a delightful meal while reminiscing about the hard times of their youth. Each man's reflection becomes more dramatic and unfathomably horrifying, to the point of absurdity. This is essentially how Chicagoans converse in the winter.

Chicagoan 1: My car got stuck getting out of the garage this morning. I spun my tires until a neighbor finally came to help. We spent 45 minutes shoveling me out of the alley.

Chicagoan 2: That's too bad. I had a pipe burst last night. Soaked my collection of Ditka memorabilia.

Chicagoan 3: Guess what happened to me? I slipped and fell on the ice and broke my collarbone. And then the 72 bus was late, so I still haven't gone to the hospital. Do you have any painkillers?

Chicagoan 4: You three had it easy. Frostbite killed my pinkie fingers this morning and then a stray dog ate them right off my hands.

Chicagoan 5: Child's play. I froze to death in my garage this morning and had to be revived by a large rat. Made me 10 minutes late to work.

Chicagoan 1: Hey, only two months 'til Cubs opening day.

26

THE FRONT PORCH

Our front porch is falling apart. Like many houses in Chicago, ours was built in the late 1890s. The current porch is easily 40 years old, and it's a miracle it's lasted as long as it has. At some point well before we bought the house, the porch was painted red, so now it resembles a rotting open wound. Spanning the entire front of the house, the porch is a non-impressive width of about 20 feet. Flanking the columns that hold the floor to the roof are what look like small wagon wheels. I *loathe* these wagon wheels, but Dave has pointed out that if we remove them, there will be gaping holes instead of wagon wheels.

Fucking wagon wheels. I am angry right now just looking at them out the front window.

Every spring since we've lived in this house, my Dave and I have this conversation:

(Dave and Melanie are standing just outside the front porch, admiring the first beautiful day of spring.)

> *Mel:* Are we going to get a new porch this year?
>
> *Dave:* Yes. We need to.
>
> *Mel:* How much does a new porch cost?
>
> *Dave:* Probably like 10 grand.

Wagon wheels. (Note also the overgrown hedge.)

Mel: Do we have 10 grand?

Dave: No.

Mel: OK, so we aren't going to fix the porch this summer.

Dave: No.

(Pause)

Dave: But I'll go to Home Depot and get the stuff to seal it this summer so that it lasts through the winter.

Mel: OK.

And then every fall comes and we have this conversation.

(It is raining. Dave holds open the front curtain, looking out into the mist.)

Dave: Well, I gotta seal the porch before it gets too cold, but I need to wait for a dry and warm enough day.

Mel: How warm does it have to be?

Dave: Like 60s.

Mel: It's November. It's not going to be 60 degrees and dry until May.

Dave: Yeah.

Thus, unprotected and raw like a pasty Irish student on spring break, the porch continues to decay.

Despite its precariousness, our rotting porch is also wonderful for parties. Before we take an axe to the floorboards, I want to have an Appalachian Porch Party in the tradition of my elder LaForce relatives. My ancestors were French Huguenots and reportedly came over from Europe in the 1600s. Supposedly half went up to Quebec and the other half settled in Virginia.

To make a long story short: The LaForces have literally been sitting on a front porch in southwest Virginia since the 1600s. Today, you will find a handful of LaForces left, aging quietly under the Cumberland Mountain in Jonesville, Virginia. My Great-Uncle Tom, recently committed to a home, is the only one left there (to my knowledge) who still bears the LaForce name. I'm told that he keeps removing his catheter and touching nurses inappropriately.

The basic porch party agenda goes like this:
  1. Sit down.
  2. Don't move for eight hours. *

You may occasionally fan yourself with a church bulletin.

Jonesville summers are hot and stagnant, so a porch gathering with close family and mullet-sporting neighbors is a common way to take a break from hoarding soup cans to cool off.

Early porch partyin' with my great grandpa and uncle Kevin in Jonesville, VA.

When my relatives originally started coming up North, hoping to find factory work during the Depression that slumped tobacco sales, they brought many of their Appalachian traditions to the Midwest with them. Porch parties translate so nicely to the Midwest, especially Ohio—the supposed "heart of it all." There are several key elements to a successful porch party:

Porch Party Element 1: A cooler of Genessee Cream Ale. In my youth, not a graduation party or wake went by where Grandpa didn't bring along a case of Genny Cream and Genny Light for the ladies. Note that if you don't like Genny, acceptable alternatives include iced sweet tea and freezer-chilled Old Crow.

Porch Party Element 2: Pickled eggs. Aunt Bette offers these up from a giant jar when we head down to Jonesville. (You can also find these in Chicago's finest dive bars.) Bette is a purist, but if you're feeling radical, go ahead and pickle them in beet juice for a scandalous pink hue.

Porch Party Element 3: Conway Twitty. There is a certain breed of country music that is acceptable to listen to, and that breed is Conway Twitty. Dad said it was actually Grandma Marge (raised in Ohio) that liked Conway Twitty, but we'll include him because he blends perfectly into the porch party environment: sweet molasses tunes for sitting still.

Porch Party Element 4: Sinning. Finally, despite the strict Baptist traditions, gambling will likely surface after eight hours of pickled eggs and Genny. You may move now, but only to play poker in the five-card stud tradition. At this point it's also acceptable to tell spiteful stories about non-LaForces. I also vividly remember the time my uncle Cal told us kids the vague details surrounding the circumstances wherein my Grandpa may or may not have committed involuntary manslaughter while running a backhoe.

While Dave and I haven't had an official Appalachian porch party, the front porch has made a tremendous home base for the annual neighborhood block party. The premise of a city of Chicago block party is simple: Find an enthusiastic neighbor to do the legwork and get the permit from the city. Then everyone moves their cars off the block the night before the party lest they be subject to public shame and/or towing. The block is closed off the next day from 9 am to 9 pm. What you and your neighbors opt to do with this sudden open expanse of road is up to you.

The best neighborhood block party happened the first summer after we moved in. Dave and I made a cooler of rum-spiked punch to share with any neighbors inclined to venture up the death-stairs to our porch. The block party invitation had suggested providing "food to share." We put sliced melon and orange smiles out on a brightly striped Target serving tray, poised on some cinder blocks in the front yard.

During the quiet morning calm, Dave and I sat on our rickety porch stairs. We spiked our coffee and observed the block calmly for a few hours, picking shards of frayed wood off our legs as the porch dissolved underneath us. We watched as the man who lives across the street from us, Elmer, set up an elaborate giant pink tent over his front yard. He seemed to be going all-out for a neighborhood block party. Local children began to ride bikes and scooters up and down the block. We watched Elmer hang streamers of pink crepe paper.

We got progressively drunker. None of the neighbors were drinking our rum punch, so by noon we were sloshed. The sun rose above the brownstones and Cape Cods. Sweat settled comfortably into a pool in my bra.

A few friends came over to sit outside with us. Cole, a skilled hairstylist and roller derby teammate, gave impromptu haircuts on the front porch. She snipped away as neighbors cautiously eyed her colorful tattoos, which include bullet holes on her neck, a pair of bloody scissors on her arms, and a full gun and holster belt around her hips. The vibe was settling into a pleasant, sticky mellow. Friendly neighbors finally began to stroll around, gifting us paper plates stacked high with fragrant ribs. One neighbor, a beefy, elderly man who smelled like a nail salon and introduced himself as both the Deacon at Our Lady of Peace and "Mayor of the Neighborhood," brought a large plate of pork and pigeon peas. Dave and I aren't really meat eaters, but our neighbor waited expectantly until we dutifully sampled the pork and peas, nodding fervently.

"MY WIFE," he then boomed, pointing at a round redhead chatting with a group of parents down the block. "SHE COOKS GOOD."

We set the meat stacks alongside the fruit slices. A chubby kid from a few houses down promptly parked himself in our front yard and proceeded to eat the entire plate of community ribs.

About 1 pm, pedestrian traffic over at Elmer's began to pick up. Men in sharp trousers and cowboy hats escorted ladies in tight sundresses under the pink tent. It became clear that this was not typical block party fare. A sour-faced cook set up a giant, weathered grill toward the back of Elmer's house and began to make tacos. Through some neighbor, we learned Elmer was throwing a double baptism party for his two young daughters.

At approximately 2 pm, I stumbled back to the front porch from a quick pee break inside and spotted the fire truck outside of our house. "YAAAAAYYY!" I yelled gleefully. Often, the city will send a fire truck to various neighborhood block parties. Firefighters open a hydrant with a giant wrench-like tool, turning it into a sprinkler for the kids.

Dave shushed me. The block had gone still. A few neighbors glared at my outburst. "Someone got shot," Dave said, pointing at the commotion toward the rear of the pink tent. My rum punch-addled brain struggled with this. "Who gets shot at a double baptism?" I asked. It didn't look like my stereotypical picture of a shooting scene. Partygoers were still milling about, unconcerned. An ambulance pulled up and a few minutes later, a young girl, looking quite calm, was wheeled out in what resembled a makeshift hand truck. We watched neighbors whisper to each other, playing telephone down the block until the story reached our house. Apparently, a teen girl, about fourteen, had a small gun in her little Forever 21 purse. She tossed her purse down on a table, nonchalantly, and the gun went off and hit an eight-year-old girl in the leg. Luckily, the little girl was fine. The gun owner herself had darted down the alley to avoid arrest, so the cops unhelpfully arrested her brother. Not ten minutes after the ambulance left, *banda* music resumed, taco meat sizzled on the grill, and tequila was once again being poured under the pink tent. I admired Elmer's strategic diffusion of any tension in the air.

Around dusk, our friends started to depart. Dave and I were waved over from the pink tent by a blurry body. We felt excited like we were being invited to the cool kids' table. Walking was difficult by this point, but we managed to amble across the street to make polite intermediate-drunk-level Spanish conversation. Elmer directed us to tacos and introduced us to his rooster, and then the rest of his family. We were welcomed warmly despite our conversational uselessness. By 9 pm we were playing musical chairs in the alley, kids and adults alike.

That day, I fell deeply in love with my neighborhood. It was the quintessential city summer experience: booze, haircuts, accidental shootings, tacos, and alley party games. In all, I'm constantly reminded of how life in major cities is timeless. Some trends may shift, but on a hot summer day, watching the neighborhood from our porch, every scene is like something out of a spastic Norman Rockwell painting. Kids eating popsicles on the curb. Old men drinking and shouting on front porches. Toddlers dressed as superheroes each Halloween.

Teen boys stealing from my lilac tree on prom nights. Good Friday church processions, complete with Jesus-flogging Roman soldiers. Neighbors hanging their laundry out to dry. Our front porch is an excellent way to drink in the history of the neighborhood as well as its community dynamics. We love to hang outside any time the weather inches above 50 degrees, slurping our Miller High Life tallboys and people watching. In those moments, it feels as though our block is the entire world.

27

PORCH PARTY PLAYLIST FOR HARDCORE FEELINGS

"Jackson"—Johnny & June Carter Cash

"Good-Hearted Woman"—Waylon Jennings (least feminist song on this playlist but that twang)

"I Fall to Pieces"—Patsy Cline

"You're the Reason Our Kids are Ugly"—Loretta Lynn & Conway Twitty

"Jolene"—Dolly Parton

"Where Does a Little Tear Come From?"—George Jones

"Fifteen Years Ago"—Conway Twitty

"Ramblin' Fever "- Merle Haggard

"When The Man Comes Around "- Johnny Cash

"Does My Ring Hurt Your Finger? -" Charley Pride

"Song to John"—June Carter Cash

"Whiskey River -" Willie Nelson

"I Dreamed of a Hillbilly Heaven "- Dolly Parton, Tammy Wynette, Loretta Lynn

(Courtesy of Bob LaForce. Dad also made a great blues playlist. Email me and I'll send it to you.)

28

THE WINDY CITY ROLLERS

LaForces are not great with pain. All of us, save my brother, who somehow was blessed with a willowy 6-foot-tall figure, have the body types of low-ranking primates. We are short, stout, and duck-footed. As such, we have a lot of chronic body pain. I was diagnosed with juvenile rheumatoid arthritis as a toddler, which means that as an adult, my knees maintain the 2018 utility equivalent of a rotary phone or a VHS player. Add that to a spine fulla herniated discs, and really I deserve an award for getting off the couch, like, ever.

The LaForce proclivity to chronic pain led my parents to be rather paranoid about physical fitness. When I began "working out" in college, they expressed concern. The summer between my sophomore and junior year, I took up jogging. This was no small feat. Our street is only a quarter of a mile long (dead-ending into a cul-de-sac), half of which is a very steep hill. Once you get to the top of the hill, you are faced with the busy two-lane Route 84. The consistent number of dead deer on that road was sufficient warning to keep me or my brother from ever attempting pedestrian activities. So I jogged for three minutes on the flat part of the street, slogged up the hill, whizzed down the hill, and jogged again briefly on the flat part of the street again. And then I would repeat—praying all the while that no neighbors would decide to engage me.

My routine wasn't the best setup for actual fitness, but it sufficed. Naturally, after jogging a meager three laps, I developed some soreness in my calves and quads the next day. Dad was *so angry* with me for this blatant self-harm. My mother maintains that you should never work out so hard that you get *sore.* The LaForce body is fragile and awkward, like a glass pot-bellied pig. Activities like running a marathon or crossfit training instill eye-rolling pity from my parents. It is difficult for them to understand why anyone would engage in such foolish self-destruction.

They were not super thrilled when I decided to take up roller derby.

———————

In places like New York, Seattle, L.A., and shit, even Miami, one is cool merely by existing. The zip code is a status symbol. One of my closest L.A. friends is Tom. A WASP-y dad with a bowl haircut, Tom wears polos and drugstore cologne, but he lives in Silver Lake so he's automatically one hundred times cooler than me. Cool kids live on the coasts. This is why monthly rents in coastal cities tend to exceed the GDP of Scotland. The Midwest, however, is the land of casseroles, unironic mom jeans, and dinner theater. (While these are objectively *awesome*, they just aren't cool.) When I travel to New York and people ask where I live, I see the telltale pretentious smirk flutter across their face when I say "Chicago," and I must bite my lip to keep from adding, "We have art museums and vegan donuts too, assholes!" In the Midwest, we must create our own cool and drag our churchgoing, white-socked selves into sophistication, kicking and screaming.

My interest in roller derby was perhaps largely yet another strategy in my quest for coolness. I had always felt that *difficult things* could make me cool, like getting a Ph.D., or playing roller derby, or successfully resetting the clock on my stove after Daylight Savings Time. Finding roller derby made me cooler than I had ever been before or ever will be again. Roller derby remains THE THING that people ask me about all the time, even though I technically retired seven years ago.

Modern roller derby originated in Austin, Texas, but has always felt like a perfect sport for the Midwest. It's gritty, it's cheap, and as women, we already felt like perma-underdogs in the sports world. I discovered roller derby at exactly the right time, shortly after I finished my doctorate. During the summer of 2007, while spectating at Chicago's Pride Parade, a skater named "Dee Monica" (most roller derby skaters skated with pun-laden monikers) rolled up to me and handed me a condom. Condoms were flying around like snowflakes at the Pride Parade, but this one was special: the label was emblazoned with a skull and crossbones. The skull had beautiful eyelashes, and the crossbones were docked with skate wheels. It read "Windy City Rollers." I clutched the condom and watched the skaters in awe—their legs were thick and strong like Michigan oak trees, clad in fishnets and brightly colored hotpants. These women held their heads high with remarkable confidence. I was hooked before I had any idea what I was hooked on. Having recently found myself with the strange phenomenon of post-graduate-school free time, roller derby seemed like a worthy outlet to explore.

At first, I quietly investigated this shiny new thing out of sheer curiosity. Luckily, 2007 was the MySpace era, and I was able to conduct extensive roller derby research via the burgeoning social media scene. I fell in love with the Windy City Rollers' personas. There was the gazelle-like Athena DeCrime. The downright terrifying Malice with Chains—statuesque with a fake-blood-splattered uniform and trophy-like mohawk. Have you ever seen videos of crazy ripped kangaroos in the Australian outback? That's basically Malice. I watched grainy videos of skaters chasing each other around a track and flying off into the audience. Roller derby looked *hard.* I liked that. It looked *cool.* I sat at the computer each night, cyberstalking skaters and imagining myself as one of them. There was just that one large caveat: my complete void of athleticism.

I played sports three times as a child. First, I'm putting every single childhood Field Day as one sports experience and I AM COUNTING IT, even though I never achieved anything but a green participation ribbon. Second, I played t-ball for six weeks in third grade. Dad was a coach, and I played a made-up position – an infielder between the first and second basewomen. I was reasonably mediocre at hitting a softball off of a stationary pedestal but quickly lost interest. I didn't have a sports brain; the one time I actually caught a fly ball, I had absolutely no idea what to do with it once it landed in my glove. Finally, my last childhood sports experience was one game of Powder Puff football in 11th grade.[1] *That* was pretty successful: I got another girl kicked out of the game for punching my head.

---

1. I pray that it's not still called "Powder Puff" when girl-identified kids play football. Although to be fair, I DID wear a ton of Wet n Wild makeup to that game.

However I did, and do, love to roller skate. I can still close my eyes and imagine the skating rink at Laura's Roller Emporium. Picture it: Painesville, Ohio, 1986. Cameo's "Word Up" plays; I have chunks of Red Vines stick between my front teeth. The brown rental skates with orange wheels hurt my feet, but it's all worth it if Keith Binnick asks to couple skate with me...

I probably never would've had the guts to actually try out for roller derby if it weren't for Dave. Dave has played hockey since he could walk. I love going to see him play, though my favorite part of the game is before the first whistle when all the players do their sexy-splits stretching on the ice. Dave was thrilled that I wanted to try a sport, any fucking sport, but especially a contact sport. Though my parents viewed contact sport as imminent demise, my husband viewed it as just another day at the rink. I tried out for the Windy City Rollers in secret. Only Dave knew. I was certain I wouldn't make the league and felt silly for trying. What would my fellow education researchers think? It wasn't the kind of thing that people talked about around the water cooler. (That was why I liked it.)

Dave had to physically push me out of the car for tryouts. I tried out amongst 30 other women with my brand-new $99 Riddell speed skates and the cheapest helmet, knee, elbow, and wrist pads I could find. *This is hard. Mom would never go for this,* I remember thinking as I gasped for breath, trying to succeed at a speed trial. Most of the trials determined how well we could skate and take coaching, as most of the women had no prior roller derby experience. Mentally ranking my skills, I decided I was in about the middle. I could skate decently, and I was fast enough to qualify during the trials. There was no contact at the tryout. It would be months, the coaches assured us, before women started hurling their bodies at us.

That night, I got the email that I had been given a spot on the league. I gagged and nearly threw up with a mix of glee and terror.

———————

During my first derby scrimmage, I split my face clean open. When I started playing, I took my body to limits I did not know could even exist. Especially for a LaForce. For example, I was shocked that a human body could produce *so much* sweat. Skaters left practices looking like we had jumped in a pool. We barfed at practice all the time. My world, my old social circles and my family, would've been appalled at some of the physical challenges I put myself through over the course of my derby career. But to skaters, it was just part of the game. Within the first week, I stopped being embarrassed by my sweaty red workout face. We regularly went to bars right after practices, caked with sweat and dust and saliva. It reminded me of going out after a Dairy Queen shift, covered in sugar muck. Prior to roller derby, I never would've considered going to a bar without a full face of makeup. It was incredibly freeing. I became acclimated to the powerful, zero fucks feeling that roller derby gave me. Who knew that confidence could come from *inside?*

Splitting my face open happened in February, about one month in. I still skated with the cheapest protective gear money could buy, including an ill-fitting helmet – the strap dangled about two inches below my chin. The twenty of us who had gotten into the league were still called "skater tots," meaning we were recruits not yet drafted to a team. We all had our new skater names, however. I dubbed myself Riley Coyote, based on Dad's love for Looney Tunes. In February, amidst the wintery gray eternal darkness that is Chicago winter, a beacon of light emerged. We were FINALLY allowed to start hitting each other!

Basic roller derby rules are as follows (feel free to skip if you know these, or find it boring):

There are two basic positions: **jammers and blockers.**

The jammer is the player who scores points for her team by passing skaters on the opposing team, while skating around an oval track. Each team has one jammer, and the remaining eight skaters on the track are four **blockers** for each team. The blockers' job is to use physical contact and skillful maneuvering to make it impossible for the opposing jammer to get past others and thus score points. The "pack" is the term for the largest group of skaters on the track. Once a jammer makes it out of the pack (i.e., she is able to skate past all of the other skaters), she can score points by passing skaters on subsequent rounds.

Ava Sectomy, a brusque, avuncular skater-tot coach, handed me a spandex helmet-cover (frequently called "helmet panties") emblazoned with a star—the star signified that I was the jammer. My only job was to get through the pack—to weave and jump between blockers, avoiding their hits.

I pulled the helmet panty over my helmet and lined up behind the other skaters, feeling a familiar a wave of panic. The recognizable tunnel-vision, heart-racing, "I'm about to faint or I'm definitely having an apocalyptic stroke" feeling hit me fast. But then a weird thing happened. The instant that the whistle blew, I didn't have time or capacity to panic. I had to just start sprinting. On skates. Swerving between women who wanted to pummel me into the ground. *That* was the only thing my brain could do. It was like theater. When I had no choice but to do the damn thing, I didn't have any mental resources left for panic. All the panic was pushed out of my brain.

Success! I skated like a beach ball and made it through the pack on my first round! Onto the scoring round. Skating fiercely around the track, I felt a surge of determination. I rounded the turn and approached a wall of skaters, hoping to use stealth to squeeze by them. Suddenly, Helsa Wayton appeared out of nowhere and gave me a sharp hip check. I stumbled, doing that thing where you sort of fall forward and then sort of fall backward, and think that you've got it under control—and then you fall on your face. I didn't yet have safe falling skills under my belt. I belly-flopped like a dachshund in a kiddie pool.

My ill-fitting derby helmet slipped up as my head connected with the cold cement floor. In those days, we skated on yellow-painted cement. It was, in a word, slippery. Yellow paint dust constantly coated our wheels and lungs.

A jarring, lightning-flash sensation clanged in my brain. Pain hadn't yet set in, just an echoing, thunderous vibration. I vaguely sensed the coaches skating over to check on me. They weren't rushing—falls are very, very normal in roller derby. I spit out my mouthguard and breathed heavily on the cement, a line of saliva dangling from chin to floor. Varla Vendetta, skater-tot coach and captain of the Hell's Belles, gently touched my shoulder and asked in a mom-like voice, "Did you hit your head? Ohhhh. Oh yep you did."

Varla pried my forehead from the floor. Warm liquid immediately oozed down my face. I rolled onto my back. But before the adrenaline had time to settle in, a surprising, soothing tingle replaced the impending panic. I felt a dozen hands on my body. My scrimmage teammates and opponents had all circled around me, looking to assist. While I laid on my back, keeping my eyes closed and pressing my sweaty palm against the hole in my face, anonymous hands lifted my limbs and gently removed my skates, wrist guards, elbow pads, and knee pads. Instead of fear or pain, I felt calm. With assistance from Varla, I managed to sit up. My face continued to ooze. At a later date, a fellow skater named Typhoid Mary informed me that the blood had created a zigzag map all down my face, and it looked "so punk rock." Ava Sectomy took my face in her hands and proceeded to methodically wrap my entire head with medical tape so that I resembled a Civil War reenactor.

Far less serious traumas (bee stings, vaccines, AP psychology videos) have been known to make me panic and faint. However, in this situation, I felt completely safe. My new roller derby family was taking care of me. Happy, tranquilizing neurotransmitters bounced around my brain and I nearly cried with gratitude. I felt a sense of communal, estrogen-laden love that I'd never before experienced.

This comforting sense of love kept me relaxed and grateful through the rest of the ordeal. When my husband showed up to take me to the hospital, he shook his head and smiled at my dopey face. (He's had more stitches than I can count.) I smiled back—I was high on ladylove. And possibly a bit of blood loss.

My teammates lifted me up. Despite the inherent competitiveness, we supported each other, admired each other's oaktree legs, and high-fived when one of us really creamed another skater. It became a strange place where, despite it being objectively the point of sports, winning wasn't my ultimate goal. Derby was about doing my best, hanging out with my best friends, sweating out my anxiety, and hopefully getting to grab Norma Lee Wright's butt in a paceline. All of the women in the league were bonded by blood, sprains, broken bones, hematomas, and more than anything, mutual respect. We were connected, and we fostered each other's self-assurance.

Derby isn't a magical fairyland. There was certainly the lion's share of drama, gossip, and infighting. Yet somehow all this existed in a community where love was the first and foremost tenet. Even my parents came around on roller derby. Sure, they still worried about me constantly and regularly reminded me that it was OK to quit. "Your knees," Mom would whisper, almost inaudibly, as though hoping to subconsciously push me back to couch potato. But they saw the joy and support that roller derby brought me. They understood that this was my Chicago family.

This unique roller derby bond permeates leagues across the world. When I meet skaters from Philadelphia, Portland, London, and beyond, we share a common energy, like a coven of the most broken-ass witches on the planet. (Seriously, the injuries were relentless.) On the track we slam each other around, intentionally knocking each other to the floor. But off the track, we hug, cry, and laugh over shots of whiskey (or tequila, depending on a given team's preference). Roller derby fits so well in the Midwest; it is, to me, defined by the warmth of its people.

I skated competitively for four years until the pressure of a full-time research position at a university pulled me away. When the stress from competing demands finally led me to leave the league, I grieved for nearly a year. I avoided all of my beloved roller derby sisters because it simply hurt too much to know that they were still together on the track and I wasn't. A

piece of my identity and my membership in the best community of women I'd ever known had died.

After a year of mourning, I gradually edged my way back
into the league. Over the past seven years, I've become a coach
myself. Like Varla and Ava before me, I enjoy an opportunity
to work with the younger new skaters. I only see them once
a month or so, but in those few hours I work hard to make
them strong skaters and to reinforce that bond of love, support,
and dedication that was so critical to my own experience. Sure,
roller derby did make me "cool." But that wasn't why I loved it.
For the first time since working at Dairy Queen, I really loved
a group of women.

Photo by Katie Stapely

When I fell, these women literally picked me up. They not
only loved me through a head injury, but through panic
attacks, insecurity, and all the struggles of adult womanhood.
I remain united with these women—whether it's a taco bike
ride or a Easter pig roast, we still get together regularly. We
spend more time nowadays talking about children, dogs, trips
to Prague, or home renovations than we do about skating.

However, that allegiance is always there. We are the Windy City Rollers.

29

THE BEST GROSS THINGS ABOUT ROLLER DERBY

Wrist guards.

Wrist guards are the smelliest of all gear. Hand sweat is ample and pungent. (The only piece of gear that even comes close to stinky wristguards is ankle braces.)

Mold.

We are not always great at cleaning our gear. I admit to having had a moldy mouthguard, as well as an ankle brace that became dotted with happy little mold lichens.

Farts.

A lot of women in derby get nervous farts. In the early years, before diet was well-connected to fitness, many women also ate Taco Bell right before practice- right there in the practice space. A lady would consume several Burrito Supremes and then spend the next two hours crop dusting her team.

Bad breath.

In derby, heads and faces are constantly smushed together. Halitosis is a fantastic distracting strategy for those skaters so blessed to have it. I have lost complete concentration in the middle of a jam when Beth Amphetamine breathed on me.

Saliva trails.

In the league's earlier years, we used awkward, chubby rubber mouthguards that you could pick up at any big box sports store. In order to talk, we took them out and tucked them under the shoulder band of our sports bras. This frequently led to a spider-web-like sinewy trail of spit from our mouths to our shoulders.

Hematomas.

A hematoma is a fancy medical word for Agonizingly Colossal Bruise. These showed up most commonly on the outer leg and ass, and were regularly the size of a dinner plate. Often, hematomas never fully heal. While the vibrant purple color will ultimately dissipate, a faint shadow of the original bruise remains, like a roller derby ghost.

Skate wheel to the vulva.

A lot of vulva owners took the occasional skate wheel (or elbow pad, or helmet – it all got in there) to the vulva. Once, I'm pretty sure a toe stop (the rubber stopper at the toe of a skate) penetrated me.

Anus falls.

It is fairly common to fall on one's rear end in roller derby. Although good skater posture should keep you from losing your balance and tipping over backwards – it certainly happens, particularly when receiving a shoulder to the chest. Usually landing on the ass is a good thing, because the ass has lots of natural padding. However, occasionally you might land *in just the right way* with your legs apart enough for the floor to directly impact your butthole. This impact would shoot waves of vibration up the anal cavity – but not in a good way. Anus falls = painful butt earthquake.

Rats.

One season, our practice space became infested with rats. Chrissy Fiction claims she saw one once, although the rest of us only knew of their existence via trails of flattened rat feces, courtesy of our skate wheels. The rats stole mouthguards out of gear bags. During a deep clean of the practice space, a pile of wood storage pallets was removed, and skaters discovered a nest of mouthguards and rat feces. The rats had stolen all the mouthguards to create their own swanky little rat bachelor pad.

Incontinence.

Sometimes when you get knocked down really hard, you pee a little. It just happens. *Usually* it doesn't make a mess. Birthday farts[1] are also known to occur.

God, I miss roller derby.

---

1. "It's a fart that comes with a present!" - the man I married, Dave Abbott.

30

LIPSTICK DATES

"Here's what I think you should do," Mariah said.

She pointed a finger at me and spoke deliberately through bright orange lipstick. We sat in her Volvo wagon in front of my house in the cold of early December. I dug my butt down into the warmed leather seat and waited for Mariah to bestow her wisdom. The topic of discussion was an important one: Mariah was spearheading my multi-year crusade to find the blouse that Beverly D'Angelo wore on Christmas Eve in the immortal 1989 movie, *National Lampoon's Christmas Vacation*.

If you haven't seen the movie the blouse in question is a perfect metaphor for D'Angelo's character: a demure, suburban mom with a splash of slut. It's a white, silky, almost prissy number —save for the gaping keyhole over the chest, excellently showcasing D'Angelo's bonkers cleavage. In *Christmas Vacation*, she pairs the blouse with a long, green taffeta-esque formal skirt, black tights, and black pumps. I have wanted to recreate this outfit for years. Whenever Mariah visits thrift stores (which is often), she searches painstakingly through all the white blouses for me. This is the type of friend that every adult woman should have: a friend who unconditionally sifts through strangers' relish-stained and yellow-pitted blouses for your half-thought-out costume whims.

"The best thing you can do to get this blouse is to call the costume designer and ask for it," Mariah said.

"You think that I should call the actual costume designer?" I asked. "Like, look up the costume designer from the 1989 movie, and call her?" I somewhat prejudicially assumed the costume designer to be a woman. Perhaps an ascot-wearing gentleman.

"Yes. That movie is like 30 years old. That blouse is probably just sitting in storage somewhere."

She paused. "Or it's in a museum."

Mariah is a couple years younger than me but tends to be the grownup in our friendship. If we were parents (a fantasy I have often), she would be the dad. Classically lovely and photogenic, she has knowing eyes and tasteful brunette bangs. I've learned most of my critical adult skills from Mariah, like how to smoke a one-hitter and how to make a halter top out of a T-shirt.

The most important adult friends have two qualities: 1) they keep you fun and 2) they keep you from having too much fun. It is a delicate balance. For example: In a party environment, my friend Deb can feed me whiskey out of a shot glass necklace while simultaneously shutting down my loud vocal appreciation of high school lacrosse players.[1] Mariah can bestow her wisdom about the artistic process while passing me a bong. I require this juxtaposition of drugs and honesty from my friends.

Mariah is the perfect case study of my roller derby sisters. While diverse in personality, a common wild power coursed

---

1. Dear high schools of the Midwest: Please stop building your sports fields right by the road I take to work.

through all of the women who skated with the Windy City Rollers. One of my earliest memories of Mariah is from my first year playing derby. She was in her second year and played for an opposing team.

I played for the Manic Attackers in those years. To say that my beloved team was awful would be giving us some credit. We were slaughtered in every single bout. Because we were so bad, I got to play a lot for a rookie. And by "play" I mean "skid across the floor with my ass in the air."

Mariah was on the Double Crossers (a team I later transferred to for several reasons, including Mariah). She was a solid blocker. A beautiful, delicate ass-kicker. I didn't know her very well yet, but I remember her poignantly from a particular bout that first year. We were losing terribly to Mariah's team, and I was on my last legs, exhausted from having been knocked down at least five times in ninety seconds. I finally got myself away from the other team and began limping around the track when Mariah glided up to me. Sweat had given me temporary blindness, and my legs were burning on a level I never thought possible. I felt like a massacred French fry that some monotone adolescent had left in a deep fryer all day. Looking fresh and effortless, Mariah eased close to me. And then she gave me this look out of the side of her eyes that I'll never forget. It was a look of slight pity, but mostly warmth, that said, "I love you. You're so wonderful and you're trying so hard! You are amazing. But I have to flatten you now."

And then she did. She tossed me to the middle of the track. My legs splayed and my face slid across the ground. Mercifully, the whistle blew, ending the play, and I dragged my beaten body back to my team's bench. But I didn't hold it against her. We never held grudges for hard hits in derby — that's just the game. You aren't really playing if you aren't getting your ass handed to you.

It took me until I was about 30 years old to truly realize how deep a female friendship can get. While there were a lot of lovely women in my life prior to my 30s, I didn't have the soul mates like I do now. I thought that my high school and college girlfriends were the most kindred spirits I would ever find. Although I loved them, I never quite felt like they understood me completely.

Although anxiety has never really left me, it took on a different kind of vague terror during my childhood, because no one had a label for it yet. In the 80s and 90s, anxiety wasn't yet "out there" as a legitimate phenomenon. Nowadays, society loves anxiety and everyone wants to claim it. I get irritated every time a new BuzzFeed article comes out, titled something like "20 Things Only People with Anxiety Will Understand." Now suddenly the universe has hopped on the anxiety bandwagon just because BuzzFeed says anxious people sometimes get nervous to go to parties. I'm competitive in every respect, right down to my mental illness. You BuzzFeed readers don't really know what it's like! You don't have a panic attack because you have to stop at Walgreens to pick up toilet paper on the way home from work.

I think about some of these moments when I'm sitting with Mariah or one of my other adult friends. There's no judgment. Last time I visited NYC, I had a panic attack at brunch in Bushwick while drinking a Bloody Mary out of a Mason jar.[2] My dear friend Lisa provided some words of comfort, and then rapidly acquired the check so we could get the hell out. She

2. Pleaseeee everybody go back to normal glassware now. Mason jars are strictly for masoning.

wasn't irritated that she had to wolf the remains of her house-made sausage frittata. She didn't care that I hung out in the bathroom until she could get the bill. I can tell my best girl-friends some of the ugliest secrets of my life, and they truly empathize with me. They love me unconditionally.

———————

It was January 2013, and Mariah was looming over me on a ladder, the printed cats on her thrifted sweatshirt looking at me curiously.

"Can you put your hand over that bruise on your leg?" she asked.

I obliged and straightened my granny-waist underwear. Mariah was photographing me topless.

Mariah likes boobs. And to be fair, I have really great boobs. Mariah is also a very talented photographer. It just made sense for her to take photos of my boobs. The initial plan for the shoot was a Catherine Deneuve-inspired portrait. I'm still not sure how she came up with this, because I look like a young Catherine Deneuve about as much as those women who get plastic surgery to look like a Barbie actually look like a Barbie. The portrait would feature a tomato-red backdrop and me, bare, from the shoulders up. Reasonably tasteful. The photo-shoot plan began in this manner and then devolved to include more graphic photos of me fully boobing out, posed with my vintage taxidermied turkey.

Mariah came over at noon on a Sunday. My hair and makeup took several hours and three people to perfect. I hadn't done this much primping at my wedding, but then again, I didn't get to be topless at my wedding! By the end of the prep, my hair was wrapped up in an elegant, neat twist, but tousled enough to give the impression that I had been rolling around in a male model's lap all day. Thick black liner coated my eyes precisely, leaving a slight rattlesnake-tail flip at the outer corners. Pale pink rouge and lipstick added a flush to ensure that it appeared as though not only had I been rolling around in a male model's lap all day, but I had really enjoyed it. I felt a bit uncomfortable being so dolled up. In between takes, I covered myself with a dirty blanket from the dog crate. This felt more "me."

After the seated Catherine portrait shots were done, Mariah set up her giant lights and ladder in our guest room. I tossed my robe on the floor and stood awkwardly with my hands on my hips, hoping my nipples were hard enough to be photogenic but not too hard so that it looked creepy. Subtle nips.

"Now," she said, readying her camera, "try to look like you've had a few too many pills with your...Chablis."

I relaxed my face into what I assumed she wanted — a sultry, stoned look—tried to give her my best "drunk Melanie at the sports bar." She cocked her head and grimaced.

"Maybe don't squint," she said.

For the next several hours, Mariah posed me under the dead turkey in our guest room, draping sheer thrift store garments over my bathing suit areas and sweetly making sure that my labial protuberances stayed tucked. After the shoot we looked through photos, and I pointed out the ones I liked best. My favorite photos were the ones where I looked most sexy and attractive. Mariah, of course, liked the ones where I looked weird.

The final portrait choice was a relatively equal combination of sensual and slightly outré. This portrait hangs on the wall in her living room. When I come over for group dinners, Mariah seats me under my boob portrait. She recently finished a new project, one where she photographs bare-chested men named David. She calls it "Modern David." So far she's gotten about at least 50 Davids. The Davids come over to her house for a portrait session, and one of the first things they often see is the portrait of me on Mariah's wall. Actually, Mariah has three photos of me up in her house. I like to think of myself as her muse.[3] But only one of the photos is topless. She says that all the Davids like it.

"They say… 'I wonder what she's thinking,'" Mariah says.

"Tell them the truth," I say, "That I was thinking about Cheetos."

Part of my adoration for Mariah comes from the fact that I think she is one of the coolest people I've ever met. Each year, she hosts a Zombie Jesus party on Easter Sunday. A couple dozen of our closest unshowered, awkward friends congregate to eat vegan potluck nachos and watch voracious zombies nosh on lusty co-eds. Mariah provides detailed table tent-style cards to identify each dish on the potluck table. "Squash salad—Gluten-free and good for you!" In the past few years, the zombie movie marathon theme has expanded. At least one undead campy gore film is guaranteed, don't you worry—but last year, Mariah took the party to a completely new level by including *Road House*. I had never seen this movie, and let me tell you- it's iconic as fuck. Stop reading and go rent it right now. *Road House* is waaaaay better than this book. You can

---

3. While she has not necessarily agreed with me on this point, she has not vigorously disagreed. So.

probably even find a used VHS copy in a dumpster outside of a tattoo shop. You will watch it, and then you will want to begin MMA lessons. Swayze's character is an in-demand bouncer at a large, rough country bar. He is convinced by a troubled bar owner to come "clean up" his joint. Apparently in Texas Hill country, quality bouncers are difficult to come by and must be cajoled to take gigs with inordinate sums of money. Swayze's ability to throw a 300-pound troublemaker over a table captivated me enough to keep me seated, even as I knew that I wasn't going to get my hands on any beet slaw before it was finished off by what looked like a stoned lumberjack.

Mariah and I go on a lot of dates—it's a very romantic friendship. We hold hands and sit on the same side of the table. She also struggles with social anxiety, so we take comfort in each other's presence. It's a beautiful coping mechanism, one of many we've learned from growing up with anxiety. Together, we can relax enough to enjoy situations that might otherwise be difficult. We stroll through fancy places, like bars that have "mixologists," and art exhibits that feature nude portraits of elderly sex workers. Sometimes during the warmer months, Mariah will drive the Matador on our dates. The Matador is a 1973 AMC wagon, "the color of money," as she says. It requires 10 minutes to heat up, even on a humid 90-degree day. While the standard wardrobe for most of our low-key dates is cut-off jeans and sleeveless T-shirts, skirts and lipstick are requisite for Matador dates.

Once while visiting my brother in LA, Mariah came to spend a couple of nights with me. We dined al fresco on shrimp salad. At night, we snuggled on the sofa bed and in the mornings she photographed me eating macarons and sipping coffee at Cafe

Lipstick tacos

Los Feliz. Our dates feel like a honeymoon in an erotic French graphic novel. Minus the sex. While I tend to think that we come off together as poised and sensual, in reality I think we resemble two little girls pretending to be ballet dancers. (We do sometimes wear leotards.)

Mariah is highly intelligent. She studied at the prestigious Art Institute of Chicago. While impulsive, she is not irresponsible. She bikes everywhere in a dense layer of reflective gear and a giant helmet — the sort of gear that overprotective parents pile on their children when they are learning to ride. When she shows up at our house, I know she's coming—I've seen her bright blinking lights and neon yellow vest coming for blocks. My dogs are also in awe of Mariah.

"They are comforted by my dull monotone voice," she says. They somehow sense that she doesn't need them, but will pet them if it is convenient to her.

Mariah is unable to lie. She's brutally honest, and I appreciate that. Recently, we both went out for Mexican diner food on a snowy Sunday night. Mariah wore cool-girl snow boots the size of trash cans, and I wore my somewhat-snow-friendly embroidered Peruvian boots.

"I like your boots!" I told her.

"Thanks," she said and looked closely at mine.

An awkward silence ensued as Mariah bluntly ignored the social norm of reciprocity when women compliment each other's clothing. She wasn't about to pretend to like my boots if she didn't like them.

Lately, she's been trying to help one of her close male friends get a date. She takes him to Brooklyn Industries and helps him pick out clothes that she believes young eligible females will find attractive—skinny pants and decorative plaid pocket squares. "If you want to touch a vagina," she tells him, "you're going to have to start trying harder."

Although polarizing, her bluntness somehow comes off as charming in many situations. You appreciate the fact that Mariah is not going to bullshit you. She charmed the pants off my parents the first time they met her in the summer of 2013. Most friends speak to senior parents with a delicate subtlety, politely laughing at my dad's Groucho Marx-era jokes and my mom's preschool teacher wit. Within the two minutes of meeting them, Mariah had managed to get my parents to pocket weed brownies.

"They're really not that potent. You guys need this in your life," she told them. It's very hard not to do things that Mariah thinks you should do.

Mariah became the cool crowd I was seeking my whole life, and I didn't even have to try. She made me realize that I had my own kind of cool, too. All those years I struggled with wanting to be conformist but simultaneously wanting to be my own person—I finally got to a place where I was cool just by being myself. Mariah and I both have our weird traits, our respective cat sweatshirts and unreasonable addiction to multivitamins. We both have our own damage, but Mariah makes me feel OK about it all. I can trust that Mariah will never judge me for anything I tell her. She has comforted me through many difficult times while managing her own busy life.[4] She's not the biggest fan of unnecessary touching, kind of like a cat herself, but will hold me close and hug me when I need it. I can tell her about all of the unethical things I've done recently, and she tells me all of the dirty shit she's gotten into. And then we feel good about ourselves, relishing in our mutual despicable-ness. Mariah reminds me that life is worth living, and in particular, it's worth fucking shit up.

When I told Mariah about this chapter, I asked her if she wanted a pseudonym. She said, "I don't know—send me the chapter."

I told her OK and prefaced it with "It might be weird to read about yourself." She replied calmly, "I'm pretty self-actualized." And that she is.

---

4. Mariah Karson has also published a beautiful photo essay book about the subculture of US veterans in the American Legion. It's heartwrenching and gorgeous. Look it up and buy it. Your coffee table will be infinitely cooler. SHAMELESS PLUG BECAUSE THAT'S WHAT BESTIES DO.

31

FLORIDA, THE PROMISED LAND

Why Florida, in a book that's supposed to be, at least loosely, about the Midwest? Because to Midwesterners, Florida is Eden, the land of milk and honey, a utopian paradise unfathomable to our frostbitten souls. Growing up in Ohio, Florida was the mythical promised land for all of us Rust Belt kids. Florida is far enough away from Northeast Ohio to be incredibly exotic—it requires a plane ticket, or at the very least, a multi-day drive. Florida is full of palm trees and perma-sunshine. Hell, Florida even has *gators*. This is a state that has prehistoric reptiles that *eat toddlers*. As a teenager, I heard there were even *topless beaches* in Miami. For winter-weathered children, Florida offered danger, sex, and sunshine.

And of course, *l'ultime*.

Florida has Disney World.

I've been to Florida a handful of times since my childhood – always briefly, and almost always involuntarily. Despite my inclination to trash Florida as a gutter state, I try to remember the magic it held in my childhood: the infinite promise of escape from our cold, gray, cul-de-sac existence. Florida lures Midwesterners seeking better lives, even if just for a few days.

Orlando Disney Universe has hosted me three times in my life. I first went to Disney was when I was eight. Walt Disney World was larger, more impressive, and more powerful than anything I could have imagined. I didn't understand why all the world's leaders weren't living there. I still sort of don't understand it. Fuck Mar-a-Lago, why isn't 45 living at Harry Potter World?

The second time I went to Disney World was in ninth grade, the first and only year that I participated in high school marching band. Our band director managed to land us a spot in the prestigious Disney Parade. My teen Disney experience was mixed: I found out that my boyfriend and my best friend were into each other, which made for a few shitty days walking around the park alone. The spinning teacups do, however, pair well with angst. I screamed into the humid Orlando air as a pastel tea cup flung me and my heartbreak around in circles.

My third time to Disney was as a fully grown adult woman. I was invited to give a presentation on STEM education that happened to be held in the Disney Yacht Club. Childless, hipster, and cynical, it had been decades since I had really even thought much about Disney.

"Ugh, Disney," I said to my colleagues. "I'll probably spend the entire time sidestepping toddlers and rolling my eyes at 25-year-old moms in too-tight Minnie Mouse T-shirts—with their sleeves rolled up." (Pause for laughter.)

I equated Disney with McDonald's, or Nike, or Coca-Cola: a siren song of addictive, mass-produced bullshit. I prepared myself to come in, give my talks, possibly take a quick dip in the adult pool, and head back to jaded, gritty Chicago, ripe with superiority.

I totally underestimated the power of Walt Fucking Disney.

Disney is a goddamn *machine*. The park has only closed down *three times* in its history, all in anticipation of hurricanes. The literal scourge of humanity traipses through Disney every single day, yet one is hard-pressed to find any litter, public urination, or even pedophiles! Just think of how the pedophiles could CLEAN UP at Disney! But no, because Disney functions like a finely calibrated communist regime. A few years ago, my friend Bill received a "behind the scenes" tour of Disney. He learned that every night, after the park closes, employees comb the entire park with jars of paint, touching up every possible scuff they can find. That is why everything at Disney always looks brand spanking new.

The Walt Disney Yacht Club is one of many Disney-owned resorts in the near vicinity of the theme parks. The Yacht Club was clearly designed for a high caliber of people; it was a far cry from the off-brand strip motel with algae-laced pool where we stayed in 1986. Disney Yacht Club was manufactured for people who typically summer at places like Cape Cod or Martha's Vineyard, not people who grew up spending leisure time near an Ohio river that once caught on fire. The staff uniforms were strictly gendered: women wore long, muted aprons atop Victorian dresses and kept their hair tucked neatly up – the look of the matronly servant dormice in *Cinderella*. At first glance, these uniforms also gave the hotel a vaguely *Downton Abbey*-meets-Cancún vibe. All of the men, however, wore light-colored sailor shirts and crisp shorts, an outfit that would be quite at home at any mother-son country club dance or gay nightclub. (It was extremely difficult for me to not catcall all of the sailors. But I didn't, because you know, feminism.)

After my cab dropped me at the door of the Yacht Club, where a Purell-fresh sailor wished me a magical day, I floated into the wood-carved lobby and inhaled every tiny Disney-fied detail. The soft background music was a pleasing, somehow nautical rendition of "It's a Small World." Tanned sailors and dormice flitted around the lobby. There was an entire cadre of staff whose job it was to merely smile at passersby and look approachable. I glided to the grand mahogany check-in area.

"Welcome to the Disney Yacht Club, Dr. LaForce," a dormouse beamed at me. How did she know my name?! Surely some Disney black magic.

"Here is your Mickey wristband," the dormouse added, unwrapping a new, blue plastic Fitbit-style device and gently placing it on my arm. "This will allow you access to all hotel areas, and you may use it to pay for visits to the park, food, drink, and souvenirs from our gift shop."

I didn't care how ugly the wristband was; I fastened it gratefully. The hotel had already triggered a strange nostalgia long-dormant in my brain, and I briefly wondered if I would look cute in the nautical-blue $50 mouse ears that teased me from the gift shop behind the check-in counter.

"Please sign by the Mickey," the dormouse added, "and then unless you need anything else you are welcome to go up to your room." I smiled and signed, tucked away my university Mastercard, and hummed "It's a Small World" as I floated to the elevator. "Good afternoon!" I called gaily to any passing sailors and dormice.

In my 24 hours at the the Disney complex, I was stunned to find no children underfoot. Kids were shockingly well-behaved. I can only imagine the pre-trip warnings that must've taken place to ensure such good conduct:

Parent: You realize we are taking you to Walt Disney World.

Child: Yes! Oh thank you, Papa!

Parent: This is a very special trip.

Child: I am so excited, Papa!

Parent: DO NOT FUCK THIS UP.

The patter of little feet throughout the hotel was minimal, and there was no noise whatsoever after 10pm. *This is not so bad,* I thought, refueling from my travels with a surprisingly fantastic bowl of room-service New England Clam Chowder. I watched the fireworks over the manmade bay from my balcony, sipping a Dogfish Head IPA. It was pleasant as fuck.

The next day, after my (completely professional and legitimate) conference presentations, I noticed a sign indicating that conference-goers would receive a special after-4pm rate of $63 to any of the theme parks. I considered this, incited by that irresistible Disney spark. It was a lot of cash to throw out for just a few hours, but how often was I spitting distance from such an iconic land of magic and commerce? Going alone would be fun, though I could certainly scrounge up a few new friends to tool around with. It's Disney, land of love!

I posted a query on Facebook: "Considering an impromptu trip to one of the Disney Theme Parks. What should I choose, Epcot or Magic Kingdom??"

The responses:

"You can drink at Epcot."

"Epcot has booze and fewer kids."

"Epcot! Way better food and drink."

"EPCOT—eat and drink around the world!"

(I have blissfully bacchanalian friends.)

Easily sold by the promise of alcohol, I walked 10 minutes to Epcot and scanned myself in with my blue wristband. Epcot is split up into two seemingly arbitrary themes. Half of the park is the "World Showcase," which hosts elaborate mini-versions of 11 countries from Canada to Morocco. The other half of the park is an exhibition of technological innovation and science, a nod to Mr. Walt Disney's uber-nerdiness for the concept of "future," and a representation of the park's original acronym: Experimental Prototype Community of Tomorrow. I was curious to see how Epcot had changed since I was nine, but priorities: I went straight to Fake Mexico and bought myself a Modelo tallboy. I was starving, having skipped the conference-provided lunch in favor of a nap, but too excited to see the park to bother sitting down and eating.

Beer in hand, I walked toward the tech-future part of the park. It began to rain. Park-goers donned cheap ponchos all around me, creating a dystopian clone ambience. A nice thing about central Florida is its low standard of beauty. I tucked my unwashed hair into a side pony and embraced the rain. The sweat and stick of Florida in July rinsed away.

Mission: Space is a spaceship ride that relies on centrifugal force to simulate a trip to Mars. A teenage boy at the entrance told me firmly that I needed to finish my beer before I could enter the ride. I told him that he was a buzzkill but chugged agreeably.

"Green?" he asked me, and I looked at him puzzled.

"Do you want an orange or green ticket?" he clarified.

"What's the difference?" I asked him, burping.

"Orange is more intense. You would spin."

"Oh, I'll spin," I said, snatching the orange ticket, irritated at his assumption of my wussiness.

As a single rider, I was able to get on immediately, paired by the authoritarian teen with a Korean mother and child that did not speak English and had no desire to be my friend. (I noticed this repeatedly in Epcot. For some reason, parents seemed hesitant to befriend the solo adult woman who smelled like beer and had mascara running down her face.) Gary Sinise appeared on a video to give a set of VERY SERIOUS instructions, warning us repeatedly that the mission would be intense and if we decided we wanted to leave now, a crew member would escort us out. I felt a bit nervous as 20 ounces of Modelo churned in my stomach. A Disney staffer reiterated that anyone uncomfortable with "dark, small spaces" should leave now. But then I looked down at the 7-year-old Korean boy next to me and decided that if he could do it, my tipsy ass would be fine.

Each of us had an assigned job. As the "navigator," I had the complex job of pressing a certain button whenever Gary Sinise told me to do so. The 7-year-old also pointed emphatically at the button for me each time to ensure I didn't botch the whole mission. His mother gripped him nervously each time the ship jolted. My silent Korean friends and I spun and whirled and managed to land our ship safely. Miraculously, no one (me) threw up.

I wanted to ride it again with some more engaged crewmates but was too hungry. I walked to Fake Norway and purchased a lefse (rolled sweet flatbread) and 20 ounces of Carlsberg beer from a dangerously attractive Norwegian college student. (Disney recruits good-looking humans for each mini-country from their respective real-world counterparts, which feels a tad exploitative. But hot.) The rain stopped and the sun had turned the park into a sweat lodge, so I downed my Carlsberg and snuck a tiny scrap of lefse to a mallard wandering between the tables, JUST LIKE SNOW WHITE WOULD.

For the next few hours, I drank and wandered and people-watched, marveling at the diversity. From the little Aryan baby in Lily Pulitzer to the lesbian honeymooners to the 70-year-old Latina grandmother wearing a shirt that read "No boyfriend? No problem" – the only thing Disney lacked was a cohort of single, hetero cis-men. Disney is absolutely NOT the place to pick up men if you are a hetero woman. It may be, however, the place to pick up men if you are a homosexual man. There were many, many groups of gay men. I tried to ingratiate myself with a few groups by sharing helpful tips ("Hey, I know where the Chinese acrobats' dressing room is!"), but none of them seemed interested in my friendship either. By this point, I was doing that suppressed burp thing that comes out sounding like farts. I resigned myself to wandering Disney alone.

Time flew and suddenly it was almost 9pm. Magically, giant torches all around the park spontaneously burst into flame. I made my way to a staircase overlooking the bay for the nightly light show. I considered skipping it and heading back to my room; my eyelids were droopy and sweat pooled in all of my groin regions. A day of work and an evening of Disney had left me exhausted. But I knew this was probably the last time I would ever be at Disney World, so I might as well watch the goddamn light show that could only be perfect, because every-thing in Disney had proven to be perfect. I sat on the stairs and leaned against the cool marble, barely noticing when a nearby toddler tried to climb onto my lap (finally! a friend!) before his mother yanked him away. Then the show started.

It didn't disappoint. It was, of course, predictably gut-wrenchingly huge and expensive and beautiful. Fireworks! Lasers! Dramatic, swelling music! Tall plumes of flames reached to the sky. A giant globe floated across the bay and projected high-quality video of Savannah lions, grassy fields, and whales swimming in the oceans. It was a beautiful way to end the day. My cynical brain got annoyed as I felt a lump in my throat, and I tried to tell myself it was probably just remnants of lefse wedged awkwardly in my esophagus.

I was happy. My joy was only partly due to the many ounces of foreign beer I had consumed. I had thoroughly enjoyed wandering the park alone, something that would've been a deep challenge for me in my younger years. Sure, booze has magical powers that suppress anxiety, but it was more than that. I felt like young Melanie would look at old Melanie and be happy about who she grew up to be. Not only was old Melanie fucking killing it at Disney, but she had turned out OK. There were a lot of years where I had assumed that if I actually lived to be an adult, I would be a weak, unhappy, anxious wreck—afraid of new people and new situations. But old Melanie had just successfully navigated a crew of three to a safe Mars landing. While drunk. After giving a fancy-ass academic presentation. I was proud of myself. I liked me, and I was rocking adulthood. Disney made my culmination of confidence all the more sweet. Watching multi-million-dollar nightly pyrotechnics blossom over the man-made Epcot bay, I felt like I had finally arrived.

Acknowledgements

I have so much gratitude for Nicole Tourtelot and DeFiore Literary, for finding me and believing I had something valuable to say. Thanks to Thought Catalog for taking me on, and Kendra Syrdal and Kristina Johnson Parish in particular for their support. Thanks also for Alex Zulauf's help early during the process. I am eternally grateful to Rosamund Lannin and Jesse Aylen for their extensive reviews. I was also lucky enough to have Kelli Joy Thompson, Kristina Rago, Tanya Pazitny, Emily Cromwell, Kara Luger, and Kate Dunn provide valuable feedback.

Thanks also to Stuart Horwitz, Sean Cusick, Seth Gersbach, Mark Denzine, Allison Fox, and Mariah Karson for reviews of early chapter drafts. God bless the irreverent @lehrerboys (Daniel and Jeremy Lehrer) for the wonderful cover art, and Katrina Zimmerman for graphics support. Many people acted as emotional handlers across this journey, including Sharon Jedel, Deb Schimmel, Megan Deiger, Liz Noble, Mary Abbott, Kristin Mayle, Lisa DuRussel, Megan McCormack, The Binders, and loads of other wonderful humans who offered words of encouragement. I'm especially grateful to Mom and Dusty for their support, and to Dad for his unyielding blind pride in me.

Last but never least, the biggest thanks to my beloved Dave Abbott, for being the best copy editor, cheerleader, personal chef, dog dad, comedy audience, and border collie to my confused sheep's brain.

About The Author

Dr. Melanie LaForce was born in Northeast Ohio and currently lives in Logan Square, Chicago. In addition to her writing, LaForce is a researcher at the University of Chicago and adjunct faculty at Northwestern University. Her hobbies include petting dogs, napping, stage comedy, and flirting.

Twitter @rileycoyote
Instagram @rileycoyote
melanielaforce.com

THOUGHT
CATALOG
Books

Thought Catalog Books is a publishing house owned by The Thought & Expression Company, an independent media group based in Brooklyn, NY. Founded in 2010, we are committed to facilitating thought and expression. We exist to help people become better communicators and listeners in order to engender a more exciting, attentive, and imaginative world.

Visit us on the web at
www.thoughtcatalogbooks.com and *www.collective.world*.

YOU MIGHT ALSO LIKE:

This Is For The Women Who Don't Give A Fuck
by Janne Robinson

Wild Mama: One Woman's Quest to Live Her Best
Life, Escape Traditional Parenthood, and Travel the
World
by Carrie Visintainer

From Excuses to Excursions: How I Started
Traveling the World
by Gloria Atanmo

THOUGHT
CATALOG
Books

CPSIA information can be obtained
at www.ICGtesting.com
Printed in the USA
LVHW08s2147071018
592761LV00020B/605/P